This book will contribute to the history of at[...] and ultimately used for peaceful purposes.

     — *Jimmy Carter*, President of the United States 1977-1981.

This is the intimate true life story of Miller Moseley, a unique personality-an obscure Texas farm boy, orphaned in childhood, Masonic Home football standout, WWII scientist and revered TCU Emeritus Professor of Physics -told by a close observer. With a remarkable sensitivity to colorful detail and an exceptional gift of verbal expression, first time author, Stella Brooks shares with us this fascinating story.

     — *Jim Wright*, Former Speaker of the House and author.

Miller Moseley was a graduate student at the University of North Carolina at Chapel Hill in the 1940s and came with Professor Nathan Rosen on the liquid thermal diffusion project being carried out at the Naval Research Laboratory in Washington, D.C under the direction of Philip Abelson. It is likely that Miller is the last surviving member of that team. Stella Brooks has written a compelling biography of Miller. Miller's generation were an elite group of American heroes. Everyone during that time performed way above standard and it is fascinating to have firsthand account of their experience. I enthusiastically recommend this book.

     — *John Abelson*, Professor of Biology (Emeritus) at California Institute of Technology and author.

A truly inspirational story. It showcases the spirit of humanity and what young people can achieve when given direction and a fighting chance. It is also a great testament to the Masons and their Home for their commitment and guidance.

     — *Gary Patterson*, TCU Head football coach and
     — *Dick Bumpas*, TCU Defensive coordinator and defensive line coach.

I was Miller's student at TCU and a faculty colleague for over twenty years, but I never really knew his story. Stella's recount of the formative events in Miller's life have helped me appreciate and respect his special qualities even more.

– *Dr. C.A. Quarles*, TCU Professor Emeritus.

I have never read a more true book about my home, The Masonic Home. This book brought back so many memories, especially watching the 1938 football team with Miller Moseley playing left end for the greatest smallest team in the history of the Home. Stella, in her book displays the true spirit of what Masonic Home was all about. The Home not only produced great athletes, but produced a great person with an intellectual mind, which happened to be Miller Moseley. When my older brother and I went to live at the Home in 1931, Miller was already living there along with his younger brother and sister. I feel so honored to have been raised in the same Home along with Miller Moseley.

– *Tom Brady*, Masonic Home Masons and class of '43.

Stella, as I read your story, it made me re-live my experience at the Home almost exactly as you wrote it. It was almost like I was living it again.

– *Richard Opperman*, Masonic Home salutatorian and co-captain for the Masonic Home Masons football team. Class of '48.

This is a great book. It will no doubt be a big success. Thanks to you, Stella for all your time and hard work on the book. Miller is lucky to have you as the author of his book.

– *Horace McHam*, Masonic Home Masons Left Guard and Class of '39.

"Wishing Miller and his wife all the best."

– *Ellen Cherniavsky* (Abelson).

Dr. Harrison Miller Moseley.
The scientist who went to war and won. Dr. Harrison Miller Moseley pushed
through fear, loneliness, abandonment and poverty.

UNBELIEVABLE

The story of a small boy who defeats huge physical and psychological challenges to become a brilliant scientist working among the Who's Who on the Atomic Bomb.

Stella Brooks

ISBN: 978-0-9996484-6-9 (hardback)
          978-0-9996484-7-6 (paperback)
          978-0-9996484-8-3 (ebook)

Dedication

I am truly fortunate to have met the brilliant Dr. Harrison Miller Moseley, and I am grateful for the privilege of putting together the puzzle pieces of his amazing life in this book. Harrison Miller Moseley is not your usual high school football star or your usual scientist. Miller has accomplished more in his lifetime than those born with a silver spoon. At 92, his recollections are exact and he is careful never to exaggerate. Listening to Miller recall his life during the Depression, at the Fort Worth Masonic Home and School and at the Naval Research Laboratory where he was part of the A-list team working on the atomic bomb was unbelievable. This may be the first time some of his recollections of the Naval Research Laboratory have ever been recorded. Dr. Moseley was among the handful of men who developed the means needed to end a cruel war.

Thank you, Dr. Harrison Miller Moseley, for giving me this unbelievable opportunity of a lifetime.

§

To my kids, Michael and Emma, who take life's tough challenges and succeed in pulling up others with them along the way.

Acknowledgments

Special thanks to those who had a personal interest in this book and made it possible:

Harrison Miller Moseley for exclusive rights to his story.

Dene Moseley, Miller's wife. She recalled the chilling day she came face-to-face with a German soldier in England. She was unable to join her friends that day because her mother was ill and needed help. As she watched her friends from her family's second story apartment ride their bicycles on the street below, her gaze was suddenly forced upward. There, on the other side of that thin piece of glass was a German pilot so close she could see his face and helmet as flames shot out from his plane. She had just witnessed the cruel reality of the war as he continued to gun down her friends. She also remembered a festive evening at a dance that turned horrific in the blink of an eye when a bomb crashed through the roof of the building and exploded, throwing her down several flights of stairs. Dene feels the atomic bomb saved the world. She hopes to see a World War II movie that ends with a handful of scientists quietly standing. After numerous visits to the Moseley home, Dene said, "Stella, you have the magic key. Miller has discussed very little regarding his life at the Home and his work on the atomic bomb. You walk in and Miller tells you things he never told family, friends or me." Dene, thank you so very much.

My Masonic Home friends. You guys were the driving force behind this book. You wanted this book as much as I did. Your encouragement pushed this book from a blank sheet of paper to completion.

Richard Opperman, 1948 Masonic Home and School salutatorian. You inspired me to keep at it. Your labor and efforts provided a wealth of information, documentation and records. As a young boy, Richard was dropped off at the Masonic Home by a couple of strangers. He was confused and very afraid. Years later, as an adult, he is proud to say he is a Mason and was an orphan at the Masonic Home in Fort Worth, Texas.

As a boy at the Home, Richard shared laundry duty with his best friend, Kell. One day, as they delivered the clean clothes to the various buildings, Kell eagerly handed a basket to Richard to deliver to the big girls' building. As Richard walked into the building, he happened to glance down into the basket and turned red as a beet when he discovered the basket was full of female products. He immediately dropped the basket and ran outside to discover Kell had left with the mule.

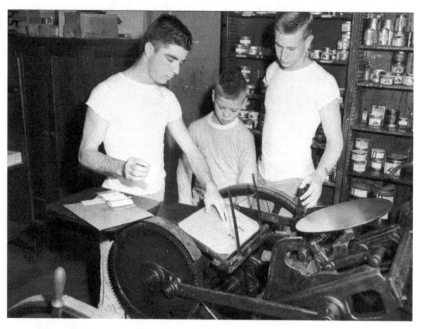

Football co-captains for Masonic Home, Richard Opperman (right), and O.L. Stephens (left) printing tickets for the game with Laneri High School while Odie Faulk looks on. *(Courtesy of the Fort Worth Star-Telegram. Special Collections, The University of Texas at Arlington Library, Arlington, Texas).*

DeWitt Coulter, a boy at the Home who would later become known as Tex, was an all-American on Army's 1945 national championship team, played for the New York Giants, the All-Pro team in 1948 and 1949 and with Montreal in the Canadian Football League. DeWitt paid Richard Opperman 25 cents to sit still so Dewitt could sketch his profile. Afterwards, Richard ran to the store and bought a pint of ice cream for

DeWitt and a candy bar for himself. "Had I gotten caught leaving campus, I would have gotten my tail whopped," said Richard. But Richard was never caught. "I received plenty of whippins, but I deserved them and a few more," Richard remembered. Today, Richard says, "I would like to ring the neck of the person who said these were the Golden Years."

Tom Brady (Masonic Home. February 1, 1931 to 1943). Without you, this book might not have happened. Your recollections, memories and details of life at the Home were invaluable. You patiently answered enough emails, calls and letters to fill a large box. Your unbelievable memory for facts nailed down exact dates, names, places and events. Thank you for your endless encouragement and support.

"I guess I can tell this now, because I am the only survivor," said Tom, referring to the night the boys decided to help themselves to Mr. Bodiford's good food and got off Scott-free while the wrong boys were blamed.

§

1940 Masonic Home Football team, Hotel Texas, February 14, 1941.

As the boys stood to go back on the field, Mr. Russell said, "Boys, Dr. Hall has a few words to say." Dr. Hall stepped up and said, "Boys, when you hit 'em, hit 'em right in the gut," remembered Tom Brady.

Tom said, "My mother never cussed, but as she was getting older she once remarked, 'This old age is the "damdest" thing I ever got into.'"

Horace McHam, (Masonic Home. January 9, 1930 to 1939) for your wonderful memories, visits, book and encouragement.

Jack Bates, 1939 Masonic Home and School graduate and Roberta Bates for the rights to Jack's book, *Proud to Be Number 23, The Story of My Life*, by Jack Kent Bates.

We arrived at the Naval Academy and once again we had to build our own buildings and classrooms, make sidewalks, pour cement and landscape the area before classes could start. We were across the Severn River from the Naval Academy at the Naval Air Facility of the Academy (NAF). Our headquarters was on the old Navy ship the Reina Mercedes. This ship is as old as the Constitution berthed in Boston. We did our usual instruction syllabus. The Midshipmen would come over from the Academy in motor launches. President Carter was a midshipmen at the time and was in our classes. Sonic, J. L. Daniels was also in attendance.

To Bill Walraven, (Masonic Home. 1933-1943) and author, for his encouragement, interest and publishing experience. Thank you for the use of "*Ziggy,*" "*Returning to the home,*" and, "*The General said, 'Nuts.'*" Bill died on December 12, 2013 in Corpus Christi, Texas. Marjorie Walraven was a huge help coordinating correspondence back and forth between Bill and myself.

Bruce Riddle, Masonic Home graduate, thank you for your memories and artifacts. Bruce is responsible for helping Richard Opperman create a Masonic Home museum at the Masonic Temple in downtown Fort Worth, Texas.

To Ellen Cherniavsky, Philip Abelson's daughter. Philip Abelson never discussed work on the atomic bomb at home. Ellen enjoyed Miller's memories of her father, Philip Abelson, especially the night Miller met her father for the first time. Ellen said, "That sounds exactly like my father. Every Friday was hamburger night at home. Mother and I would have a hamburger and father would always have steak. She remembered a time when her father dropped a cat out of the second story window because it had been sleeping on his pillow. The cat wasn't harmed. She said, "Once father collected 91 bags of leaves from neighbors for compost in his garden."

To Dr. John N. Abelson (Philip Abelson's nephew), Emeritus professor of Biology at the California Institute of Technology and author. Thank you for your generous gift, "*Uncle Phil and the Atomic Bomb,*" and the use of your wonderful research and memories of your uncle, the amazing Philip Abelson. And thank you for the memorable conference call between you, Miller and me.

To Dr. C. A. Quarles, Emeritus Professor of Physics at Texas Christian University for the memories, pictures and eagerness to assist.

Reverend Andrew Leigh Gunn, Charles Rowley Gunn and Ross Gunn II. A special thank you for the personal conversations regarding your father, Ross Gunn. "The Arsenal" was the name Ross Gunn bestowed on his home, the place where the Gunns were kept. He named his 38-foot cruiser the *GUNNBOAT.* Ross Gunn was apparently unaware that he may have invented the first microwave. Gunn had built an antenna inside the laboratory, and every time anyone went to the restroom, which was located close to the antenna, they began to sweat and feel extremely warm.

To Cheryl Castells and Karen Messick for your continuous support, assistance and stories about growing up in the Moseley household.

To all those whose names are too many to mention: librarians, museum personnel, military archival assistants, authors and historians. Kai Bird, author of *Tragedy of J. Robert Oppenheimer,* for words of wisdom. Dick Vallon, Burkburnett Chamber of Commerce, thank you for confirming Miller's story and for the use of your quotes, "A friend is a person you do not have to explain to or for," and, "History does not belong to only a few of the 'doers,' it belongs to those of us who read about it." Amy Leslie, TCU Special Collections; Brenda McClurkin, UTA Special Collections;

Susan Diamond, Daughter of Louis K. Diamond; and the many widows and children of Masonic Home orphans—Mrs. Harold Ferguson (Mary Lu), Lucille Torres (Poppy) and more.

David Hughes, who offered encouragement, knowledge of the industry, and a quick eye for my grammatical slipups while juggling the publication of his books, *The Epiphany of Joy* and *Melted Clowns*. I never understood why an author praised their editor until now.

CONTENTS

PART I

Contents

PART II

PART III

PART IV

PART I

one

Dundee

The sound of footsteps drew closer. The boy lay motionless, not making a sound. He had crawled under the house to escape the intense Texas sun, and as he sprawled on the cool, soft, brown dirt, playing with the small, unusual looking creatures living under his home, he heard the footsteps stop. Peering out from the darkness into the bright sunlight, the boy saw a pair of scuffed brown shoes covered in dust standing in a small patch of dry, yellow grass several feet away. The boy hid in the darkness, his attention diverted away from the gentle creatures and becoming fixed on the shoes. Suddenly the stillness broke when the man in the shoes rushed toward him. He felt the man's strong hand grab his ankle and he heard him laugh, "I wish I could fit under there." The man gently pulled the boy out from under the house into the blazing sunshine.

As the boy lay flat on his stomach, still managing to keep his arm straight out while holding one of the small creatures in the palm of his hand, he turned his head toward the man, squinted into the sun and giggled with delight. All he could see was a dark silhouette, but he knew who it was. "Hi, Father!" the boy said.

"Miller!" the boy's mother called. "Time for supper."

In the summer of 1926, Harrison Miller Moseley was a joyful five year old boy whose happy life would soon take several fearful and overwhelming turns. Harrison Miller Moseley was Mildred Lucille Miller Moseley and John Harrison Moseley's firstborn child. He was born on December 14, 1921, in a small room in the same simple house. Just two months earlier, on October 5, 1921, the World Series was broadcast on the radio for the first time. Two years later, on September 15, 1923, his brother Cecil Ray Moseley was born, followed by a sister, Dorothy. John Harrison Moseley had an average build, light brown hair and tanned skin. He made a scanty wage as a cook for roughnecks on a rig. Mildred Moseley was an elementary school teacher in Dundee, Texas. She was a small woman with a round face, thin nose and the corners of her mouth turned down slightly. She had short, dark brown hair with large loose curls and was rarely seen without a hat.

Their house was no more than a meager set of walls and a roof for protection. It was located on a farm near Dundee, in Archer County, 27 miles southwest of Wichita Falls, which, at the time, had an approximate population of 400 people. The house glared in the hot sun; there was nothing around to provide shade. Nor was there a fireplace, just a simple wood burning stove occupying the corner of the front room for cold winter nights. No roads led up to Miller's home.

Next to the house lay a small, dry, crisp garden Mildred had planted. It desperately needed water. From the front porch, all Miller could see for miles around was hard, dry, cracked ground and a large grain field. On the other side of the field stood Miller's maternal grandparents' house. Their house was also modest, but larger than the Moseley home. His grandparents' house was built such that a breeze would flow from one end of the structure to the other. The sheer, white curtains would move with the breeze, and the beige pull-down shades would flap. His grandfather was a short man with white, thin hair and dark brown, weathered skin. He bred horses, farmed and owned many of the buildings located in the middle of Dundee, including a rooming house, a drug store and the only two-story building in town.

As Miller struggled to scoot out from under the house, he heard his mother call again: "Miller! Time for supper! Come wash your hands."

Once freed, he raised to his knees holding what looked like a fierce horned creature about three inches long with a short tail, flat body and rough exterior. But looks were deceiving—the horny toad was completely harmless. Miller stroked its soft underbelly until it fell asleep. Then he released it to feast on a bed of luscious red ants. After he knew the horny toad saw the ants, he stood, brushed the brown dirt off the front of his shirt and watched the toads dart around, making their way back under the house where they lived.

Miller was an extremely bright, quizzical five year old boy with brown eyes, light brown hair bleached from the sun, olive skin, a strong jaw, and easy smile. In his eyes you could see the wheels turning with expectation and the desire to learn everything life threw his direction. If he did not have a book to read, he did not sit still. He ran into the house, covered in dirt from head to toe. Even the creases in his neck were filled with soil. He headed to a bowl filled with clean water to wash his hands. The smell of chicken frying in the cast iron skillet made his stomach growl. Earlier that day, Miller had helped his mother catch the unfortunate chicken and he'd watched, fascinated, as she wrung its neck within seconds of its capture. Now the house smelled wonderfully of fried chicken, and he hoped for the leg. To make it fair amongst the three children, his mother pulled pieces of straw from the broom and held them up. The one who chose the longest straw got to pick the first piece of chicken. He chose the second-longest straw, which was perfect since there were two legs.

In the mid 1920's, American farmers struggled as the United States imported cheap crops from Europe. As a consequence, the value of farmland fell drastically. But the Moseley's never considered themselves' poor; after all, everyone else was in the same financial condition. The house, a basic shell standing against the glaring sun, featured neither electricity nor running water. One small mesquite tree guarded the emaciated front yard, and an outhouse stood twenty feet behind their home. Around the outhouse door horseflies swarmed, making trips to the restroom an adventure. And when a north Texas storm rolled through, the worn path, usually a strip of hard, dry ground lined with dry, yellowed grass, became a slippery path of mud which pressed between Miller's toes. A towel hung on the doorknob to use to wipe his feet before entering. On Halloween, pranksters would turn the outhouse over and everyone had to pitch in to stand it upright again.

Miller idolized his father. Every day he waited eagerly for him to return home from work. John Harrison Moseley was extremely talented. He was an accomplished pianist, violinist and organist, and his old, foot-pumped organ stood in the front room where Miller and Cecil would lie on the floor and listen to him play while his mother cleaned the dishes. Cecil was a sweet three year old boy with sandy blond hair, round face, chubby cheeks, brown eyes, and a ready smile. He was also very intelligent, like his brother.

When Miller visited his grandparents in the early morning hours, he usually found them sitting at the kitchen table, drinking coffee and eating grits or oatmeal. When Miller's grandfather left for work, the house became very quiet except for the creak of the wood floors when his granny walked calmly down the long hallway in her laced-up shoes, cotton dress and apron. No one ever yelled. If anyone had something to say, they walked into the next room and spoke in a quiet, friendly voice. A wooden porch ran the length of his grandparents' house, fronted by a white railing. Several chairs and a couple of rocking chairs sat on the porch, welcoming family and visitors. A weathered wooden bench swing which had never been painted hung near the front door and swayed gently in the breeze.

Sometimes, in the evenings, Miller would join his granny as she sat and rocked on the front porch. She was a small woman with white hair and pink cheeks, and her feet barely touched the porch deck as she rocked. As he sat on the porch, he could hear his Aunt Edie, and his two cousins, Chester Franklin Miller and Bud, who were close to Miller's age, behind the house hanging clothes. Miller's mother had lost her only brother, Uncle George, and his widow and children had moved in with Miller's grandparents, filling every room in their large house. Despite the number of people living there, his grandparents' house was a peaceful place to be.

One day, as they relaxed on the porch, his granny slowly rocked, tapping the porch with the toe of her shoe. She turned to Miller and said, "I suspected someone was stealing my chickens. The size of my flock was dwindling." She continued to rock back and forth. "And just as I had suspected, I heard a commotion in the chicken coop. I stepped in front and pointed my gun inside. Then a deep voice said, 'Put the gun down lady. There isn't anyone here but us chickens.'"

Miller laughed.

One hot August day around 1927, Miller ran through the hay field to his grandparent's house for a visit. He stopped in the shade of the porch to cool off his hot bare feet. As he lay on his back and waved his feet in the air like a fan, he heard his granny mention the name "Papa Doc." He had no idea who she was talking about until his grandfather walked out onto the porch to get on his horse. At that time his granny stepped outside and said, "Papa Doc, don't forget to buy salt while you are in town."

Aunt Edie added, "Papa Doc, don't forget to stop by the feed store."

"Papa Doc, don't forget my candy," Bud called from the house.

His grandfather did not practice medicine, but that's what Miller's granny decided to call him one day and the name stuck. As he lay on his back fanning his throbbing feet, he smiled and added a farewell to Papa Doc as well.

After Papa Doc left, Miller ran as fast as Babe Ruth stealing third base down the road to a large hill close to the main highway in Wichita Falls. It wasn't Miller's first time to race to this hill. He had been informed that someone had been buried in that hill and there was only one way to awaken the spirit. Directly above the mound was a wire. All Miller had to do was pull that wire and the spirit would awaken and it would supposedly make a sound. But every time he pulled the wire, it cut off the lights downtown, and before the spirit had a chance to speak, a repairman would show up to get the lights back on. On one occasion, shortly after the repairman had arrived, his superior showed up and told the repairman to hand over his license.

Not long after, Miller stood next to a busy street in Holiday, near Dundee, waiting for an opportunity to run across. A man approached, also waiting for a break in the traffic. Miller looked up at the man. "Aren't you the same guy that had his license taken away?"

"I knew you were the same S.O.B.," the man said.

Miller ran home. The burnt yellow grass from the relentless sun jabbed his bare feet like needles and the hard, dry, cracked ground burned his soles. Miller ran as fast as Ty Cobb after Babe Ruth. If he stepped in a bed of stickers, he would be forced to walk on the sides of his feet until he could find a clear spot on the ground to sit and pull the painful stickers out. Sometimes a thorn would break off the end of a sticker and lodge in his foot. When that happened, his mother would heat up the tip of a sewing needle in a flame and use it to dig the thorn out of his foot. His ankles were always swollen from multiple chigger bites; big, red, itchy whelps covered his ankles and itched like chicken pox.

The Moseley's did not own a car, which was typical for those days. Almost everyone walked where they needed to go, whether to the store, the doctor, or to school. Every Sunday the family walked to the local Methodist church. They followed the railroad tracks until they met the road that led to the church. The Moseley's walked through the doors of the church with his baby sister, whom they call Dot, on his father's shoulders. On hot summer days, Mr. Moseley would arrive at church sweating profusely, and once inside in the shade he never could cool off enough to get comfortable.

Regardless of the heat, John Moseley always wore a suit to church. Constant streams of sweat ran down the sides of his face, but he never complained. One Sunday, the pastor asked John to play the piano prior to the service. John sat on the piano bench and began playing as the congregation looked on. The bench did not quite suit John, so without missing a beat, he pushed it out of the way and squatted as if he were actually sitting on something as he continued to play. The congregation had a hard time keeping a straight face. Miller was proud of his father and loved that he was the life of the party.

For extra income, his father set traps in hopes of catching any edible animal for money. Miller would sit patiently on the porch waiting for his father to return from work so they could check the traps together. When he saw a figure off in the distance walking in the direction of the Moseley home, he knew it was his father. He would run as hard as he could to accompany him. After catching up to his dad, the two walked the lines quickly to check the traps before it got too dark.

Miller enjoyed trapping with his father; in fact, he enjoyed helping his father with any chore. One summer evening the temperature had not yet dropped below 100 degrees even though it was eight o'clock. Miller jumped over the wide cracks in the hard ground as he and John walked the trap lines. As Miller and his father approached one of the traps, Miller saw an animal stuck in one of them. In anticipation, he ran ahead to check out their prize, but he suddenly turned away, covering his nose and mouth with his hand. They'd trapped a skunk! His father tied a handkerchief around his nose and mouth, released the skunk from the trap and buried it.

During the long walk home, Miller kept a good distance behind his father. He smelled awful.

A couple of weeks later, in the fall of 1926, Miller's mother enrolled him in the first grade at the small school in Dundee, where she taught. The school was a small simple, white building. A weathered outhouse stood a short distance further down the hill. Miller enjoyed being inside the old building and learning from the moment he walked into the classroom, and he performed well despite being the youngest in the class. He was meticulous like his father, with an "I can" attitude.

But he soon ran into a problem. The head of the school discovered a girl in the first grade whose mother had misrepresented her age. Her daughter was not seven years old, the minimum age any student was allowed to be registered for school. The head of the school told the mother to bring her daughter back when she reached the proper age of admittance.

This angered the girl's mother and she decided to take out her disappointment on Miller. In front of the class stood the girl, the girl's mother, Mrs. Moseley, and the head of the school. The students watched from their desks as the girl's mother pointed her long, trembling finger at Miller and firmly stated, "If you will not allow my daughter to attend school, then Miller must leave as well. Miller is even younger than my daughter!" The children fixed their gaze on Miller, who sat very still and quiet as the woman ranted on and on. He took a deep breath as she continued to stand her ground. It seemed as if she would not stop arguing until she won. And she did, or so she thought. The head of the school also de-enrolled Miller from the first grade. However, shortly after the woman left, Mildred convinced the Dundee school authority to allow Miller to continue to go through all the motions, without taking credit. That was good news to Miller as school opened up a new world and he longed to continue studying and expanding his knowledge. He never knew how his mother was able to convince the authorities to let him stay, but she did, and that was all that mattered to Miller. Each day, Miller continued to sit in the back of his mother's classroom determined to learn as much as he possibly could.

§

Work in Papa Doc's two story garage came to an immediate halt. The loud roar from the large farming equipment spun down with a cough and fell silent. The workers in the garage had no choice but to sit on the dirt floor and wait.

Miller and Cecil watched as men leaned their heads against the walls, lowered their hats to cover their faces and took naps. Others cleaned and arranged tools.

The dirt on the garage floor was soft and fine, unlike the hard, cracked ground outside. Farming equipment stretched from one end of the garage to the other, and the owner of each piece of equipment sat waiting for the signal which allowed the men to return to work.

As Miller sat on the floor, he traced the imprints where doodle bugs had burrowed into the soft dirt. Miller and Cecil let the fine granules run through their fingers as they silently waited.

This building was the only two-story structure in Dundee and Papa Doc owned it. The bottom floor contained a garage where farmers and ranchers brought tractors and other farm equipment in for repair. But the meeting taking place on the second floor that day demanded quiet and a temporary cessation of all work in the garage. The mysterious meetings held on the second floor would soon prove supremely beneficial to Miller's future welfare, but for now, what took place upstairs remained shrouded in a complete mystery.

John Moseley and Papa Doc were Master Masons at Lodge #994; Lodge meetings took place on the second floor of Papa Doc's building. On that particular day, Miller and Cecil waited patiently for their father so they could walk home with him. Finally the meeting ended and the Masons filed out of the little room and down the stairs. John smiled and said, "There are my boys." Miller and Cecil got to their feet and the three walked home together. It had been a particularly hot, clear afternoon and as they walked, clouds began to form overhead and the sky grew dark. By the time they reached the porch, it had begun to rain. They watched the rain fill the dry, two-inch-wide cracks with water, and steam rose from the ground. The air became an unbearable steam bath with no escape.

Growing up, Miller learned quickly the meaning of the popular saying, "If you do not like the weather in Texas, just blink."

Summer soon passed and Christmas of 1927 was quickly approaching. It was an unusually cold winter already, and on December 14, 1927, on Miller's sixth birthday, the men kept busy cutting fire wood which had been delivered earlier that day into smaller pieces to fit into the stove.

As John and Papa Doc chopped wood the children took full advantage of the scrawny mesquite tree in the yard. Dot and a group of kids ran around the tree playing a game they had made up called "Christmas Tree." Under the tree, the children had piled a stack of rocks and pretended they were presents. The child who played Santa spied an ax the men had been using to cut firewood, fetched it, and presented it as a Christmas present to Dot. As she reached for the ax, the imposter Santa accidently dropped the present on Dot's foot. Fortunately the blade missed her toes, but the gift exchange cut her foot. She ran to her father and declared she did not want Santa to bring anymore presents. Miller looked up at his father with concern. "She will be just fine," John assured him. That was all Miller needed to hear. If his father said it was so, then it was so. Little did any of the children know this would be the last Christmas they'd spend with their father.

two

Tragedy

The fall of 1928 would have a horrific impact on Miller's mental and physical security. Life as Miller knew it took a terrible turn as sadness surrounded his home, an unexpected and unwanted invader. His father, a strong man, had contracted typhoid fever. No one knew what to say or do. On the morning of September 30, 1928, Papa Doc took him to the hospital in Seymour, Texas. No one could eat or sleep. Miller walked outside, lay on the porch with his hands behind his head, stared at the stars and said a prayer. He was a scared little boy.

When Papa Doc returned the next day, he stepped inside the door, took off his hat and lowered his head. John Harrison Moseley died October 1, 1928 at the hospital in Seymour. Miller was only five years old and his father, the man he idolized and counted on, would never return home. The man who was the light of his world had left them. The uncomfortable stillness in the home continued throughout the next day and over the next weeks and months. His mother, busily working through her own grief, never noticed Miller holding his emotion inside. In one brief, catastrophic moment, Miller's world suddenly became unpredictable.

Miller continued to hide his feelings from the world, and without adult intervention to assist him with the expression of fear, loss, sadness, confusion, and uncertainty, he dealt with it by burying everything deep inside.

A few months after John Moseley's death, Papa Doc thought his daughter needed time to grieve and asked her to visit The Rooming House, a local hotel owned by Papa Doc not too far from their farm. Miller, his mother, brother and sister stayed at The Rooming House for a short visit. However, Miller and his brother, Cecil, continued to bottle up their emotions. They were too young to know how to grieve, and no one discussed it. Silence became their way of coping, and silence would eventually define them as they matured.

At The Rooming House there wasn't much to do, so the boys just sat and watched the guests come and go, their chins resting on their fists. That is until a particular guest walked in with a baby in her arms. The baby started crying. As the infant's cries grew louder and more insistent, the woman raised her hand and spanked the child. The baby began to cry so hard it fell silent, as if it couldn't catch its breath. Miller sat up straight as his mother marched over to the lady, took the baby out of her arms and informed her that when she learned not to spank babies she would give her child back to her. Miller's mother must have left an impression on the woman because days later, as they were leaving the hotel to return to Dundee, the woman thanked his mother and gave her a beautiful glass pitcher. But the trip did nothing to erase Miller's loneliness for his father.

By that time, the nation's economy was essentially dead. Countless stories filled the newspapers and air waves about bread lines and soup kitchens. Thousands of desperate industrial workers around the country staged protest marches for jobs. Mothers needed milk for their children. People had forgotten what a dollar bill looked like, and President Franklin Delano Roosevelt raised the price of a stamp to three cents. The school where Miller's mother taught closed and she began working for a family by the name of Ross as their housekeeper, but it would not prove to be a steady source of income.

Miller, then six, stood alone and watched quietly as his family loaded their packed belongings onto a horse drawn wagon. More of his world as he knew it got pulled out from under him. Through it all Miller stood in silence, never complaining and never understanding how to express his feeling of loss and his need for consistency and stability. At that age no child understands how to express fear, grief, and sadness without adult intervention, and in 1928 bereavement assistance for children was non-existent. Miller dealt with the pain with the strength of an adult, the stoic expression on his face hid the hurt and pain. No one knew how afraid he felt.

In early 1929, the Moseley family left their home in Dundee for a new life. As they neared their new house, all Miller could see from the wagon was acres and acres of cotton and grain fields in all directions. They arrived at their new home, a ranch. Leaving his childhood home included leaving behind memories of his father, and to Miller it was as if he was being torn from his father a second time. Papa Doc signed a lease with the ranch owner guaranteeing Miller's mother secure employment. After the first day on the job, his mother laughed as she realized her "secure employment" was cooking for the hired hands, keeping the books and picking cotton. The ranch hands were large, burly men who worked hard. At first they were a bit intimidating to Miller, but he soon got used to them as his mother served everyone lunch every day.

Cecil was too young to attend school, so he stayed behind and helped his mother pick cotton while Miller went. Cecil enjoyed picking cotton beside his mother and he enjoyed his mother's gratitude for his hard work. Mildred pulled Dot around the cotton field on a cotton sack while they worked.

The farm was about five miles outside of Seymour on a country road. Day after day, Miller walked the long journey to Seymour where his school was located. On the first day of school, the teacher gave the students a tour of the restroom. Most had never seen an indoor restroom before, and the children marvelled over it.

One cold day in January of 1929 the temperature dropped below freezing. As Miller walked home from school, he ducked his head, pulled his coat up to his ears and began to push against the wind, but the strong wind pushed back. His ears grew cold and his fingers turned red and numb. "Miller, climb on," someone yelled over the howling wind. Miller slowly raised his head from under his coat and stood up straight. Papa Doc held out his hand. Miller grabbed it and his grandfather pulled him onto the back of his horse. Miller sat behind Papa Doc and wrapped his arms around his waist. The Lone Ranger did not seem as heroic as Papa Doc did that day. Miller hid behind his grandfather, shielded from the blasting wind, and he wished Papa Doc could pick him up every day. That would never happen, though, because Papa Doc had to catch a freight train with accommodations for his horse each time he came to visit.

When the two finally reached the ranch, they found his mother busily cooking for the ranch hands. As they walked in, closed the door against the frigid wind and began to warm themselves over the wood stove, Mildred informed Papa Doc she needed money. She asked him if he would make the trip to Dundee and collect the $5.00 rent from the family staying in her house. Miller held his hands and feet close to the fire as Papa Doc left the house, got back on his horse, and headed to Dundee.

Later that evening he returned and walked briskly through the house, directly to the north room without saying a word. Mildred followed close behind as Papa Doc began bundling firewood. Miller could hear the worried tone in his mother's voice as she asked where the money was. As Papa Doc continued loading the firewood, he told her the renter could not afford the rent and did not have any firewood to keep warm. He left the house again, and as his grandfather rode off to deliver the firewood, Miller heard something outside the window.

He ran and pressed his face to the screen and saw a couple of wild turkeys walking close to the farm house. He knew they had left their eggs unattended. Miller ran as fast as he could to rob their nest, and as he got to it he saw two large eggs sitting in it. He grabbed them both, one in each hand, and he ran home, hoping to make it to the house without breaking an egg or running into the turkeys. He reached the house safely, and without breaking an egg.

After John Moseley died, Miller, now seven, sat on the porch, closed his eyes and tried to remember the thump of his father's footsteps as he walked in the door, or the creak of the rocker on the hardwood floor when he was finally able to sit down for the first time in the evening, or the raucous organ music he played in his entertaining style, or his adoring smile he willingly gave Miller. In Miller's mind, he could see him walking through the dry grass on his way to work early in the morning. But he knew he wasn't there any longer, and he wasn't coming home. The pain became unbearable and he began to wonder if it would ever go away.

One evening, Miller mentioned to his father's brother that he had found his father's birth certificate, and the certificate indicated he had been born in Mobile, Alabama. His uncle turned to look at Miller out of the corner of his eye and laughed. "Well I guess that is close enough," he bellowed. He laughed for a few more minutes while shaking his head in disbelief. Miller never learned where his father was actually born. All he knew was the location was somewhere near Mobile, Alabama, or close enough.

In the late spring of 1929 the weather turned hot. Miller continued to walk to and from school day after day in the blistering sun. Shortly before reaching the ranch, he passed a lady's house with a loose dog that terrified him. As he neared the house his heart pounded harder as he walked past the dog. Every day he contemplated what his chances would be of outsmarting the dog and living to tell the tale. As he passed the house, the large yellow dog would stiffen his front legs, lean back, lower his head, bare large, yellowed teeth, and growl with a low, vicious grumble as if he was ready to attack.

One day, as Miller approached the lady's house, he saw the dog off in the distance, sniffing the ground. The dog slowly lifted his head and looked straight at Miller with a wild, cold stare. Suddenly it bolted toward him, barking viciously. Adrenaline shot through Miller's body as he realized, sickeningly, he was on his own and there was no one who could help. As the dog barreled toward him, head lowered, spit flying, Miller saw an opportunity and took it; the dog had turned his head for a split second, giving Miller time to race through the adjacent corn field. His heart pounded in his ears as he ran as fast as he could. He heard the dog plowing through the corn behind him, but Miller just increased his speed. Just a little further and he would be in the cotton patch where his mother was working. As he burst through the edge of the corn field and flew into the cotton patch, he no longer heard the dog. It had given up! Miller dropped to his knees beside his mother and took a deep breath. The plan had worked. He had beaten the dog. "Miller," she asked. "You okay?"

Miller nodded as his heart beat out of his chest. He stood, brushed the dirt from his knees and walked to the house for a glass of water.

One day soon after winning the race against the neighbor's dog, the County Commissioner, who lived down the road from the ranch, was driving to work when he spied Miller walking to school. He pulled over and gave him a lift. From that day on Miller got up extra early, grabbed his books and lunch and ran to the road as hard and fast as he could, hoping to catch a ride to school. Once he got to the road, he would slow to a melancholy stroll, always looking back over his shoulder to see if the Commissioner was on his way. The Commissioner owned a big, black Ford, and he drove with the windows down on hot days. The wind felt good on Miller's face as they bounced and jerked down the country road to school.

School let out at 2:30 in the afternoon, much too early for the Commissioner to drive by after work, so Miller was on his own for the return trip. Fear of the dog continued to overwhelm his thoughts and each day he either outsmarted or outran the dog as his speed and endurance continued to increase in spite of the dehydration from the long, hot walk. The dog never caught him.

The economy grew worse. On October 29, 1929, the stock market crashed. A public run on banks resulted in a wave of bankruptcies. Cotton prices dropped between five and six cents per pound. Mildred and Cecil had to work even quicker because cotton provided a seasonal income and had to be picked in autumn. Pickers had to work fast and put in long hours to get all the cotton harvested by the deadline, and if that deadline was missed and if the land did not get plowed by a certain time, the soil could become contaminated with cotton weevils. And if it rained before all the cotton was picked, the bolls turned yellow and the value of the cotton would fall even more. Cecil worked hard for a little boy and he picked enough cotton to pay for a new set of clothes for both Miller and himself. They were growing boys and needed a new change of clothes at least once a year.

One warm autumn evening after school, Miller reached his mother in the field as she and Cecil had just finished picking cotton and his mother needed to hurry back to the farm and cook dinner for the hands. She stood up, brushed the dirt from her dress, rested her hands on her hips and stretched her back. She leaned down, lifted Dot off the sack and carried her on her hip. Though Miller had just walked about five miles, he helped take the cotton to the truck to be weighed. He dragged the sacks across a railroad track and up the hill to the truck. Every day a gentleman arrived at the farm like clockwork to settle up with Miller's mother. He weighed the cotton on a scale which sat on the back of his truck and paid her in cash. Before leaving that evening, he looked at Cecil and said, "Did you pick all this cotton by yourself?" Cecil nodded once, before lowering his chin to look at the ground. "Why you're the best cotton picker I have ever seen." Cecil continued to look at the ground without saying a word. "Can I see your hands?" the man asked. Still looking at the ground, Cecil held out his hands. He had worked so hard his fingers were close to bleeding. "Oh my goodness," the man said.

"They don't hurt" Cecil insisted. That evening, they lay on the floor and listened to the radio. Mary Pickford won an Academy Award for best actress in *The Divine Lady*. She had successfully crossed over from a silent movie star into "talkies" and had become the world's first movie star. But these few minutes of rest weren't enough. Mildred Moseley was working non-stop with nothing to show for it. The Great Depression had begun.

The next morning, Miller dressed and walked into the kitchen for breakfast and found the usually busy kitchen empty. He was surprised to find his mother and Papa Doc engaged in a deep conversation on the front porch of the ranch. Their voices floated on the quiet air in a soft whisper. When Miller arrived they quickly stopped talking and turned and wished him a good day. Miller didn't think anything else about it. He was more concerned about making it to the road in time to meet the Commissioner and he ran like Jim Thorpe with his eye on home plate.

three

Shattered

Later that evening, as the sun settled on the western horizon, his mother
told Miller and his siblings to sit on the top step of the front porch. The
fading sunlight lit up his mother's face as she sat down on the step in
front of him. He noticed her nails were stained and cracked from picking
cotton, the back of her neck was blistered from the sun and she had been
crying. She picked up Dot and sat her on her lap, put her arm around
Cecil and looked Miller squarely in the eyes, as if he were an adult. Her
voice was shaky and faint as she explained that she had tried her best, but
it just wasn't good enough. She could not make enough money to provide

for Miller, his brother and his sister. "Tomorrow morning," she said, "I am enrolling you at the Masonic Home, an orphanage in Fort Worth."

This caught Miller off guard. He was just getting settled into this new life. He had done everything asked of him. He had never complained. He had become a master at hiding his frustration, sadness and loneliness. How could this be happening? Was it his fault? Could he have done more? He stood in silence wondering if it was something he did or didn't do. His father had abandoned him, now his mother, grandfather and granny were deserting him as well. As his mother continued, Miller sat with an elbow on one knee, his cheek resting on the palm of his hand.

She had a plan, she assured the children. Mildred intended to go back to school to become a nurse. Once she graduated, she would return for them. *But this is our new life,* Miller thought. He sat there, agonizing over the fear of the unknown. The thought of leaving his mother, grandparents and cousins seemed catastrophic. He bottled his confusion deep inside. Mildred told them the Home had been founded in 1899 and had a sound reputation for providing a haven for widows and orphans of Masons. She said he would never have to worry again. All of his needs would be taken care of, including many opportunities he never would be given living on the ranch.

Miller did not understand how to deal with the terrifying insecurity, or how to even talk about it. His mother was dumping him off to live with a bunch of strangers no one knew anything about. Everything about this situation scared him. Cecil and Dot were too young to realize that this would be more than a short visit. She planned to register Dot at a Masonic Nursing Home in Arlington, Texas, because she was too young for the Masonic Home and School and did not meet regulations.

The Moseley's left the following morning. Miller wasn't prepared for another heartbreaking loss. All he could think about was trying to figure out any reason this was happening. *Why?* he asked himself over and over. He had done everything asked of him.

He felt he was leaving Dundee and the farm forever. They climbed into an acquaintance's car, and when the engine started it sounded different this time. So loud and definite. With the sound of the engine came a sickening feeling of loneliness. Then the car began to roll. Miller jumped to his knees and stared out the back window. He watched the dust build into a big, brown cloud behind them as they drove down the dirt road. The same road he walked every day to school. The dust made it hard to see. But he had to see. He had to see clearly. He had to remember everything. He had to.

As the car rumbled down the road, they passed the house where the vicious dog lived. It was lying on its side in the grass. As the car passed, the dog raised its head and looked at Miller staring out through the rear window. It quickly jumped up and started chasing and barking at the car. Once the dog got close to the cloud of dust, he began to cough and he suddenly stopped. He stood motionless, his eyes fixed on the car like a wolf fixed on its prey. Miller continued to watch the dog until it and the farm were no longer in sight. Everything in his life was about to change. Nothing would be familiar. He was heading into the unknown. Nothing, not one single aspect of his life would ever be the same. He closed his eyes, concentrating, forcing the memories to stay forever in his thoughts. He felt unwanted.

When they reached the halfway point, they stopped to stretch their legs. The back window had become coated with dirt and he could barely see out of it. He slid out of the seat, climbed onto the car's trunk, and began wiping the dirt off the back window with his bare hand, fast and deliberately. He had to see clearly. He had to remember everything. As they got closer and closer to Fort Worth, his heart pounded harder. He kept his eyes fixed out the back window.

As they approached the city, they became lost and were forced to stop and ask directions to the Masonic Home. They continued as directed. Upon arrival, they piled out of the car and walked inside to find it was the wrong Masonic Home. This home was for retired Masons, not young children. But the residents of the retirement home knew exactly where the Moseley's needed to go. As they passed Wichita Street and Poly High School, Miller wondered if that was the school he would be attending and what about vicious dogs?

September 6, 1930, almost two years after the death of John Moseley, Miller entered the gates of the Masonic Home, located in southwest Fort Worth on East Berry Street. Harrison Miller Moseley was eight.

There it was. He could see the Masonic Home down the red brick road as the car turned the corner onto Wichita Street. Two huge wrought iron gate doors guarded the entrance to the Home. To add a welcoming appearance, the fences on either side of the gate had been lavishly embellished with a decorative wrought iron design twisted into a simple pattern similar to the letter S. Miller stuck his head out the window to get a better look. The gate doors stood open as if they were expecting them.

Inside Miller's head, he screamed, *Slow the car down! I'm not ready!* He sank into the seat as far as he could. They slowly turned into the entrance, drove past the gate and rolled down the red brick road, which he would later learn was referred to as "the Pike," to the front of the Masonic Home.

They had arrived.

four

They Had Arrived

From his sunken position in the seat he slowly raised his chin and glanced out the window. Miller had never seen such beautiful buildings before. They were huge, made of red brick with grand entrances and large steps. *This must be what heaven looks like*, he thought as the car came to a stop.

When the car engine died, Miller's curiosity took over. He opened the door and jumped onto the hot pavement with his bare feet. His fear had changed to curiosity. He ran around the car to the other side, stood on his toes so he could see through the rolled down window, pulled at Cecil's arm and insisted he hurry out of the car, and run up the steps with him. Miller's curiosity now burned so intensely he forgot the bottoms of his feet were sizzling. He was both scared and hopeful. He climbed the steps with enthusiastic wonder, finally reaching the large, heavy wooden doors. He pulled them open and the Moseley family entered the vast offices of the Masonic Home.

As his mother began filling out the enrollment paperwork, Miller sat very still and quiet. He was excited yet confused. He felt like a tiny boy who had been dropped off in the wilderness to survive on his own. The first person Miller met was Mr. Fletcher, the superintendent. He walked over to Miller and Cecil and said, "We're awfully glad to have you with us." His warm manner comforted Miller a little bit. "The first thing we'll do is go over to the hospital and let the people over there meet you."

The Home had a private dentist and hospital which was fully equipped with an operating room right on the campus. Miller learned later that Dr. Hall, the staff doctor, had been treating the children at the Home since he had first arrived in 1899 riding in a horse drawn buggy. While Mildred filled out the paperwork, a group of older girls helped entertain Dot. They sat in a circle and rolled a tennis ball back and forth while Dot sat in their laps.

As Miller and Cecil walked toward the campus hospital, Mr. Fletcher laughed and joked so much that Miller thought he was attending a regular get-acquainted exercise rather than a physical checkup. The school had to protect the children and the staff from chickenpox, measles, mumps, and other childhood diseases common to the era. Once Miller and Cecil received a clean bill of health, they continued to follow Mr. Fletcher around the campus. Mr. Fletcher was known for leading a sound, conservative administration which brought the Masonic Home to the top of the list of similar schools. He and his wife worked hand-in-hand and were the father and mother to all the Masonic Home children. They loved every child the same. Mrs. Fletcher was good at comforting the children's fears. She wore a crisply-starched cotton dress regardless of the temperature and lack of air-conditioned buildings. Mr. Fletcher always wore a suit. The Masons took pride in taking excellent care of widows and orphans, and they referred to all the orphans as "Their Jewels."

Miller saw there were kids everywhere. Boys ran around the Home, others tossed a football and others huddled around the radio. Miller noticed that every boy wore the same grayish blue coveralls.

A boy ran up to Miller and asked, "Who are you? Have you ever played football?"

Miller shook his head slowly. No, he had never played football.

The boy handed him a football and said, "You will now."

"And now," said Mr. Fletcher, "we'll go down to the dormitories and find a place for you to stay. You'll like it down there."

If a boy was sitting on the steps or banisters when an adult approached, every boy stood up, and one would run and open the door. If they did not, it would be the last time they forgot.

The huge, red brick buildings continued to amaze Miller. "You see," said Mr. Fletcher, "each building is named for its specific function, such as little girls' building, large boys' building, auditorium, etcetera. No building is named after a specific individual because the Masons are a brotherhood, and everyone is treated equally."

Miller listened to every word Mr. Fletcher said while marveling at the campus. They arrived at the small boys' building and climbed numerous steps which seemed huge for his small size. When they reached the porch, which spanned the length of the building with inviting tables and chairs, they walked inside.

The two-story red brick building was shaped like the letter "H" and contained a large basement. Mr. Fletcher led them down the biggest hallway the boys had ever seen. It ran down the middle of the building, with four dormitories on each wing. Both the first and second floors contained four dormitories each. The dormitory rooms were labeled for use just as the buildings were. The number on the dormitory doors correlated to the boys' grades in school. Dormitory #1 was home to the boys in pre-school through first grade, Dormitory #2 housed the second grade boys, Dormitory #3, third grade, and so forth, with Dormitory #8 for the eighth grade boys. Miller's dormitory room was massive, with 30 beds arranged in four or five rows across the span of the room.

Mr. Fletcher handed Miller and Cecil three pairs of coveralls, two towels, a comb, and two pairs of shoes. The low quarter shoes were their Sunday shoes and the other pair was for everyday use. He also handed them a toothbrush made with a bamboo handle and hog hair bristles, and other essentials. "Put these in your locker and don't leave them out and expect someone else to pick up after you," he instructed the boys. "You are responsible for your own things." Every boy had their own locker in which to keep his personal items. Each locker was about six feet tall and about a foot-and-a-half wide and a foot-and-a-half deep. "Here is your locker and here is a key," Mr. Fletcher continued. "Be careful and hang onto your key, because if you lose it you'll have a hard time getting to your clothes. You can put your coveralls on anytime you want."

Large windows lined the dormitory, each window containing small, square glass panes trimmed with white paint. All stood open in hopes of a small breeze. But there was no breeze. It was a still, stifling hot afternoon.

The Masonic Home seemed wonderful, but nothing in his life seemed to last. Not yet, anyway. Questions overwhelmed Miller. *How long will this last? Where to next? Will they like me?* But Miller asked nothing. That seemed the safest choice.

After Miller stuffed his personal belongings into his locker, Mr. Fletcher led Cecil and him down the hall to Cecil's dormitory and got him acquainted with his room, bed and locker. As they walked to the end of the hall, Mr. Fletcher said with a smile, "This is the lavatory you will use." He pushed open the brown, wooden door, and Miller could not believe his eyes. He had never seen anything like it. The floor was covered with tile arranged in a pattern and it felt cool to his bare feet. There was one large shower with three shower heads that gave five small boys plenty of room to shower together, and a mirror so large it covered the full length of one side of the room.

There seemed no end to the miracles this place offered, and Miller followed Mr. Fletcher in a haze of wonder. Next, the superintendent led the brothers to the swimming pool. Miller marveled as boys splashed and played in the crystal clear water. He had never heard of such a thing. It was so incredibly hot that day and the water looked so cool. He wanted to stick his hot feet into the cool water, but didn't. Mr. Fletcher explained that in previous years, the boys would take off running to swim in the creek at Sycamore Park. The boys felt anxious to get there as often as they could because they feared it would dry up. The Masons worried the boys would get injured playing in the creek, so they funded the cost of a campus swimming pool.

Mr. Fletcher saved the best for last: the print shop. He handed Miller the school newspaper and told him it was called the *Master Builder*. It had great significance to the Home and School because the entire process of putting the newspaper together, from writing the articles to printing the paper, was accomplished by the Home's staff and the students. Everyone at the Home referred to the *Master Builder* as "our paper" because almost everyone out at the Home had done something for it. The articles were written by students of all ages. Some were amusing, others informative.

Hardly a day passed that someone didn't walk up to one of the editors and ask a question about the newspaper. "When does the *Master Builder* come out?" "Is my name in it?" "Do we get the *Master Builder* today?" As they walked into the print shop, Mr. Fletcher told the boys, "This is where it all happens." Miller gasped at the roar of the machines and the hustle of students running from the copy room to the typesetting room. The proofing, typesetting, printing, folding, trimming, assembling, and binding for a completed job was happening before his eyes. He hoped to be a part of this exciting process one day. The room was unbearably hot, but the heat did not seem to bother the boys. "All of this happens in this modern printing plant," Mr. Fletcher told them as he pointed to the paper he had previously handed to Miller.

Miller opened his first *Master Builder,* and on page three the title read, "Our Object for September 30, Beat Bridgeport."

The *Master Builder* was not free. Each student who wanted a copy was required to pay $1.00 a year. "I know, you are probably asking yourself, where can a small child get such a large sum of money? It's easy. After the boys complete their assigned chores, which were assigned during roll call, they can make a fairly nice income picking up various jobs around the campus." Assisting Mr. Dobust, the groundskeeper, with the lawn was one of the available jobs. Any boy interested in helping trim shrubs, trees and gardens could make ten cents an hour. The boys loved driving the mower pulled by Mr. Dobust's horse, Coaly. Coaly also had the job of pulling the milk wagon. Kitchen duties paid 35 cents an hour.

Miller began to feel a little better about his new "home."

"Let's walk back to where your mother has been waiting anxiously for you to return," Mr. Fletcher said. After they arrived back at the office, he assured Mrs. Moseley, that "the success of the Home, at the end of the forty year span, must be determined by the success of those who have been reared in it and have been furnished with its advantages and opportunities. This is the final test of the efficiency of any educational institution. Our experience leads us to conclude that the Home has satisfactorily met this test."

Mr. Fletcher continued, "We hold to the doctrine that the Home, if it is to discharge its obligations to the children committed to its care, must train them so that they may be self-supporting members of society. They must have good habits and sound characters. Never has our country had greater need of soundly educated youth. Our Board of Directors has been liberal in its provisions for well-trained teachers and adequate equipment for carrying out a wholesome educational program. Our per capita cost for care and training may seem high, but we believe that the quality of the product turned out justifies the cost."

He smiled and said, "Mrs. Moseley, why don't you join us as we walk over to the pens?" Miller, Cecil and Mildred followed Mr. Fletcher out of the office building and across the lawn. As they walked, the superintendent continued to describe the Home. "The pens, Mrs. Moseley, is a 'Boys' Town,' a village of huts." He lifted his hand. "To your left is the small boys' building, and located behind the dormitory you can see for yourself, Penville. Every boy," he explained, "reaches a stage where he feels the urge to build something. Out here Penville is the answer. The village belongs to the boys alone. They are given a free hand to build whatever they please from the material they can assemble."

They approached Penville. "During the past year," Mr. Fletcher said, "various national organizations dealing with boys' work have been interested in the progress of the pens, and it is an interesting project. As you can see, Mrs. Moseley, the pens are each unique in size, material and function. Some are no larger than a dog house. One roof is patched with tin, one has screened windows and a padlocked door. One has a little shed to the side, where the boy stores wood to use on a makeshift stove inside. There, the boys have fried eggs and have attempted to make candy out of molasses. The materials were picked up from junk piles formed from individuals who disposed of their trash in the vacant fields west of the Home's property." Miller hung on every word Mr. Fletcher spoke.

"Once in a while a boy will burn his house down," Mr. Fletcher continued, smiling. "But, we don't let that worry us, Mrs. Moseley; they can always build another."

They continued to inspect the shanty town and the superintendent continued to talk. "Oh, it's a fascinating world in Penville. One boy keeps a white rat and ten baby mice at his house. Another has nine chickens in his mansion and has an abundance of eggs. One boy's hut boasts a radio aerial. That boy owns a crystal set inside. There was a boy a few years back that used his house as a roosting place for a covey of pigeons and as I recall, the boy made quite a bit of spending money. The Pens, in many respects, are just as important as reading, arithmetic, typing, printing, and all other studies the school equips its students for a profession."

If Mr. Remmert, the dean of the large boys, ever found anything in a pen that did not belong to that boy, he would burn down the pen. On one such occasion, a fire truck rushed to the home. Firemen jumped off the truck and ran to the sight. Mr. Remmert turned and calmly explained the situation to the firemen. They immediately dropped their equipment and watched it burn to the ground.

When Mr. Fletcher and the Moseleys returned to the office, they found that the girls had fallen in love with Dot and they asked Mr. Fletcher if they could keep her with them in the large girls' dormitory. They promised to take care of her. They begged Mr. Fletcher to let her stay. They were not going to give up. Mr. Fletcher said, "No children that young are allowed to attend school, therefore she is too young to stay at the Home. Those are the rules." But the girls didn't give up. They negotiated and pleaded and finally broke him down. He agreed, and Mildred was relieved to have all of her children together in the same place.

Before leaving, Mildred fell to her knees and gave Dot a hug. As Mildred stood back up, the big girls took Dot by the hand and walked off with her. She then turned to Cecil and said, "After nursing school, I promise." Cecil smiled up at her while squinting in the sun. Then she turned to Miller. "Watch after Dot and Cecil for me. I think you are going to like this place." As one tear rolled from her eye, she hugged Miller goodbye. He watched his mother walk briskly to the car, not wanting her children to see her cry. Miller stood in front of the Home and stared as the car drove away. He remained motionless, a small boy left by his mother in a strange place with strange people. Alone.

five

New Beginning

Boys began running up to Miller with a barrage of questions. "Where did you live before coming to the Home?" a boy asked.

"Dundee, Texas," Miller said.

"Where is Dundee, Texas?" a boy asked with a quizzical look as he leaned his hand on the outside wall.

Miller remembered the answer his Papa Doc gave: "It's a mile and a quarter south of Powder River Bluff where the west begins and the pavement ends." Miller didn't exactly know what that meant, but the boys seemed to be satisfied with the answer.

A boy walked up to Miller, looked him straight in the eye and announced, "You will be called, 'New Kid.'"

"What do you mean?" asked Miller.

"That's what we all call the new kids around here, and you're a new kid. We're the old-timers."

"How long have you been here?" Miller asked.

"Two weeks."

Miller laughed as he shrugged his shoulders.

About this time, Mr. Fletcher and Cecil came walking up. A bell started ringing. Cecil grabbed Miller's hand and Miller looked up at Mr. Fletcher. Mr. Fletcher put his hand on Miller's shoulder, smiled and said, "It's time to eat." They walked into the dining room and boys of every age ran and quickly found their places in line according to age. Mr. Linn, the dining room manager, called out "March!" and the boys began marching into the dining hall.

But the boys could not stop talking, so Mr. Linn made them march back outside and try it again. Miller found his place in line and followed the boys to the table. Once everyone was standing in front of their tables, another bell rang. Everyone immediately pulled out their chairs which caused an eruption of scratching and squealing as chair legs scraped across the tile floor. Two big boys were assigned to each table as table captains, one sitting at each end of the little boys' tables. Their job was to teach the little boys manners, and to make sure they ate everything on their plates. After grace had been said in unison, the table captains began to dish food onto each boy's plate. But a few of the big boys abused their authority: if they knew a little boy did not care for a certain vegetable, they loaded the little boy's plate with that vegetable, knowing if the boy did not eat everything on his plate, he wouldn't get dessert. Boys instantly began trading food. One boy turned as yellow as his squash as the gooey vegetable had apparently stuck in his throat and refused to go down. If a little boy chewed with his mouth open, did not sit up straight or burped, one of the older boys would kick him in the shins or bop him on the head.

Then the boys leaned across the table and the questions started all over again. "How old are you?" "Where are you from?" and the inevitable question: "Say, do you like football?" "Wait till we have 'slimy okrey and spinach.'"

At the end of the meal, every boy bowed his head and said, "We thank you, oh Lord, for the gifts we have just received."

The boys jumped into action. Every boy had a job. One picked up trays, one carried out the knives and forks, one gathered the glasses, another plates. Boys were in the kitchen waiting to wash dishes, others drying them. Dishes for 350 people were washed, dried and stacked in 30 minutes. The boys worked like a machine.

The boys enjoyed every minute of their meals, including their fascinating conversation. However, on the faculty side of the room, their excitement during the meal wasn't as appreciated. The following article appeared in the *Master Builder:*

Co-operation in the Dining Room.

Can you concentrate on what is being said with the hubbub of noise in progress? If so, you have been gifted with such powers as Thomas A. Edison possessed. There are very few people in the world or that have lived, who have been able to fix their minds and concentrate in such a hubbub as we often have to listen to at our own Masonic Home dining room. Every boy that eats in the dining room knows that at the beginning and at the end of each meal he is individually expected to be quiet. Obviously the boys have not yet heard of this, or else it is too complicated for them. Such a bedlam of noise as arises from the Home dining room is equal to that which issues forth from the print shop when all the machines are running. Try to correct this misdemeanor, for at any rate the required period of quiet is only about two out of thirty minutes each meal. I am sure that Mr. Linn will greatly appreciate any co-operation that is directed in quest of absolute quiet at the required time in his vicinity.

Mr. Fletcher walked over to Miller and said, "I know you are going to like this place. In a day or so, after you are enrolled in classes, you will be assigned a job."

Horace McHam, a tall slender boy with a head of thick, wavy hair was standing close and added, "Miller, when you get to high school, you can try out for the job of Milk Slime. Everyone wants that job, but you must try out just as you do for football. I hear it's a pretty tricky process, but the rewards are many."

Don Stephens, a small boy with a square jaw, thick neck and brown hair that laid flat on his head offered, "Everyone wants the position of Milk Slime."

"Yeah," said Horace, "and ten boys get chosen for the Milk Slime team."

"Four cows are yours for two years," said DeWitt Coulter, an unusually large boy who towered over all the others.

"No, they are not your cows," said Horace.

A.P. Torres, a dark-skinned Hispanic boy with a wide, toothy grin piped up. "In a way. Those four cows know who you are."

"One Slime wakes up the other Slimes before he leaves to get the wagon that carries the Slimes to the milk barn," said Woodrow Pittman, an intelligent looking boy gripping a model airplane. Miller had never seen a model airplane before. It fascinated him.

"All the kids think the Milk Slimes job is very important," said Horace. "We like our milk." The boys laughed.

"And at the end of each month the Slime receives a half a cent per gallon," continued Don Stephens. Miller's eyes widened with interest.

"The best part of the job is a Slime gets to move to the large boys' building," Horace McHam said. "Instead of 30 kids to a room, there are only two, unless you have a corner room, then three. You have your very own table."

"And your very own chair," said Don.

"And your own personal closet," said DeWitt. "There is one more significant bonus," DeWitt continued. "When you move to the large boy's building, you are under the authority of Mr. Remmert. That is every boy's dream come true. Mr. Remmert doesn't have any children of his own, but he has us figured out."

"Okay," said Mr. Fletcher. "Enough talk about a job that is far out in the future. We will find a job suitable for you right now."

"Where is the school?" Miller asked. He couldn't wait any longer. He stood quietly, listening and learning about the Home, but no one mentioned where the school was. "Where is the school?" he said again. "It says Home and School, so where is the school?" The fear of vicious dogs filled his every thought. He had seen a couple of schools out the back window of the car on the way to the Home, and he wondered how far the walk would be.

One of the boys pointed to a building and said, "It's right there. You will attend school in the gymnasium through the fourth grade."

"You don't mean it?" Miller said. He could see the building from where he stood.

At that moment, he thought, *Man, this place is going to be something good!* "You mean all I have to do is walk past the dining room and I'm there?"

"Not exactly," said Horace. "If you walk across the porch of the dining room, you will be on the girls' side of the campus and boys are never allowed on the girls' side of the campus." Miller looked around and noticed for the first time that, indeed, the girls resided on one side and the boys were on the other side.

Mr. Fletcher interrupted, "Okay, you are getting ahead of yourself again."

After dinner that night, Miller watched Mr. Fletcher as he supervised the boys leaving the cafeteria. He watched as the man smiled and encouraged the boys as they left. The boys looked up at Mr. Fletcher and smiled or grabbed his hand as they ran out the door to join the others. Miller felt at home. But he didn't dare put his guard down too soon.

As Miller thought about it that evening, the mysterious Masonic meetings on the top floor of Papa Doc's two-story building suddenly made sense. He was standing on the lawn of the Masonic Home and School because of his father. He felt a small part of his father still with him as he began to walk across the campus toward the small boys' dormitory. It felt good and he began to feel this would be the start of something even better.

Miller returned to dormitory four. As they did every night before bedtime, each boy undressed, wrapped his towel around his waist and sat on the small stool by his bed with his toothbrush in-hand, waiting for the matron, Mrs. Gannon, to call their rows up to shower. There were four rows of beds with five beds in each row. The bathroom contained one large shower with three showerheads which was plenty of room for five small boys to wash up at the same time. As one row finished showering, the matron called the next row. The boys stood, walked over to Mrs. Gannon and held their toothbrushes for her to load with toothpaste. They brushed their teeth and showered.

"Hurry up in there!" the matron yelled. "Time's up. It's time for the next row to shower."

As the next line stood, one-by-one receiving their dab of toothpaste, one boy held out a large back brush for Mrs. Gannon to cover with toothpaste. She smiled and he held his toothbrush for paste. Every three to four days each boy received a clean towel.

§

It was 6:30 in the morning and no one had mentioned to Miller that he would be abruptly awakened by the sound of *Reveille*. Miller learned quickly that the boys playing *Reveille* could always be counted on to wake everyone up on schedule with the blasting of their bugles. Miller's heart pounded as he sat up in bed in response to the blast. He'd had a hard time getting to sleep that first night at the Home as he worried about Cecil and Dot, and he hoped they hadn't cried themselves to sleep. Up and down the dorm room boys scrambled out of bed and Miller watched as they started getting ready for breakfast. He tried to mimic the boys' routine. "Hurry, Miller. Make your bed look like new," said Jack Bates. Unbeknownst to Miller at this time, he and Jack Bates would share a historic moment as adults.

"Yeah, no wrinkles," said Horace.

"And get dressed fast," said Norman Strange, a lanky boy with platinum blonde hair and a wide, toothy grin.

"And make sure everything is in your locker," said Buford Hudgins, a small, skinny boy with dark brown hair and a thin face.

Miller changed into his coveralls and made his bed. He quickly stuffed his night clothes into his locker and followed the boys down to the cafeteria. It was just like lunch and dinner the previous day. Boys ran in from every direction, followed by "March!" Chairs screeched on the floor at the sound of the bell and food traded across the table.

Every boy at that table had experienced the loss of at least one parent and had been thrown into a world of uncertainty. They were all scared. Where the boys had come from and the bigger question, how long this situation would last, was a common thread which bonded them into a brotherhood, one they would never forget.

Some cried when they came to the Home. Many remained homesick for a very long time. Others screamed and kicked as they were dropped off, and others would step out of the car, look back and see their mother was already gone. Sometimes the matron (house mother) would try to comfort them, but she was also charged with trying to comfort and look after about nineteen or more other boys. It was a very traumatic experience, and boys generally did not console one another. Once a boy began to settle down and relax another boy would be dropped off and the situation would create a flashback of their own personal nightmare. Miller witnessed this same scenario play out in one fashion or another over the next nine years.

§

Sunday finally arrived. It was the only day of the week the boys were allowed to visit with their sisters. It was also the only day of the week family members were allowed to visit following Sunday school. However, few family members ever visited. Miller and Cecil stood waiting for Dot. As Miller waited he remembered his father and their long walks to church each Sunday. It had been a week since he had seen Dot. She ran down the sidewalk and hugged her brothers. "Miller, Cecil", she said. "I saw mother hiding behind a tree watching me play."

They no longer had the long walk to church. Though the Home did not have a church building per se, they met each Sunday in the school auditorium for Sunday school. Miller had been raised Methodist, which wasn't an issue because every other Sunday a different minister from one of the many churches in Fort Worth came to the Home and delivered a message to the kids. This gave each child an opportunity to hear a sermon from the denomination he or she had been accustomed to. Religious faith was a requirement in the Home and every child was taught that faith was the key to man's inner peace, and that God loved all of his children equally. In addition to the Sunday sermon, the children were taught during devotionals the basic values of a good life: placing a high regard for personal integrity, the needs of others, accepting responsibilities as citizens, and the real meaning of the Brotherhood of Man.

Miller sat in the auditorium each Sunday wearing his nice, new Sunday shoes. Each year shortly before the first day of school, the boys received a brand new pair of high top shoes. They called their low top shoes their "Sunday Shoes" because they seldom wore them anywhere except to church at the Home. Twice a month he watched as a preacher walked in the side door and removed his hat. The room remained quiet. The preacher quietly placed his hat on the rack with one hand while holding his Bible to his chest with the other. He walked up the four steps on the side of the stage and stood behind the podium. Miller could hear the onion skinned pages of the preacher's Bible as he searched for his lesson. The preacher leaned forward, with one hand placed on each side of the podium as if the podium was holding him up. A faint ring encircled his head where his hat had been. He looked up and across the auditorium as if making a mental note of each child in the audience, smiled and began his sermon. From where Miller sat, he looked seven feet tall. When the preacher concluded, he removed a handkerchief from his pocket and wiped his forehead. At the completion of Sunday school, Mr. Fletcher took the stage and gave a little update regarding the various Masonic Home interscholastic teams and individual competitions for the week as well as the outcomes.

When the boys filed out of church, it was quiet and peaceful. Every shop in Fort Worth stayed closed on Sunday so there were very few cars on the roads, creating an unusually peaceful and noiseless atmosphere.

Miller's mother followed through with her promise and applied for nursing school at Fort Worth's Methodist Hospital, now Harris Methodist. However, the Depression forced the nursing school to close. Disappointed, she packed her bags and returned to Dundee, leaving Miller, Cecil and Dot at the Masonic Home.

§

1932 and 1933 were the worst years of the Great Depression and farm prices fell 53%. Mrs. Moseley probably knew at this point that the chances of returning for her children would never happen.

In the fall of 1932, Miller had developed a considerable amount of interest in football and airplanes. He sat watching the first team practice when the sound of footsteps tapping the gravel road that weaved its way behind and around the campus made him turn and look down the road. It was Mildred Moseley. As she continued towards him, he stood up, dusted the dirt and dead grass from his clothes and ran to her. He was just getting used to his new life at the Home, and her first visit was a great comfort. He took her hand as they walked to the football field and watched practice together. She asked, "Miller why are they calling you Lacy?"

"No one calls me Lacy."

"The lady in the office pointed your way and said, 'Your son, Lacy, is on the field.'" At that time both Miller and Lacy Brady were fairly new to the Home. Miller arrived just a few months ahead of Lacy and Tom. But it could have been that Miller and Lacy's mothers looked similar and it was their parents rather than the boys that had confused the office personnel. Mildred watched as Miller sat fixated on this football thing.

Mildred contacted a former girlfriend of John Moseley and informed her that John had died. Up to this point the former girlfriend had never been involved in their lives. Mrs. Moseley probably needed someone who knew her late husband to understand her hardship. Apparently the lady felt her pain and allowed her to stay at her house whenever Mildred came to visit her children. The Home had created a nice, convenient visitation area upstairs in the small boys' building which included meals and sleeping accommodations for children fortunate enough to have a relative stop by during visitation on Sunday. His mother never stayed on campus, however, which disappointed Miller; he never mentioned how much it would mean to him for her to stay there, so she never did. Mildred loaded the kids into the lady's car and took them to her house for the visit. Though disappointed, Miller knew he was fortunate because the rest of the children might receive a visit from a family member once every few years, or maybe never.

six

This is Home

Slowly Miller became accustomed to his new world. One day he was minding his own business when a boy started pushing him around and telling him what to do. Miller stood his ground and refused to do as the boy demanded. Frustrated, the boy started swinging. When he landed a few blows, one to the eye, Miller swung back. Suddenly another boy yelled, "Get out of here! Mr. Leberman is coming!" Miller ran to the back of the building to hide.

"Confound it," Miller said. Instead of parking in front of the building, Mr. Leberman, the Dean of Small Boys, had parked around back in the garage. Miller stood frozen. Mr. Leberman got out of his car and slowly walked over to where Miller stood.

"Miller, what are you doing back here?" he asked. "And what happened to your eye?"

"I was stung by a swarm of bees," Miller replied.

Miller thought the ordeal was over until that night after he had gone to bed. Mr. Leberman called him into his office and laid the belt on him for lying.

On a Friday night in September, 1932, Allie White, a boy who was a few years older than Miller was out of money. Allie desperately wanted to go to a movie. As he sat on a step trying to figure out a quick way to make a dime so that he could go to the Poly Theater, he noticed a group of boys huddled together. He ambled over to the huddle and found they were fascinated with a small snake they had found on the lawn. Then one of the boys said, "I dare someone to bite the snake's head off."

"Yuck!" the boys cried. Suddenly another boy piped up and said he would pay ten cents to the person who would bite off the snake's head. Allie wanted to go to the movies badly and biting off the head of the snake might be his only opportunity. He shoved his way to the center of the group, confirmed the stakes and to the horror of every boy in the group, bit the snake's head off. Allie walked over to the boy and held out his hand for his ten cents. He put the dime in his pocket and walked to the movie. The boys stood motionless looking at the poor headless snake.

Twice a month, on Saturday night, an up-to-date talking picture machine played the latest movie for the small boys. It was one of Miller's favorite nights. The older boys were allowed to leave campus and walk over to the Poly Theater. The gates were left open during the day, so one evening, Bill Mercer and Horace McHam, though not allowed as of yet to walk over to the Poly Theater, decided to leave the campus and go anyway. Miller didn't think it was such a good idea and decided not to go.

The movie consisted of singing, dancing, comedy, and pretty girls. Horace referred to the flick as a "Gold Digger" movie. They enjoyed it so much they decided to sit through the second showing. After the movie finished, they ran back to the Masonic Home as fast as they could. They quietly and carefully opened the large doors and tiptoed through the small boy's building around 11:30 p.m. But the house matron, Mrs. Mitchell, spotted Horace as he snuck in. She kept her door slightly ajar to watch the boys, and quickly informed Mr. Leberman. She worried about the boys as a mother would, and knew anything could have happened to two little boys out on the streets that late. Mr. Leberman walked into Horace's dorm and said, "Horace, come to my office." Mr. Leberman walked with quick, deliberate steps as they headed toward his office. Then he said, "Now, let's go get Bill Mercer."

After they collected Bill Mercer, Mr. Leberman sat down at his desk and looked the boys straight in the eyes. "Where have you been for the past five hours?" he asked. Neither could offer an "acceptable" explanation. "Are you ready to take your medicine?" he asked. The boys looked at each other and then took their medicine, which consisted of six or eight licks from a razor strap. Afterwards, Horace decided next time he would think the matter over very carefully before agreeing to go to the Poly Theater with Bill Mercer, or with anyone else for that matter.

"Of course, the exception to this rule would have been if another 'Gold Digger' film played," said Horace.

§

Christmas Eve, 1932, was Miller, Cecil and Dot's second Christmas at the Home. But it was Tom Brady's first Christmas there. Cecil watched as Tom hung his socks at the foot of his bed for Santa to fill with goodies, as he had done every Christmas before coming to the Home. Cecil wished he had something to put in Tom's socks. Christmas morning, Tom jumped out of bed to see what Santa had stuffed in them. "Well guess what? They were empty!" said Tom. It was at that moment he realized there was no

Santa Claus. He knew he would have discovered that fact sooner or later, so he considered it as good a way to find out as any.

But all was not lost. Christmas at the Masonic Home was not a gathering of the family by fireside and singing Christmas carols around the piano. But there wasn't any moping around either because they had the Oak Cliff Christmas Tree. Every year, the Oak Cliff Masons presented the same Christmas program and the kids would have been greatly disappointed if any part of that program had changed. The night began with Christmas carols followed by the same skit year after year performed by a Dallas businessman who pretended to be a drunken magician. The children knew the jokes, and yelling out the punchline was an anticipated thrill for all of the kids. Then Santa Claus appeared. The Oak Cliff Masonic Lodge members drew names and every child would receive five or six presents. The children watched in anticipation as names were called and presents were opened. The children intently studied every shape of every present held in the air.

If the box was flat, then it most likely contained socks or a tie. But if the box was a small square, then it grabbed the children's attention. They gathered around the recipient to see if it contained a Mickey Mouse watch or a pocket knife. If a child received socks and a tie, he didn't fret because the next morning everyone celebrated around the Home tree. Under the Home tree, the school filled one huge box with clothes and wonderful treasures like footballs, roller skates and other items a boy would hope for. On Christmas morning each boy received a gift from the box under the tree, a gift he was pleased with.

§

Boys lined up to participate in the intramural boxing program. Boxing was one of the most popular of the intramural sports at the Home, and while the boys enjoyed the sport, it also proved to increase the children's coordination, balance and physical stamina.

On Sunday night, July 24, 1933, the boys fought in the championship bouts of the Home's featherweight division boxing tournament. The reward for all this fighting was a trip to the Poly Theater. Mr. Leberman, who judged the bouts, also set up the prize. The lawn next to the small boys' building and the tennis court served as the arena. That night, Miller fought a terrific battle against Toy Crocker for the championship bout for Dormitory 3, but lost the bout. Dormitory 1 was a draw between Charles Templemeyer and Vester Villines. Cecil Moseley won Dormitory 2. Bill Bennett whipped James (Freckles) Holman in a slugging battle for Dormitory 4. Dormitory 5 was postponed because one of the contestants had a broken hand. For Dormitory 6, Don Stephens and Herbert Thornton fought to a draw, and Robert Cook was announced champion over Dorms 7 and 8.

Mr. Fletcher, the Home's superintendent, was so impressed with the results of the boxing tournament that he added a special flavor to the program: he promised additional awards such as movie tickets, steak dinners and special outings to the winners, giving the boxers extra incentive.

On June 1, 1934, Mr. Leberman resigned as Dean of Small Boys. This was a big loss. The boys thought he was exceptionally kind, and he had invented a breakfast cereal sold on the grocery shelves that they thought was very good. Shortly after the dean resigned, Miller and the boys sat in the auditorium waiting to meet their new dean. He was new to Miller and the rest of the boys, but he was not new to the Masonic Home high school football coach, Mr. H.N. "Rusty" Russell.

Mr. Russell, a tall, thin man wearing wire framed glasses, a brown suit coat and matching tie, walked onto the stage with his hat in his hand. A younger man followed him onto the stage. Mr. Russell cleared his throat and began: "Before I came to the Masonic Home, I coached high school sports in Temple, Texas, and while there I coached a very enthusiastic athlete. This athlete excelled in every sport he undertook, and he played above average in all kinds of high school games." Mr. Russell put a hand on the young man's shoulder and said, "That student was Frank Wynne, your new Dean of Small Boys. Mr. Wynne comes to the school with a great background and education from T.C.U., where he received a Bachelor of Arts and a Bachelor of Education in 1932."

Not long after the announcement, Mr. Wynne realized just how much he had bitten off when he accepted the position of Dean of Small Boys. His job was to care for and supervise 145 small boys between the ages of six and fifteen, an overwhelming responsibility for one person.

He was determined to give the boys an opportunity to play all sports and to teach them how to channel their wild energy toward achieving goals in sports rather than running around without any direction. He sacrificed his personal time to improve the current program, which included building an indoor boxing ring and organizing and kicking off an expanded intramural program for the boys that comprised of boxing, wrestling, tumbling, baseball, softball, basketball, and track. He split the boys into teams according to weight in the same manner Mr. Leberman had. This program would result in the development of one of the most memorable football teams in Masonic Home and School history.

seven

Boys

It took years for a boy to feel safe after being dropped off at the Home, to feel he would not be uprooted out of the blue again. But those fears never vanished completely. Every time a new kid was dropped off at the Home and Miller witnessed the hurt and fear in the boy's face and actions, old memories and fears tumbled out of his memory and sank back into his stomach.

If a boy cried, the others never consoled him. They were afraid to. But one way they fought off fear and sadness was to giggle and talk. After the boys were in bed for the night, they usually fell asleep within minutes, but some nights talking, giggling and numerous trips to the restroom would begin to annoy the matron. Her job was to make sure each boy was safe and had plenty of sleep, and to enforce her mission, she would sometimes resort to using the switch.

Bedtime was the worst time for Miller and the boys. As they lay quietly in the dark, fear took control of their thoughts. A boy desperate to stop thinking, to stop remembering, made up innocent shenanigans to shoo the fear away, to occupy and fill his thoughts with something other than real life. On one unsettled night, the boys quietly climbed out of bed and tiptoed to the door. They peeked around the door and saw the house matron was nowhere to be found; the coast was clear. They slowly and quietly walked down the hall to the dorm room next door. Once in the neighboring room, they tiptoed with extra effort, hoping the floor would not creak. It was all they could do to refrain from giggling. As the boys took positions on each side of the beds, they simultaneously lifted the mattresses up in the air with the boys fast asleep on top and dropped the mattresses on the floor. The hapless boys rode their beds all the way to the ground. As soon as all the mattresses thumped to the floor, the pranksters ran back to their own beds as fast as they could, pulled their covers up and pretended to be asleep. In the meantime, the boys who had been rudely awakened with a thud began kicking and screaming. It would not be long before the favor was returned and the pranksters found themselves abruptly awakened and lying on their own mattress on the floor.

§

"Miller, please go to the supply closet and bring me my notebook," the teacher commanded. It was recess, but Miller did as he was told. He ran back to the building as fast as he could. Once inside, he slowly walked down the hall and opened the door to the supply closet. There in front of him was a box of pencils. He froze. At that time, the school was holding a contest: whoever used the least number of pencils won a prize. The teachers were keeping a tally of the number of pencils each child requested.

As he reached for the notebook, the thought of winning the contest was too much. He grabbed a handful of pencils and slipped them into his pocket. On his way back, he buried several pencils in a pile of dirt and kept a few in his pocket. He handed the teacher her book with a wide grin. As she took the book, she asked, "Miller where did you get those pencils in your pocket?" He knew not to say he had found them floating in a bucket. That excuse had been used by another child who had received licks for not only stealing but lying as well. Miller told the teacher that he had found them in a pile of sand. The teacher didn't buy that excuse either and Miller got licks. Miller then told another boy where the other pencils were hidden in the dirt pile and that he could have them. After the boy found them, the teacher asked him where he had gotten his pencils. He said he found them in a pile of sand. He, too, received licks.

§

Mr. Remmert, the Dean of Large Boys, was sitting behind his desk when he looked up to see who was knocking on his office door. "May I speak with you regarding the behavior of the small boys?" Frank Wynne asked. "They seem to have no direction or understanding of rules and consequences when they do not obey adult authority."

Mr. Remmert agreed, and for the rest of the afternoon both deans discussed their concern for the lack of established rules and guidelines for the boys. After several hours they emerged from Mr. Remmert's office with a list of rules to follow, consequences if not followed, and rewards for the boys who obeyed the rules. "Mr. Wynne took pleasure in whipping if someone did something wrong," Miller later reflected. "He would wield that old strap pretty well."

"I do not have time to coordinate games and activities for those who cannot follow the rules," Mr. Wynne later announced to the boys. Constantly running after the few boys who could not follow the rules was not fair to the others who wanted to participate in the planned sporting activities. Wynne expected everyone to participate in as many intramural sports as possible. After Mr. Wynne presented the options and laid down the ground rules, he urged the boys to sign up for their sports. The boys chatted amongst themselves for several minutes, then they walked over to the table Mr. Wynne had set up and signed up for boxing. All 142 of them.

One-by-one they weighed in to ensure fair and accurate tournaments. Boxing was scheduled to begin outside on Monday, but that Sunday, as the fall weather turned cool, it began to rain. Mr. Wynne decided to start boxing inside, that very day, instead of waiting until Monday. He had spent hours setting up a boxing ring in the basement of Dormitory 3 in the southwest corner of the building. Buck Witt and Sanders Jernigan, two employees who worked in the power house, served as referees. A few of the older boys refereed the smaller boys from time to time.

The boxing tournament was a huge success. 142 boys fought a total of 738 bouts. The winner of each division was determined by the most fights won by an individual. The boys had fun while working off extra energy, some of which was due to being healthy boys, but some extra energy was due to their emotions and fears related to their pasts and their futures. Athletics, it turned out, was an excellent tool to release mental and physical energy. The finale was held on the high school stage where the first runner up would box the second runner up.

Miller participated in as many different sports as he could, but no other sport matched the energy he felt when he stood on the football field. In the fall of 1934, Frank Wynne formed the intramural football teams according to weight. He had a 75 pound team, a 90 pound team, a 100 pound team and a 120 pound team. Once Miller discovered the sport of football, he found his passion. He was a natural and hard to catch. When he caught the football, it remained clutched in his nimble hands. Even though the boys did not have a father giving personal advice, instruction, one-on-one practice, or the fundamentals on the rules of the game, they all played well. So Mr. Wynne decided to form and coach a special 85 pound team to play in the city league at Sycamore Park. They named themselves "The Sonics." "We played just about every hour of every day," Miller remembered.

As equally impressive were the girls. The young ladies won ribbons and medals in swimming, typing, shorthand, and tennis as well as other events against the city schools, but the boys rarely kept up with what the girls were doing.

"The purpose of having an intramural program is to keep the students out of trouble and to have them prepared for Rusty Russell when they reach high school," Mr. Wynne announced to the students. Before each game the Sonics walked as a group in their matching coveralls toward Sycamore Park with determination in every step. They were glued together by a sense of purpose, competition, and above all, excitement.

Mr. Russell, the high school football coach, seldom had any extra time to devote to attending the small boys' football games, but he was able to squeeze a couple of practices into his schedule. To the west of the laundry building, Mr. Russell watched quietly as he leaned on the side of the building. He would periodically take his hat off and wipe the sweat with his handkerchief. Miller knew why he was there.

This was Miller's chance to showcase his talent in front of Mr. Russell. The taste for football was now in Miller's blood and it was all he lived for. He ate, drank and slept football. When he wasn't playing it on the field he played it in his mind. With Mr. Russell watching practice, Miller's goal was to impress him enough to one day land a starting position on the Masonic Home football team. But with the insecurity Miller felt despite his confidence on the football field, he kept a protective wall around him by thinking very carefully before he spoke. Because of this, he would miss out on well-deserved events. Unlike a lot of children who might have run up to Mr. Russell yelling, "Pick me! Look at me!" Miller was content and hoped his new life at the Home would remain just like it was.

No one hogged the ball as they demonstrated genuine team spirit. As they walked to Sycamore Park for a practice game, their bare feet tramped on rocks, stickers and small twigs, yet it never seemed to slow them down. The neighbors enjoyed watching the little boys play.

One day Miller noticed Mr. Russell glancing at Mr. Wynne and nodding with a slight smile, as if they knew a secret. Mr. Russell called Miller over with just a look and a nod. Miller immediately ran over to the big boys' coach with wonder, his heart beating. "Miller, how did you acquire such speed?" Mr. Russell asked.

"Running from vicious dogs," Miller replied. Mr. Russell smiled with a nod and Miller ran back to the game where the boys were waiting. But Mr. Russell had very little time to spend with the small boys—in addition to coaching football and teaching, he had taken over as principal of the Masonic School when Mr. McCauley, the school principal, became ill and suddenly left.

§

Tom Posey and his brother Cam were given the duty of keeping up with the small boys and were paid for their efforts. Any time they felt a boy needed correcting, they ran and told Mr. Wynne. The boys called them "squealers."

One day, Tom Posey drove the Home's truck, filled to capacity with boys, to a movie in downtown Fort Worth. The truck was so crowded no one could move. He allowed them time to see a movie and the short comedy or cartoon which followed. After the show, the boys did not return to the truck. Tom walked into the darkened theater and stood with arms crossed waiting for the boys to follow him out, but the boys never knew he was waiting because they were so absorbed in watching the movie for a second time.

Frustrated, Tom cupped his hands and roared, "All right, everybody out! *Now*!"

His voice roared off the walls of the theater, and before the echoes had died, everyone in the house was rushing for the exits. In a matter of seconds the building stood empty. The boys climbed onto the back of the truck while the ushers came running in to find out what had happened. They urged frightened patrons to return to the theater while Tom Posey and the truckload of boys rumbled home.

§

In 1934, Miller entered 8th grade. The 8th grade was a major milestone for all the boys in several ways. Upon entering 8th grade, the boys got to practice with Mr. Russell and the Varsity football team, which was a very exciting year for the boys. Official practice began August 20 each year without fail, and on September 1, 1934, the coaches allowed the boys to put on pads for the first time. Also upon entering 8th grade, it was mandatory that every boy spend two years in the print shop. Upon reaching the 10th grade, each boy could then choose between sticking with printing or learning Gregg Shorthand.

That same year in English literature, each student was assigned a play to perform in front of the class. It was a little difficult to portray a part in a play which a child did not understand. Miller's role involved an individual who had inherited some money and later changed the pronunciation of his name. The teacher explained it was a fairly common practice in those days for an individual who came into wealth to change either the pronunciation or the spelling of their name as a status symbol of "upgrading."

It was now clear. After several years of bewilderment over a conversation which had taken place years ago, Miller finally understood. A friend of Papa Doc's had stopped by one day for a visit. It was a hot summer day and everyone sat around the kitchen table drinking tea and discussing old times. Papa Doc shelled peas while he visited with his friend. His friend looked over at Miller and said, "Miller, I knew your dad when Burk Burnitt pronounced his name Burk Burnett," and everyone laughed. Miller must have looked perplexed as he wondered what was so funny about that statement. They explained that Miller's grandfather had changed the spelling of his name from John Gentry Miller to John Jentry Miller. He never understood why anyone would change the spelling or pronunciation of their name until now.

Frank Wynne set ambitious goals for the boys. He created a reading room and cleverly set up a schedule so each boy had a fair opportunity to read at least two magazines apiece. "My goal is to develop each boy's mind as well as his body," he said. But regardless of the physical and mental activities the school provided, a few boys continued to have difficulty following rules, and when Mr. Wynne swatted a boy with the razor strap, the boy had trouble sitting down for a few days. He was quick to give a boy licks but equally quick to show his appreciation for good behavior with picnics, swimming parties and outings when a group stayed out of trouble.

It was a choice, licks or rewards. Miller liked the Home and the boys and he worked hard to "stay put" for once.

The boys adored Earl Bodiford, the Home's cook, who, in their estimation, was the best cook in the world. The dining room manager, Mr. Linn once told Earl to borrow a ladder and clean the exhaust fan. "I can reach the fan by standing on the potato peeler," replied Earl. Mr. Linn agreed. As Earl cleaned the fan the potato peeler shifted and he immediately grabbed the vent. His left thumb was cut off. Mr. Linn rushed Earl to the home physician, Dr. Hall, and after 52 stitches Earl returned to work. His missing thumb was never found. He later revised cooking utensils to accommodate his missing thumb. Earl invented another unique kitchen gadget that interested the boys. To speed up the pie baking business for 400 children, he cleverly cut a piece of wood into the shape of a pie and drilled numerous nails through the disk. Instead of cutting thousands of steam holes in pie crusts one at a time, he simply pressed the nails into the pie crust.

§

The boys thought Earl made the best comfort food on the planet. One evening around 7 p.m., Tom Brady and four other boys decided to sneak into the dining hall and help themselves to cakes, pies and some of the richest ice cream ever made. They ran across the lawn in their night clothes, giggling with every step. They entered the kitchen through the door on the girl's side of the dining hall because they knew it was left unlocked.

Once inside, they quietly scampered through the dark kitchen and began helping themselves to a feast. Their smorgasbord was suddenly interrupted before they had an opportunity to take a bite of anything when they heard the night watchman, Mr. Hanson, whom the boys had nicknamed "Nighty," prowling around in the dining hall.

Mr. Hanson wasn't a young man. He always wore a hat and always wore glasses. The boys crouched behind the sink room table where they felt safe because the night watchman had come into the dining hall on the opposite end of the room. The boys crouched in absolute quiet, but just as Mr. Hanson turned to leave, Tom Brady accidently kicked a trash can. Mr. Hanson snapped around toward the noise, and Gordy Brown started meowing. "I see you, come out!" Mr. Hanson yelled. The boys took off running back to the small boys' building. They jumped in bed and pulled the covers over their head, hoping against hope Mr. Hanson hadn't pursued them. After an hour the boys breathed easier. The staff never did figure out who was sneaking around in the kitchen that night. "Mr. Remmert blamed the wrong boys," remembered Tom.

Mr. Hanson made the boys feel secure. They knew "Nighty" was outside in the fearful dark of the night guarding them.

eight

Another Tragedy

The boys packed onto the back of the Home truck, standing up so as many as possible could squeeze on. Miller climbed up and stood smashed together with the other boys like pencils in a pencil box. There wasn't room to sit, turn or fall, but it was well worth it. The three-foot sideboards around the bed of the truck held the boys together like a giant rubber band. "When the truck went somewhere it was usually packed full," Miller remembered. That day Mr. Wynne was driving the boys to Lake Worth for a day of fishing, swimming and a picnic as their reward for good behavior. Soon Mr. Wynne, the only adult accompanying the boys, started the engine and guided the fully-loaded truck down the Pike and through the gate. The sun beat down on the boys so intensely that their hair grew hot to the touch, but you would never know it by their laughter.

Mr. Wynne drove the truck over a long, wide bridge with water flowing over the top. When he reached the dam, he thought the water under the falls looked level and peaceful—a nice place for the boys to swim. "We camped at a place called 'Inspiration Point' which is just below a small dam on the East end of Lake Worth," said Jack Bates. "At this point, the water rushed over the rocks and flowed into the North Fork of the Trinity River. The water was swift and churning with white water forming big whirlpools."

After Mr. Wynne parked the truck, boys began to jump off the back and run toward the water. "Stay close to the bank and avoid swimming out further until I find a safe place to swim," he hollered to the boys. After unpacking and setting up camp, Mr. Wynne began grilling the hamburgers. Miller came running up to the picnic area to join him and most of the boys for lunch. Mr. Wynne had just sat down to eat and had taken one bite of his hamburger when he heard boys screaming in distress. A few of them had not followed his direction and had swum out further than instructed. "Once Mr. Wynne had each boy's attention at the table, he spit on his hamburger and said, 'I will be back for it.' But, he never came back for it," Miller said.

The swift current had carried several boys away from the shore and they were trapped in the big whirlpools. No matter how hard the boys tried, they couldn't escape and were being dragged under. Boys held limbs out for the victims to latch onto. One of the boys caught in a whirlpool had gone under twice before Mr. Wynn located him. Mr. Wynne jumped in with his clothes on and swam out to him. The dean gave the boy a big push upward and shoved him out of the whirlpool. Within minutes Miller heard Mr. Wynne yell "Help me Don! Help me!" Don Stephens yelled back, "I need help myself!"

Miller jumped up from the picnic table and ran to the river bank as the tragic scene unfolded. Mr. Wynne had successfully pulled a couple of boys to safety, but was then forced under by the same current. Leo Tiberman, a 13 year old boy, pulled a couple more boys to safety. Miller frantically searched for a pole or long limb to hold out to Mr. Wynne. Boys ran across the bridge from the other side and witnessed the horrific event. Miller continued to search for a pole while others tried to hold limbs they had found for Mr. Wynne to grab onto. But when Miller looked back, he could no longer see Mr. Wynne. The boys were horrified, scared and suddenly alone.

But they didn't give up. They stood, staring at the lake, straining their eyes on the water as the sun glared off the surface, hoping, wishing, praying Mr. Wynne would appear and everything would be all right. They searched for any sign of hope, silent so as to hear the slightest movement in the water.

Miller walked over the bridge and joined the other boys. They were afraid. Some stood, others sat. Sheer panic and nerves swept over every boy. They had been left with no adult supervision. The weight of the world had just been dumped on their small shoulders.

Hours later, help arrived. A group of friends and family stood vigil near the accident scene. They waited and watched, trying not to give up hope, but with every hour that passed without a sign of Mr. Wynne, hope faded that he would ever return home. After two long, hot days of intense searching, authorities found Mr. Wynne's body two miles downriver. On May 28, 1935, Frank Talley Wynne, son of B. T. Wynne, died in Tarrant County at the age of 25. Frank Wynne had planned to get married just days after the accident.

The Masonic Home printed the following in his honor:

There is no more honorable token of love for another human than one who sacrifices their life to preserve another's life. "Greater love has no one than this, than to lay down one's life for his friends." Gospel of John 15:13.

No one remembered how they got home that day. "It took some time to get over it," Miller recalled. Another adult who promised to watch over him was taken away tragically.

"This was a great loss to the Home and to the boys on that trip," said Jack Bates.

Slowly, over the next few months, the boys began to regain normalcy and worked to recapture their hope and faith, immersing themselves in football to squelch the pain. The nights and intense quiet were always the hardest hours to get through.

§

As the boys struggled with yet another powerful loss of another parental figure, a new, strange replacement for Frank Wynne was thrust into their lives. The boys' everyday existence would soon be dramatically altered. Again. The Home environment afforded no opportunity for the young boys to become acclimated with the overwhelming change, nor did they have a voice in the matter. They were expected to accept, obey and get on with it. Otha Tiner, a former T.C.U. football star and graduate, immediately accepted the position of the Dean of Small Boys and picked up where Mr. Wynne had left off. He was much stricter than Frank Wynne, he was ornery and he had a booming voice the boys could easily hear across the practice field. Tiner gave licks with a strip of garden hose for any and all infractions, including unintentional infractions and mistakes. Rusty Russell always seemed to hire young men straight out of college to watch over the boys.

§

One morning the new edition of the *Master Builder* had just hit the newspaper box in the school hallway, and Tom Hurst, who was a year ahead of Miller, had every Home kid laughing and elbowing the student who had been honored with Tom's recollection of how an occurrence had actually, or not so actually, taken place. No one in the Home ever knew if they would make the newspaper's hit list until it was printed, and those who were exposed and reported were good sports about it. They all enjoyed the attention.

Winchellisms
by Tommye Hurst

Red Norman was pruning a tree from a tip top branch. In his excitement, he sawed off the very branch upon which he was sitting and fell headlong onto the ground. He still thinks someone pushed him out.

Miller Moseley asked, "On what day do we have Christmas Dinner?" I imagine Moseley has found that we eat it on Christmas Day.

J.W. Stephens devised an ingenious method of making his money go a long way. He hadn't enough money to buy each of his folks an expensive present, so he bought a lot of cheap stuff. He then took some tags off expensive articles in a jewelry store and pinned them on his presents.

Truman Graham has just finished the book, "How to be Charming."

It is reported that a certain T.C.U. student sat in the Chapel and listened to the preacher say. "Verily, verily, I say unto you." Finally after the preacher had repeated this several times, the student could hold his curiosity no longer, "Who is this guy, Verily, anyhow?"

Holy Smith still believes that hypotenuse is a disease. Holy, if you can read, look it up in the dictionary.

J.W. Stephens recently received a post card from a relative of his. This showed a famous cliff from which the early Greeks threw their mentally defective children. On the back the writing disclosed this coincidence: "This is a famous cliff from which the mentally defective children were thrown. Wish you were here."

Billy Pickens is still trying to get into the Palace Theatre for ten cents. His recent failures have discouraged him, and he proposes to walk up to the girl at the ticket booth on his knees, so as to look smaller and younger. Somebody had better tell him to shave first.

Miller Moseley once sent off for a free sample of hair oil. Upon receipt of his sample, however, he found to his dismay he had filled out the wrong side of the coupon which he had taken from a popular magazine. His free sample was a box of gall bladder pills, which Miller readily gobbled down, "to get his money's worth."

Soon it was time for study hall and the boys shuffled inside.

§

It was a quiet Sunday afternoon in July and Armando Torres and Oliver Peoples sat under a shade tree just outside the hospital building entrance, enjoying a cool breeze. As they sat, passing the time, they observed Dinky Hopkins and Rex Bozarth exiting the clinic with an apple and an orange.

"Hey, how did you guys get the fruit?" yelled Armando.

Rex and Dinky walked over to where they were sitting under the tree and joined them. "I cut my foot and had gone to the clinic," Rex said. "Mrs. Huntly bandaged it and gave us the fruit."

Oliver and Armando suddenly got a brilliant idea. "Hey, Oliver," said

Armondo. "Let me cut the bottom of your foot so that we can go over to the clinic and get some fruit." Oliver agreed and Armando sliced open the bottom of his foot with a pocket knife.

They ran to the hospital and Mrs. Huntly, the nurse, quickly patched Oliver's foot and sent them on their way. As they walked toward the door, Oliver asked, "Can we have our fruit, please?"

"What fruit?" asked Mrs. Huntly.

"You gave an apple and orange to Rex and Dinky."

"Oliver, did you cut your foot on purpose just to get an apple and orange?"

"No, ma'am," replied Oliver. "Mondo Torres cut it."

Armondo and Oliver spent the night in the ward wearing hospital gowns, and went without supper and without any fruit.

§

Not often, but occasionally, a quarrel between two boys erupted. They lived like brothers, felt like brothers and sometime fought like brothers. Miller and a large group of boys watched as two of them tussled, swung at each other, grabbed each other's coveralls, and gasped. One of the spectators shouted, "The teacher is coming!" The teacher pushed his way into the circle and pulled the boys apart.

"Okay! Break it up," the teacher commanded. "What is the problem?"

Both boys scrambled to tell their side of the story, and the truth finally spilled out: each felt deserving of the same and only piece of gum.

"Calm down and finish your dinner," advised the teacher, who then returned to his seat. The boys complied.

After dinner, the teacher marched the boys down to the back of the school behind the black oil furnace.

"Okay. You two want to fight? Go at it, but fight fair," the teacher commanded. The boys had to fight. When the boys had had enough, they each took half of the piece of gum and walked off as if the disagreement had never occurred.

§

"DeWitt! Stop it! Wake up!" Miller demanded.

Each child at the Home dealt with the feeling of desertion or overcoming a horrific event in different ways. Miller kept everything bottled up inside and developed into a boy of constant thoughts but few words. DeWitt Coulter, on the other hand, had not found a way to deal with his pain and was having a hard time working through his anxiety. Through the years, the dean became frustrated because no one could break DeWitt's habit of sleepwalking and losing his way to the restroom. Their only solution was to create special sleeping arrangements until he could work through his pain. They found an area on the balcony of the small boys' building and fenced it in for his protection. The Home staff set a bed out on the balcony to protect DeWitt and confine any accidents outside.

But as the weather turned cooler, the administration could not leave DeWitt out in the elements, so they moved him back inside the small boy's building and placed his bed right beside Miller's. It was DeWitt's first night back inside and Miller woke up horrified to find DeWitt standing next to his bed peeing on Miller. Miller instantly jumped out of bed, woke DeWitt up and got him to stop. "DeWitt never did it again," remembered Miller. Throughout their stay at the Home each child helped the others through their unique struggles with an empathy that only they could understand. A friend is a person you do not have to explain anything to.

§

Sitting in alphabetical order was an advantage for Horace McHam. It gave him easy access to Miller's homework. Miller allowed Horace to copy his homework in General Science class and Horace always made a better grade since Miller always made the honor role. But the seating arrangement did not thrill Katy Opperman. She was annoyed because DeWitt Coulter's huge, bare feet were under her desk. The boys sat on one side of the classroom or behind the girls in class.

The teachers devised an incentive plan. If a student made the honor role, he or she did not have to attend the two hour study hall until after report cards were issued. Miller always made the honor role and listened to great radio shows, such as "Gangbusters," "The Shadow", "The Green Hornet", and the all-American pastime, baseball. Lou Gehrig led in home runs and came in second on runs batted in. By the time study hall ended, the only radio programs were "The Lone Ranger" or "Jack Armstrong the All-American Boy." Listening to the late show was not an option either as lights went out at 10:00 p.m. sharp.

§

Anyone passing the Home truck as it made its way downtown with a truckload of 9th grade boys standing shoulder-to-shoulder in the back would stare with curiosity. Miller was on his way downtown to Washer Brothers Clothing Store, an old-line Fort Worth store, to pick out a nice dress suit—every boy who reached the 9th grade received his first dress suit. As the boys jumped off the back of the truck and herded into the department store in such a time of economic distress, the salesman smiled from ear to ear.

§

It was a little after 8:00 in the morning and several boys rushed to the supply room. They only had a few minutes between breakfast and school to load up on any needed provisions. There were two supply rooms. The supply room in the small boys' building was stocked with toothpaste, toothbrushes, shoe strings, and other basic supplies. In the supply room in the large boys' building, Mr. Remmert kept enough new shoes, underwear, socks, and other personal items for all the boys at the Home. Mr. Remmert worked the supply room in the large boy's building and hired a senior boy to work the supply room in the small boys' building.

§

Early each morning one boy, a Milk Slime, walked the gravel road. The Home assigned one Slime the job of rising 30 minutes earlier than the rest of the Slimes. He was required to walk the gravel road from the large boys' building to the barns, hook the horse to the wagon and return for the rest of the milkers. After the Milk Slimes had climbed onto the wagon, the boys began to wake up, talk and laugh as they rode to the barn. After the boys had washed, fed and milked the cows, then loaded the milk onto the horse drawn wagon, the same Slime delivered the milk to the dairy while the rest of the Milk Slimes walked back to their building.

Once or twice a month, a different Slime would accompany Mr. Remmert to the milk parlor to reduce the growing population of rats. Mr. Remmert and the Slime would quietly enter the building while the rats feasted on the sweet feed. The boy would flip on the lights, which was immediately followed by three or four shots from Remmert's pistol. He never missed. The boy took the dead rats to Tiger the cat for a hearty meal.

nine

Profession

In 1937, at a meeting of the Board of Directors of the Masonic Home and School, Mr. Fletcher, the superintendent, stated, "I want every child who leaves the Home equipped with the necessary training to earn an honest living in the business world with or without further education from a University. There were numerous trade options deliberately put in place to insure each child finds one of interest. I want to know every child is gainfully employed when they leave the Home. Times are hard. Citizens can't find work. Millions of people are without work due to the Great Depression and dependent upon national, state or local governments.

Government programs such as the **Works Progress Administration,** the New Deal agency, created employment for millions of unemployed unskilled men and women to carry out public works projects, such as bricking roads and constructing public buildings. However, it is important that every child be able to obtain a living without dependence upon anyone but themselves."

In August of 1937, as Miller prepared to enter eleventh grade, he chose the Printing Press as his vocation. He knew the distribution of knowledge was vital to the world and it was a guaranteed, safe profession. Excitement lit up his face and his demeanor as he counted down the days to the first day of printing class.

The Masonic Home owned a state-of-the-art printing shop. The boys knew that by the time they graduated, they would be able to step into one of the world's top industries at that time. Everything had to be perfect before going to the pressroom and ultimately to the end customer. The work was tedious, fingers were burned, hands were almost smashed, paper was wasted, and the heat in the metal room was intense, but the boys learned together and developed a stick-to-it attitude. With each other's help, they knew they would be able to walk out of the Masonic Home and straight into the printing industry as a skilled printer. Miller rose to the occasion as the secretary of the Masonic Home graphic arts club and school reporter. They printed all of the Masonic literature and publications for every lodge in the State of Texas as well as outside customers, a large task for a group of boys with numerous school activities. No one complained.

§

Teachers and other staff members at the Home encouraged the children to write and submit articles for the school's newspaper. Miller was thrilled when Cecil's report came out in the September 1937 edition. Miller congratulated Cecil as he slapped him on the shoulder for his article in the *Master Builder*. Cecil beamed. He could not believe it, though he had earned it.

Robbing the Hogs

Cecil Moseley

About a week ago John Mayo was hauling garbage. One of the cans was full of old stale peanuts. Pete got two tow sacks full of them and took them back to the building. He gave about everybody in the building all they could eat. After we had eaten them, Pete told us where they came from. They tasted good until we found out where they came from. Pete has not come out of his hiding place since that day.

The Boaster takes a Bow

Miller Moseley

When the rodeo came to Cow Creek it caused much excitement. It was the talk of the town. The boys talked about it at school, the women only hinted, asking their husbands, "Have you heard that the rodeo is in town?" and the men talked about it at their hangouts. It was in one of these hangouts that Bill Bradford, the man who could out boast anyone in town, spent most of his spare time. When I said he could out boast anyone in town, I only told briefly the truth. It seems as though Bill had spent about the first ten years of his life in one of the western states and this was his main topic of conversation. He told of the time he saved his dad's whole herd of cattle by putting out a forest fire with a tow sack. He told of the time when he had ridden a horse at full speed for five miles to get to the post office ahead of the train. He told of the time when he was a ten-year-old, rode and tamed a horse that had thrown the best of riders. As has been related, the rodeo caused much excitement, and more excitement was shown at this hangout than at any other place in town. The men had just gathered around and started their daily session when Biff Littinghorn noticed one of the rodeo trucks outside. He remarked; "Bill seeing that you are well versed in the knowledge of the West, just why don't you join the rodeo and show us some good riding." "Well," returned Bill, "I've never given the matter a thought, but you don't think for a minute that I couldn't show those cowboys up. Did I ever tell you of the time I rode _____." "Never mind, " cut in Biff, not wishing to hear of how he had probably ridden in and shown up a trick cowboy when he was in the middle of his act. "I just wanted to make a bet with you. I'll bet you two dollars that you can't stay on a bucking horse for one minute." "Say, listen here, Biff, are you insinuating that I ___." "No, I'm just saying," Bill cut him off. "Well, er__, er __, I'll ___ I'll___ I'll take that bet," burst out Bill. So, to settle the argument, they agreed to go to the rodeo. Bill finding himself in a jam, was thinking fast, "Why did I take that bet? Why couldn't I have told him I was going someplace? Why couldn't I have kept my mouth shut?" It was in this state that a thought struck Bill. He had met a cowboy the day before and struck up a speaking acquaintance. Here was a chance to take advantage of it. Telling Biff that he had to telephone his wife, he went to a telephone, but instead of telephoning his wife, he called the number of rodeo headquarters and asked for Skeeter. He said, "Listen, Skeeter, this is Bill, the man you met yesterday at Sander's grocery. Well, look here, in about thirty minutes I'm going to come up to you at the main entrance gates and ask you to lend me a bucking horse and you point out a tame one, see?" "Yeah, but why?" came over the line. "Never mind why, just do it and you'll profit by it." "O.K.," answered Skeeter perplexedly. The timing was right. Skeeter and Bill and the boys met at the gate. After going through the preliminaries which Bill had outlined, they were shown a "wild" horse. Bill, turning and smiling, said "Well, Biff, get out your two dollars." He then started for the horse. Grasping the reins in one hand he put one foot in the stirrup. At the same time two horse hoofs caught him and sent him ten feet high and twenty feet down the lot. He landed on his side and momentarily lost his senses. When he had come to his senses and paid off his wager he turned to Skeeter, roaring. "A fine friend you turned out to be! As soon as I touched that horse he started bucking like a cyclone. I thought I told you to show me a tame horse." "Wal, Podner," drawled Skeeter, "he is a tame horse. Wouldn't have kicked ye' either if you'd of had sense enough to get up on the other side."

Miller preferred presswork to the many branches of the printing trade, and he planned to spend enough time in the pressroom upon graduation to work his way through college. It was a challenging and fast-paced job, and learning this skill made entering the outside world a little less scary for him.

It came without saying: the boys worked as a tight-knit team to consistently produce a quality newspaper, but not at the expense of losing one member of their team. If a boy had difficulty, the others would step in until the task became easy for the ones who were unsure. It came naturally and with no hesitation. They would never allow even one of their brothers to feel unworthy nor risk the chance he might be uprooted to another field of study. As a team they grew confident in the printing trade.

The Master Builder was a major link between fellow students and it provided a listing of upcoming events, as well as coverage of past events. The students remained the focal point of the newspaper, and humor at the expense of a fellow student painted a somewhat true picture of an event.

Master Builder

No title

Eugene Smith's many recent disappearances from public sight were finally accounted for. Late one evening he was discovered listening to the lovelorn radio programs. He pretended that he had fallen asleep while listening to some other program, but we know better. Who is she, Holy?

Red Norman took a cute brunette girl out to a dance while on his vacation. After the dance was over and he was ready to take her home, she gave him her number upon his request. Red phoned her number only to find that he had been duped, for the only thing he could hear as he stood dumbfounded at the booth was "Police Department."

Ed Cotton and Steve Belt were recently caught at the creek in a pecan tree. The excuse they offered is a new one and a novel one, indeed. Ed Cotton said, "We weren't thrashing, we were just pickin' 'em."

You should see Eugene McKelvey's toiletry haven when he prepares himself for his weekly journey to the Poly Theatre. He has a line of toilet articles as continuous as the long shelf under the mirror in the bathroom. He has more bottles lined up here than King Solomon had wives. He gargles his throat, cleans and polishes his fingernails, puts Jergen's Lotion on his face, spreads Italian Balm on his hands, sprinkles perfume on his clothes, and finally combs his hair, after putting enough lard on it to cook several bowls of hominy. He is now ready for his journey and business at the Poly Theatre.

Maybe you have often wondered why Eugene Smith acquired the old nickname that has stuck to him for some twelve years. Well, your reporter has brought it to light. When but a small tot, Eugene visited the creek. While gazing into the water, Eugene said something that was to mark him in the history of the Masonic Home. "Watch me make this water Holy," whereupon he spit in the water.

That year, 1938, the kids enjoyed songs such as *Nice Work If You Can Get It* sung by Fred Astaire, *Jeepers Creepers* sung by Louis Armstrong in the film *Going Places* which starred Ronald Reagan, Dick Powell and Anita Louise, and *Whistle While You Work* featured in Walt Disney's first full length cartoon *Snow White and the Seven Dwarfs*.

It was August, 1938. Several years had passed since Miller had seen Papa Doc's farm in Dundee. For children fortunate enough to have family to visit, they could return to their point of origin for two specific weeks out of the year. As Miller walked up the dirt road toward the old farmhouse, it looked smaller than he remembered, but just as well-kept. He sat in the shade of the porch as he had done years earlier as a small child. He did not have a chance to sit long before Papa Doc and Miller's cousin, Bud, needed help storing hay. It had been a really good year and there was more hay than they could find storage for. Papa Doc said, "Bud take the extra hay to the old place." Miller had no idea where this place was, but rode along with Bud.

His cousin opened the door to a small, simple, house. It was completely empty, and as they walked across the wood floor, the house sounded hollow, echoing their footsteps. "Okay, Miller," Bud said. "Papa Doc said to store the hay in here." They worked hard, stacking every room with hay from floor to ceiling. As they threw bales, Bud said, "Miller, did you know this is the house you were born in?"

"No, I did not know that," Miller replied as he looked at the house with greater interest. He had remembered his father playing the organ and tried to picture where the organ sat. He stood in the doorway and looked out across the grounds where his father had caught the skunk. Miller laughed, "He sure stunk." Bud looked at him, puzzled.

As they pushed the last of the hay from Bud's truck into the house, it barely fit through the door. It was hard work, but the weather was unusually cool for August, which helped. They stood back on the porch and looked in the door; all they could see was golden hay piled from floor to ceiling. The tricky part was getting the door closed. As the two pushed with all their strength to shut the door, Bud added, "As a matter of fact, this is the very room you were born in."

Miller laughed, "I was born in the manger because there was no room in the inn."

Snap. The door closed. Bud locked it and they walked off. Miller noticed a lonely mesquite tree off in the distance and his heart felt heavy. "Come on, Miller," Bud called. "They are waiting dinner on us."

A few days later, Miller, Cecil and Dot returned to the Home. Most of the Home kids did not have a family member to visit and had stayed behind. They were eager to hear the details from Miller's visit. But those like Miller who were lucky enough to have relatives to visit had a tough readjustment period upon return. It took several years for the kids to adjust to the pangs of homesickness after returning to the Home from visiting family.

In 1938 Miller turned seventeen and was old enough to attend movies off-campus. The Poly Theater played movies which were 60 days behind the theater in downtown Fort Worth, but the boys didn't mind; they could easily walk to the Poly Theater from the Home as well as afford it. It was about a four mile walk, not counting the long walk down the Pike. The boys created a shortcut through a long row of hedges that lined the Pike from both boys' buildings, but it was still a long walk. And Miller never missed a chance to catch a movie.

In the early 1930's, Mr. Archibald, the theater owner, offered to let the Home kids into the theater for free, but Mr. Fletcher flatly refused. He wanted to instill the value of saving money and the virtue of self respect. But Mr. Fletcher did allow a price reduction. When Miller stepped up to the ticket window, he said, "One Masonic Home" and was charged a nickel. Mr. Archibald and his wife ran the theater, and when he saw a

Home boy sitting on the back row kissing some Poly girl, he reported the incident to Mr. Remmert, the dean of the large boys.

On days Mr. Remmert knew the boys planned to see a movie, he warned them, "Now that roll call is over, I do not want to hear that any of you were kissing those Poly girls."

On their way back from the movie, they passed an old tavern directly across the street from the Home. A few of the boys thought it would be funny to turn the saddle around backwards on a drunk's mule. The boys watched from a safe distance as the drunk tried to use the mule's tail as a bridle. The mule went wild for a couple of minutes, then, as if the mule knew the drunk was out of his mind, walked off toward the drunk's home.

A day or two later, the boys decided to walk down to a pond. Since it was such a hot day, they decided to go skinny dipping. When they were ready to walk back to the home, they panicked. Their clothes were gone. They had been stolen. One boy offered to walk back to the home and bring back clothes. As he ducked from a bush to behind a tree and darted across the street, he spied the clothes wadded up on the street where the drunk had dropped them. The drunk had won. They never found any interest in messing with his mule after that.

§

Miller's brother, Cecil, was given the nickname "Mo" by his friends. An older boy called him "Crazy" because he was so quiet. But his friends knew Cecil was smart like his brother, Miller.

Miller's bestowed name was "Dundee Moseley," or simply "Moseley" by his fellow Sonics. Mr. Remmert called him Socrates.

"All the Moseleys were intelligent," remembered Richard Opperman. Most of the boys were bequeathed their nicknames, like them or not. Richard Opperman was Little Dick, and his older brother was Big Dick. Shorty, Stinky, and Buster were others. One kid went by the name of

Skinny Well-Fed. One day a postcard he intended to be sent directly to his mother had been intercepted by a fellow student and read aloud to the other boys. "Dear Mother," the boy had written. "I came to the Home skinny and now I'm well-fed." Skinny Well-Fed's last name was Allen, and his other nickname was Fats Allen.

A couple of boys nicknamed themselves. Hardy Brown never wanted the kids to address him by his legal name, so he called himself Gordy. John Mayo named himself AZP because he thought Arizona was two separate names: Ari Zona. He tacked on "Pete," thus AZP. AZP was particularly proud of his nickname, and carved his initials all over campus, including into the huge concrete sides to the steps at the entrance to the building.

The boys would agree to any name except one. They did not appreciate the moniker "orphan." The newspapers and neighbors would refer to them as orphans. "The Masonic Home wasn't an orphanage to us, it was our home," clarified Miller. "We were brothers."

§

The neighbors living near the Home loved the boys. One couple invited them over regularly to pick cherries. "We laughed so hard," recalled one neighbor. "We enjoyed watching the boys crawl on their hands and knees into our yard with their rumps sticking up in the air." The couple watched as the boys stuffed their pockets full of plums from trees growing in their yard and run off as fast as they could after loading up. The boys thought they were really clever. "One day, we had to wipe the tears from our eyes we were laughing so hard as we watched a boy sneak into the backyard. He stole a few of our eggs, then walked around to our front door, knocked on the door and sold us our own eggs." The couple was thoroughly entertained, and it was hard not to giggle while they paid the boy.

The faculty, in many instances, had to teach lessons beyond the classroom, lessons most people learn at home while growing up. Because there were so many children, it was sometimes easier to post a lesson in the school paper and hope as many children as possible would read and grasp it.

Stop Wasting

Writer unknown

Have you ever stopped to think how much you waste each year? Just because you get everything free that is no reason why you should use more than the minimum of anything. If you see a little hole in your trousers, do not tear them up just to get a new pair. When you graduate and leave this Home you will have to buy your own clothes. Nobody is going to look after you and supply you with all the clothes you need.

Learn to save now so that you will be fully equipped to take care of yourself later in life. The boys that go out of here to go to college do not waste their clothes. They cannot afford to because they need all the money that they can possibly get to complete their education.

Let's see if we can stop wasting and we will receive more enjoyment both now and in the future.

But the kids preferred humor.

Will burying a black cat in a graveyard at midnight do away with warts?
Yes, if the warts are on the cat.

It is better to look for a white spot on the soul of a sinner than to search for a black spot on the soul of a saint.

There are lots of people who would be millionaires but the alarm clock went off.

Ben: "Where ye goin', Bill?"
Bill: "I'm goin' to see a doctor, I don't like the looks o' my wife."
Ben: "I'll come wi' ye. I don't like the looks o' mine, either."

Do not take life too seriously. You will never get out of it alive.

PART II

ten

First Practice

"We always called Mr. Russell, 'Mister,' never 'Coach,'" recalled Miller. "The only people that called him Coach were the sports-writers. We would have done anything for that man."

H.N. "Rusty" Russell was the Masonic Home and School high school football coach. It was a miracle that landed him at the Home. Years earlier, Russell had made a plea to God, "Please restore my eyesight and I will give my life to helping others and make a difference in a child's life." That was his prayer as he lay in the infirmary with no hope for the recovery of his eyesight. During World War I, Russell was injured during a gassing incident and the trauma had left him blind. He was given little to no chance of ever regaining his sight.

Over the course of his stay in the infirmary, scared and alone, he continued to pray. To the amazement of many, his eyesight began to improve in one eye. He gradually gained enough sight in that one eye to live a quality life. In 1927, determined to live out his commitment, Mr. Russell accepted the position as football coach at the Masonic Home and School and the Masons began playing football. He followed through with his promise to God and gave a bunch of fatherless boys hope and something very few other boys would ever have a chance at: being a participant in an unbelievable football program.

It was 1938, Miller's senior year and his last year at the Home. He had earned the opportunity to stand on the Mason practice field with the 1938 Masonic Home Football team. The first day of practice had finally arrived. Nowhere else in life would Miller rather be than right there, right now. Mr. Russell stood on the practice field beside his assistant, Otha Tiner, as the boys walked onto the turf without saying a word. The boys studied Mr. Russell as they slowly formed a circle around him, thirsty to learn, thirsty to play football, thirsty above all to make this father figure proud of them.

They saw hope in his eyes. This would be the smallest team in terms of weight and height Rusty Russell had ever coached. Yet he appeared confident as he looked into the eyes of each and every boy as they formed the circle around him, eager to hear his instructions. He had watched them work all summer to get the practice field in good shape. Now, not only was the field in good shape, but so were they. For the first time in their lives they expected to win, and the man who would help them win was standing in the middle of them. They studied him from every angle. They knew this man was not going anywhere. He would stick by them. He would be on their side. Mr. Russell's football record as coach at the Masonic Home was stellar. But his past teams consisted of large, strapping boys. This team was a whole new ball game in terms of weight. But with

Rusty Russell as their coach, size did not factor into the big picture. They expected to win. And that was big.

During the summer, the Masons had worked in the orchard, in the garden and with the farm animals. They were in magnificent physical condition from their chores. Russell immediately put them to work focusing on plays while coaches at other schools were forced to spend valuable time working to get the kids back into shape after summer break.

Mr. Russell could have thrown his hands up in the air and walked away from the team because of its small size. He could have thought of a handful of excuses why this team couldn't or shouldn't play football. But instead of giving up on them, he kept his promise to God to make a difference in a child's life, and if any group of boys needed and deserved a break, it was this group; he was determined to keep his promise. There they stood, a group of fatherless boys looking up at him, hardly blinking, waiting. Russell must have felt a twinge of stress as he looked into each boy's face. They were depending on him. They had faith in him. There was not a hint of doubt on any face. This was the moment they had dreamed of since they were little boys playing at Sycamore Park.

Russell put his pen to paper, and through God's continued grace, invented plays that would complement each boy's talent and strengths. Each year, the Masonic Home had to be voted into the league by the Fort Worth Independent School District for approval to play, and every year the school district agreed. 1938 was no exception. To complement the team's small size, Mr. Russell cooked up the most imaginative plays, plays never seen before, and he hand-tailored the play sheet specifically for the Masonic Home Masons, or MHM.

Miller was small compared to most regulars on the Fort Worth and Dallas area high school football teams. His weight ranged between 126 and 132. 128 would be his steady weight. In fact, the entire Masonic Home team was smaller than any other team in Dallas/Fort Worth area.

The first day of football training was the most anticipated, appreciated and exciting day of the year. Behind the red brick Masonic Home buildings, on a nice green practice field successfully cultivated all summer by the boys, the tough little Masons practiced. Twice a day in 100 degree or hotter temperatures, they practiced. They were accustomed to the heat.

When Mr. Russell first arrived at the Home, a practice field existed in principal, but not in reality. He indeed found a strip of land with goal posts at each end, but the land was in such bad shape he had to renovate it from the ground up. The field was either muddy when it rained, or so hard when the weather was dry that the players were injured when they hit the ground. It was so painful to play on such hard dirt the boys would rather play in the cow pasture covered in stinging nettles than on the practice field. After years of trial and error, Mr. Russell, with extensive help from the Home and from the boys themselves, managed to coax a respectable practice field out of the reluctant North Texas soil.

Mr. Russell was not only clever on the gridiron, but in the classroom as well. In an attempt to provide labor for the renovation while simultaneously creating an efficient system of maintaining good conduct in his classes and study halls, Mr. Russell devised a plan to take care of both concerns: he would sentence a boy to an hour's work on the football field if caught talking without permission or misbehaving. But there were many students who happily volunteered their labor without having gotten into trouble.

The football team took care of the practice field. When the field was not in constant use, two boys were given ten-yard strips to take care of as a team. David Pillans and Miller worked as a team and their responsibilities were to mow, pull weeds, fertilize, and water their ten yards. At the beginning of the past summer, Miller and David Pillans returned the rake and hoe, hot and tired but very proud of their accomplishment. They had successfully pulled all the weeds and for the remainder of the summer all they had to do was keep it mowed and watered.

So on August 20, 1938, practice started on a nice bed of grass.

The football field was located west of the laundry building inside an oval track that encircled the field. The boys worked to strengthen each other physically and mentally. Mr. Russell set a great example for the boys to follow and look up to. The Masons practiced until Mr. Russell felt each and every boy understood the plays, and the boys enjoyed every minute of it.

It wasn't long after training had started when Mr. Russell announced that Miller would be #6, the left end starter. He knew Miller was fast. He had the endurance, talent, and speed, and would be able to play 100% of every game that season. To receive a jacket, a Sonic had to "letter," that is, he had to play a determined amount of time. If he lettered the following year, too, he would receive a pullover sweater.

Mr. Russell continued calling out players, positions and numbers: #43 Jeff Brown — Right Tackle, #37 Horace McHam — Right Guard, #22 AP Torres — Center, #23 Jack Bates — Left Guard, #40 James Holmans — Left Tackle, #33 Norman Strange — Right End, #24 Gene Keel — Quarterback, #32 Buster Roach, #28 Phillip Earp, #25 Frank Bonds, #41 Don Stephens, #35 Buford Hudgins, #20 Earl Webster, #20 Hardy Brown (Gordy), and #33 Harold Ferguson.

The injury to Mr. Russell's eye left him colorblind. During practice, "Mr. Russell would have us run sprints on the football field," Miller said. "Mr. Russell would yell, 'Everyone line up at the starting line and get ready to run the 100 yard dash.' At the other end of the practice field stood a little GREEN tool shed. Mr. Russell would say, 'Run down to that little red shack as hard as you can.'"

Despite his colorblindness, though Mr. Russell proved to be passionate about living out his promise. There wasn't a father standing on the sidelines that cared any more for his son than Mr. Russell did for these boys.

§

"There were a few major differences in the way high school football was played in 1938 compared to the game today," Miller explained. "We did not have different 'teams.' There were no defensive and offensive teams.

There was no possible way to have one defense team going off and one coming in. We played offense *and* defense. We played the entire game. Had they played two teams," he said, "we would not have had enough guys to make two teams. The public schools had enough players. They could substitute if a player needed a rest. We had to be in better condition than our opponents because we had to play the entire game without a rest. Unlike today's high school football rules, in '38, if a player was taken out for any reason, he was not allowed to return to the game until the next quarter."

Miller continued: "We had to stand five yards behind the line of scrimmage before it was centered, that is, before the center could throw it to someone in the back field. Today, you can stand in the center, raise your hand and throw the football if you want."

1938

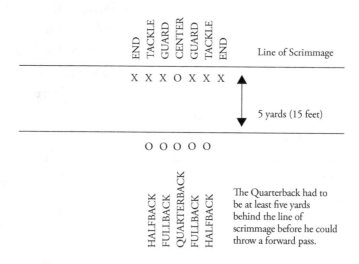

1938 high school football lineup, offense and defense.

Their formations were generally single wing, double wing, put formation, spread formation, and unbalanced line to the left or right.

Miller played left end, which has since been redefined as tight end. Players wore no faceguard and broken noses, black eyes and loosened teeth were all commonplace. According to the Home boys, a boy a year or two following the '38 team broke his nose so many times the Masons did not know which direction his nose would be facing by the end of each game. "If we won, we smiled, and if we lost, we did not smile," recalled Miller. Following a game, Mr. Russell would never point out a specific player. No child would be held publicly responsible for causing the team to lose or win a game.

eleven

Smallest Team

The 1938 Masonic Home football team was the smallest team Mr. Russell had ever coached. In Russell's mind, however, he had not been handed a group of broken boys, he had been given a team of rising stars.

The September 16, 1938, season opener pitted the Masons against the 1937 defending State finalists, the Wichita Falls Coyotes. The little boys would begin the season against a large, outstanding team, a group of boys who outweighed the Masons fifteen pounds to the man, and the non-district game would be played in Wichita country.

The bus sat idling on the Pike. The noise from the engine could be heard across the lawn. The other kids lined the Pike, yelling their support and excitement as the football players climbed onto the bus.

Each boy quickly found a seat and poked their faces through the open windows, smiling and waving back at the Home kids. As the bus slowly moved toward the gate, the rumble of the engine rose an octave, adding a layer of seriousness to what this trip represented to these boys.

The Masonic Home did not own a school bus. They had a contract with a company called The Texas Motor Coach. Mr. W.E. (Pete) Purnell was the Masons' bus driver for over eight years and he never missed a game. The boys would be greatly disappointed if he had missed a trip, because the team believed he brought them good luck. Mr. Russell could see well enough to drive, but he had other important business to take care of before each game, and left the driving to Pete Purnell. The horrible World War I gassing accident might be the reason Mr. Russell never drove the boys anywhere.

Every student and faculty member was very proud of the boys, and each said a prayer as the bus rumbled out the gate. Mr. Fletcher and every other member of the faculty and staff knew the mental and physical baggage these small boys carried, and they also knew the hard work they put into building, honing and polishing their team.

Almost two hours later, an eternity to Miller and the other boys, the bus pulled into Coyote territory. The boys could see a long line of more than 6,000 fans slowly filing through the gates of the stadium. The boys could not wait to get onto the field and they began standing and scooting into the aisle before the bus came to a complete stop. Mr. Russell stood and said, "Hold on, not so fast. Remember, grab every opportunity and make the best of it," and they bowed their heads in prayer. They walked with an air of confidence onto the field.

It was the moment Miller had waited for.

There they all stood. The stadium was full. A gasp from the crowd could be heard. The fans were familiar with the Masons' great track record and their less-than-pristine uniforms, but the small size of each

Mason player surprised even the most devoted Sonic follower. Standing on the field, on a cool late-summer evening, Miller glanced up at the large crowd who had paid money during this time of economic hardship to see him and his team play. He lowered his gaze back at his teammates. They glanced at each other as if to say, "Let's do this."

Little did they know, high in the stands, after the Masons had walked out onto the field, Wichita Falls supporters had leaned back in the bleachers with their elbows resting on the bleacher behind them, as if bored before the game even started. "This game will be over fast," they said. "Someone forgot to tell the little boys they can't play football with the big boys from Wichita Falls," they laughed. "They shrunk." "Are they big enough to play football at all?" With heads shaking they said, "This will be the end of the Masons." "I'm not going to get my money's worth." "Russell finally chewed off more than he can swallow." Then, as if to solidify their assumptions, the large defending State Champions burst onto the field in their sharp matching red and black uniforms. The fans rose to their feet, cheering loudly and stomping their feet. The Wichita Falls Coyotes had quite a following.

Back at the Home, the girls sat in a circle around the radio listening to the game.

They held hands, closed their eyes and concentrated sending positive energy to the team. If a Sonic made a mistake in the game, Miller's sister, Dot asked, "Which one of you did not concentrate?"

Amazingly, the Masons stood on the field unfazed by the crowds or the huge champions. They gave each other a nod and the game began.

COYOTES	Position	MASONS
Parker	L.E.	Moseley
Huff	L.T.	Holmans
Deynolds	L.G.	Bates
Riddles	C.	Torres
Mickle	R.G.	McHam
Bearden	Q.B.	Keel
Swanner	R.T.	Brown
Levell	R.E.	Strange
Holder	L.H.	Bonds

1938 Sonics season opener starting lineup, Masons vs. Wichita Falls Coyotes.

Though the first quarter featured plenty of action, neither team scored. No one had taken this little team seriously until now. The Masons successfully had denied the defending State Champions from crossing the goal line in the first quarter. One of the highlights of the first quarter was the Masons own Miller Moseley as he stopped the aggressive hulk, Orus Bearden, after a 7-yard gain off the right tackle. The crowd stood in disbelief.

During the second period, the crowd rose to their feet again, only this time they yelled wildly for their strong, wooly boys, as Curtis Holder and Orus Bearden carried the ball to the 3-yard line and tried for a touchdown two different times. With unending fight, the Masons blocked both attempts. Then Ben Collins, the Coyote's captain, finally got an opportunity to plunge through the Mason defense to gain the necessary inches for a touchdown. Johnston's kick from placement was good and now the Masons found themselves down to the Coyotes 7 to 0. It wasn't the huge margin the puffed up Coyotes had planned against the little Masons, but they had started feeling a little whipped and were happy to get a touchdown.

Late in the second quarter the Masons proved to the crowd they should not be taken lightly as they began a spectacular offensive show immediately after Gene Keel had taken Ben Collins' punt to the Mason 34. He followed with a 35-yard pass to Norman Strange. Then *whoosh!* Keel blasted a long pass, hitting Strange on the goal line for a touchdown. Jeff Brown's kick for the extra point was good. The score was now tied 7 to 7.

Unbelievable! The Mason's touchdown and extra point sucked the wind out of the Coyote fans, and now they were in an uproar. They were no longer leaning back on the bleachers, but rather leaning forward or standing with arms crossed. The little Masons now had the crowd's attention, whether in anger, in disbelief, or in awe, and in the third quarter, the State Champs could not score against the poor little Mason boys.

The Coyote crowd looked as if they had tasted some bitter fruit; unless the crowd had seen it for themselves, they would never have believed it. The Coyotes were so desperate to pull out on top of this small team in the fourth period that Holder got caught crawling with the ball and was penalized back to his 44.

The entire Mason team impressed. It wasn't a one man effort, it was a team effort.

When the final whistle blew, the score remained the same as it had been in the second quarter: the 1937 defending State Champions 7, the lightweights of the Masonic Home 7. Despite playing an aggressive and exciting game, Wichita Falls did not keep their crown. The little Masons, simply put, played spectacular football. The Coyotes were a great ballclub and they had played very well, but in spite of their weight, the Masons had stopped them.

The Masons exited the field in silence and with no signs of being worn out from a hard-fought game. On the other hand, the Coyotes left the field haggard, and the crowd had not only gotten their full money's worth, they had been convinced to think twice before insulting this little team.

Statistics leaned toward the Masons, though they could not gain with the ground game, even with their talented fullback, Don Stephens, careening through the Coyotes. The Coyotes led in first downs, 11 to 10, and in yards gained rushing 185 to 94, but lagged in passing as the Masons made 147 yards with their overhead mayhem.

After the elated Masons climbed back onto the bus and had found their seats, Mr. Russell stood at the front of the bus and said, "The spectators now know we can play ball with the big boys." He took a seat directly behind the bus driver who looked up at Russell in the reflection of the mirror. Miller saw that both Mr. Russell and Mr. Purnell could not stop grinning.

Sports writer Frank Tolbert congratulated the new kids on the team, Miller Moseley, A.P. Torres and Horace McHam, for an impressive game.

As the bus slowly turned out of the parking lot and headed toward the local hotel, Gene Keel asked, "Hey, Dundee Moseley, do you feel any grudges toward your mother for putting you in the Masonic Home?"

"The only grudge I have is the name she gave me, Harrison Miller Moseley. H.M.M," he shot back. "If she had just named me Miller Harrison Moseley, M.H.M, my initials would be the same as the initials of our football team, the Masonic Home Masons." The boys laughed.

§

When the bus approached the large, black iron gate the following morning and proceeded down the Pike, the boys stuck their heads out of the bus windows and were thrilled to see a wonderful homecoming welcome: lining both sides of the Pike all the Masonic Home kids jumped up and down and cheered. They never doubted the courage of this small bunch of boys.

The Masons were a machine and each team member played a vital role in making the machine function. Every part had to work. They were a fierce little band of brothers who played clean and fair, and in doing so won the hearts and admiration of thousands across the United States. The expanding fan base exploded.

With the assistance of one of the best coaches in the history of high school football, Rusty Russell, never before had the appeal of schoolboy football been so convincingly demonstrated.

Many saw the Masons as a modern-day David fighting against a formidable Goliath, and the analogy was quite fitting. The Biblical

Goliath, a Philistine warrior, had great height and his uniform consisted of a bronze helmet, a beautiful coat of scale armor and greaves on his legs. David, a small son of a farmer in plain clothes, overcame the giant by faith and impeccable skills.

The notoriety of the Masons soared as sportswriters touted the Masons with colorful illustrations such as "tempestuous aerialists," "lateralists of the Masonic Home," "those amazing little Masonic Home Masons," "The Russellmen," "The Plucky Masons," "Versatile Masons," "The salty kids," "Gallant Little band," "Little Masons," "the Sonics," and many, many more.

The prosperity and satisfaction the Masons brought seemed to irritate the Interscholastic League. The League lacked compassion when it came to decisions that were best for the kids. They worked feverishly behind the scenes with efforts to demote the Masons, one of the State's finest football outfits from Class A to Class C. Instead of putting the children's needs first, the League took the game from the children and turned it into a "symbol." They had to satisfy their own egos of creating the biggest, toughest teams, not for the children, but for themselves.

Mr. Russell was in the game for the kids, the smallest, most disadvantaged kids in the league. When the Masons won, instead of the league cheering for the advancement of underprivileged children, the Interscholastic League had steam shooting from their ears. They wanted to prove small teams could not compete in Class A. The Masons continued to prove them wrong.

§

On September 23, 1938, at 8:00 a.m., the Masons rolled down the Pike, through the gate, and headed toward Dallas for the much-anticipated non-district game against the Highland Park Scots. Riddled by injuries, Rusty Russell had been forced to hold off on any blocking and tackling practice in preparation for the game. The Highland Park team, being in sounder physical shape, could deliver a terrific blow to the Masons' willpower. Despite being in better health and larger than the Masons, Highland Park never took any challenge against the Masonic Home Masons lightly.

Highland Park		Masonic Home
Seay	Le	Moseley
Swank	Lt	Holmans
Waters	Lg	Bates
Shaw	C	Torres
Harkey	Rg	McHam
Borgeson	Rt	Brown
Germany	Re	Strange
Jordan	Qb	Keel
Welle	Lh	Hudgins
Bishop	Rh	Earp
Munnell	Fb	Stephens
Substitutions:		
Harris		Bennett
Leftwich		Manson
Giddens		Roach
Maher		Webster
Cox		Bonds, Land
Hemmingson		Crocker
		Lowrie

September 23, 1938, starting lineup, Masons vs Highland Park Scots.

Before the game, two teams stood on the gridiron, two teams from backgrounds worlds apart. Highland Park was an extremely affluent school district. Mixed in the crowd of approximately 5,600 fans were the very vocal Highland Park Scots fans, and they were there to see their Highlanders trample over the little boys from Fort Worth. The Highlanders had triumphed with fourteen wins and one defeat over the previous two years, which had advanced the team to recognition as one of the most outstanding high school football clubs, and there did not seem anything a rival team could do about it.

Amon Carter-Riverside would be the Masons next brutal challenge following this game. The towering assistant coach, Mr. Judy Truelson from Riverside, was among the 5,600 fans packed in Highland Park stadium that day to watch the highly-anticipated Highland Park team trample the Masons. He had been seen shuffling down the row to his seat with his scouting notebook tucked under his arm.

As with the Masons' previous game, neither team scored in the first quarter. But Highland Park started the second quarter strong after the Highland eleven had been pushed deep into its own territory. Through a mixture of tackles and aerials, the Highlanders fought their way 70 yards down the field toward the Masons' goal line and Highlander fullback Munnell scored from the 5-yard line when he took the ball from the center and handed it to Harris, who threw to Grady Jordan, who forced his way through the right tackle for a touchdown. Dick Dwelle kicked wide and missed the extra point. The score was 6 to 0.

The first opportunity for the Home came later in the game when Masons' fullback, Phillip Earp, intercepted Dwelle's aerial after the Highlanders had worked the ball all the way down to the Masons' 37.

From there, Gene Keel and Miller Moseley stole the limelight when Keel faded back and showed the crowd what he could do as a passer when he hurled a 30 yard bullet to Moseley, who then ran 13 more yards for a total gain of 43 yards. They were stopped on the Scot 20. Five plays later, Don Stephens and Keel had driven the ball to the 7-yard line, which set the stage for Keel to shoot a pass to Strange, but two oversized Highlander backs attempted to get to the ball first and knocked it high into the air. Just before the ball hit the ground Strange nabbed it. Jeff Brown's kick was good. The Mason's now led 7 to 6 at the half.

As the teams exited the field for the half, fans slowly stood, stretched and raised their hands for warm bags of peanuts. As the Masons made their way into the dressing room, they plopped down on the bench one at a time as Tom Posey, the "squealer," gave each a cup of water and a towel. It was hard to be too appreciative after the squealer had caused many a boy to receive licks and Tiner whipped them with a piece of garden hose that had left red lines on their backsides. However, their main focus at that moment was on Russell and game strategy.

During the third quarter the Masons thrilled the crowd all the way down the field on reverses which ended in a touchdown when Don Stephens shattered the line. This touchdown now put the Sonics ahead 14 to 6 against one of the finest clubs in the state. Highlander fans yelled, "We wus robbed," according to sportswriter Ross Bedell.

With only eight minutes left in the game, the talented Highlanders came right back with a vengeance and scored a touchdown of their own. But the Masons immediately went to work and were within seconds of scoring yet again when the final horn sounded.

Game over. The little team caught Highlander fans off-guard. The Sonics won 14-13, which boosted their respectability. The Highlanders' impressive record of fourteen wins and one defeat over the previous two years had just changed.

Masons Edge Out Dallas Scots, 14–13
Game At A Glance

Highland Park		Masonic Home
13	First Down	17
138	Yards Gained Rushing	213
2	Yards Lost Rushing	26
83	Yard Gained Passing	75
6	Passes Completed	4
10	Passes Incomplete	8
2	Passes Intercepted by	2
8 for 280	Punts (yardage)	230 for 8
45	Penalties (yardage)	20
2	Fumbles	4

Highland Park 0   6   0   7–13
Masonic Home   0   7   7   0–14

Scoring:
Highland Park – Touchdowns: Jordan, DWelle. Point after touchdown: DWelle (placement kick).

Masonic Home – Touchdowns: Strange, Stevens. Point after touchdown: Brown 2(placement kicks).

Coach Truelson closed his scouting notebook, tucked it under his arm, crossed his arms in front of his chest and stood in amazement. He had just watched the smallest team Rusty Russell had ever coached solidly defeat Highland Park. The entry in his scouting notebook concerning the game read,

For in addition to an excellent ground game, they are very skillful with the passes. That's the word for those Masons; skillful. This Gene Keel's as good a passer as you'll see in high school. And that Don Stevens (aka Stephens) makes me shudder same as he made the Highland Park line shudder last week.

When Don Stephens wasn't running himself, he was shooting bullet passes a la Sammy Baugh.

Following the game, reporters compared Don Stephens to Sammy Baugh, a local Fort Worth hero and two-time All-American at Texas Christian University from 1933-1936. In 1937 he was the Washington Redskins' number one draft choice. He was known as the "league's first big–yardage passer and spurred an offensive revolution in the NFL." He was an All-NFL selection seven years, and captured a rare "Triple Crown" in 1943 by leading the NFL in passing, punting and interceptions. Sammy Baugh led the NFL in passing six times and registered a total of 21,886 yards, 187 TDs passing, a 45.1-yard punting average and intercepted 31 passes as a defensive halfback.

As the bus pulled into the gate and preceded slowly down the Pike, the Home kids who had been waiting patiently for the boys to return began to yell, cheer and clap. The small boys ran up to the players with wide grins. Miller hit Horace on the shoulder as he walked past his seat. Horace opened his eyes from a deep sleep and stood up.

The children in the primary grades who were too young to read tore through the pages of the *Fort Worth Star-Telegram* for pictures of any member of the team—they were rarely disappointed. The next day the editors followed their every move from the practice field "outback" to the game. There were plenty of articles with pictures for the kids. A few of the headlines read: "Masons Edge Out Dallas Scots, 14-13." "Hard-Charging Masonic Home Eleven Upsets Highland Park in 14-13 Battle," and "Masons in Rally to Turn Back Scots D. Stevens, 162-Pound Back, Tears Up Hi-Park Line."

Miller held that morning's newspaper up to Don Stephens and said, "Look at the paper. Who is Don Stevens?"

"They always misspell my name," Don replied. "By the way, who is Morris Miller?"

"Someone forgot to tell my mother she had another son," laughed Miller.

Despite the newspapers' continued insistence on spelling the boys' names incorrectly, they now had Fort Worth and Dallas fans almost convinced they were a force to reckon with.

twelve

Mason Fans are Too Many
for Baseball Field

The Masons played their regular season games at LaGrave Field on the north side of downtown Fort Worth. The Masonic Home team drew such large crowds that customers were repeatedly and reluctantly turned away as there was just not enough room for them in the stadium.

The magnetism of the Masons was probably a driving factor in the construction of a new, larger, football stadium. On November 9, 1937, the evening edition of the *Fort Worth Star-Telegram* provided the following sketch of the proposed $244,000 All-City High School Stadium to citizens across Fort Worth. The Fort Worth City Council conveyed 38 acres of land to the Board of Education, but with a hitch: if the school system abandoned the use of the tract for an athletic field, the title would revert back to the city. Fort Worth City Councilman, Mr. Elder, told school Athletic Director, E. S. Farrington, "We're not selling you this land; we're giving it to you."

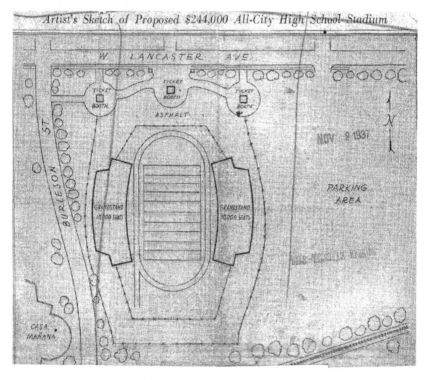

Artist's sketch of the proposed All-City High School Stadium. *(Courtesy of the Fort Worth Star-Telegram).*

The Work Progress Administration rarely funded construction of higher-end projects which employed musicians, artists, writers, actors, and directors in large arts, drama, media, and literacy projects. But the WPA approved construction of the new high school stadium, and

Miss Evaline Sellors was hired to sculpt statues to adorn the sides of the facility that was scheduled to be completed by the next year, in time for the kickoff of the 1939 football season. The stadium was to be located at the corner of West Lancaster Avenue and Burleson Street, later renamed University Drive, and named after E. S. Farrington, the Fort Worth Independent School Athletic Director.

Evaline Sellors carving one of the 8 ½ foot bas relief statues which adorn Farrington Field in Fort Worth. (Courtesy of the *Fort Worth Star-Telegram*). Special Collections, The University of Texas at Arlington Library, Arlington, Texas.

While Farrington Field was under construction, rumors spread that Miss Sellors was using the likeness of Sammy Baugh as the model for the 8 ½ foot bas relief football statue to be placed on either side of the façade over the stadium's west entrance. Though most residents were thrilled with the possibility, a young 1937 graduate of Polytechnic High expressed an interesting perspective on the use of Sam Baugh as the face of the stadium's façade. She described herself as a "very enthusiastic football fan," and undoubtedly admired Baugh greatly. However, she felt "that his figure on this stadium was something of an imposition, for he was not a Fort Worth product and knew nothing of our high schools. He did not work with our beloved Mr. Farrington as did our own high school athletes." She thought locals, such as Terry Patrick, a versatile Poly star, or Allie White of Masonic Home, or Marion Pugh of North Side should have been considered for the likeness, since the stadium was specifically designated as a Fort Worth high school stadium.

Miss Sellors assured the girl via an article in the Aug 3, 1938 *Fort Worth Star-Telegram* morning edition that there was no need for concern. "The bas relief figure which would adorn the facade of the new high school stadium would not depict Sam Baugh, but is representative of a typical football player," she responded. "I did not use a picture of Baugh. The bas relief I am preparing is that of a typical football player, and represents no person."

It did not seem to matter that the sculptor herself declared that the figure was not modeled after Sam Baugh. Maybe there were those who wanted the figure, which shows a football player poised to throw a forward pass, a signature pose of Baugh's, to have been patterned after Baugh's because the controversial sculptures were honored with a special designation in the Smithsonian Institute: "This piece was modeled after Sam Baugh, a football star in Texas and later played for the Washington Redskins."

The controversial statue. *(Courtesy of Susan Kline).*

§

Until the new stadium was built, however, the Masons continued to play at LaGrave Field. On Thursday, September 28, 1938, the Sonics were scheduled to flex their cunning against the Amon Carter-Riverside Eagles. Norman Earl, the new Fort Worth Athletic Director, wanted to accommodate the expected crowds as much as possible, as the revenue was much appreciated in such difficult economic times. He decided to open the gates earlier than usual, at 6:45 p.m., hoping to give workers time to process the tickets and get the crowd herded through the gates to keep the commotion to a minimum before kickoff. He encouraged fans to purchase tickets before arriving at the park and arranged additional ticket availability at Renfro's stores at Seventh and Main and in Poly, at Ben Weekes in Arlington Heights, at Lewis Furniture Store and Greines Dry Goods

Store on North Main, and at Scott's Drug Store at Six Points in Riverside. Students could purchase tickets at their schools, and reserved seat tickets and 25 cent grandstand tickets would be sold at the park on Thursday.

At 8 o'clock that evening, the Masons faced the Riverside Eagles. Both Masonic Home and Riverside were scheduled to make their local debut of the season at old LaGrave Field. There was nothing better than a home crowd, and the throng attempting to get an eyeful of these two great local teams was expected to reach over 10,000.

Though the Amon Carter-Riverside fans had voiced concerns regarding the weight difference between the two teams, it did not appear to concern the Masons, just as it did not concern them during the first two games of the season. Of course, the Masons were not expected to win. However, it was amazing the little guys had pushed through both of the previous powerhouses with no serious injuries.

In between football practice and the games, Miller was able to hold onto his ranking as the top student in his class. The Masonic Home did not caudle their athletes. Everyone was required to do well or attend summer school. No exceptions. They lived with reasonable curfews, were watched and monitored.

Late into the evening prior to the matchup with Amon Carter-Riverside, the Masons worked out behind the red brick school buildings on the practice field, perfecting the timing of their plays against Riverside. Likewise, Riverside's players perfected their own strategies to ensure a win against the small boys from the Masonic Home and School.

"Riverside's husky, red-shirted gridmen were taking a final drill on defensive tactics to use against the tricksome, unorthodox attack of the Masons," said sports writer Frank Tolbert.

The game was expected to be nothing less than an all-star show for those lucky to attend. Many of the All-District prospects would be playing together on LaGrave field. The list of stars included A.P. Torres of Masonic Home and Jack Dearmore of Riverside; Tackle Jeff Brown of Masonic Home and Guard Jack Pool of the Eagles; Mason right end

Norman Strange and left end Miller Moseley, and Don Stephens and Gene Keel, Mason backs; and Al Hollis, Walter Johnson, Bob Jarrell and Coon, Eagle backs. Those who could not afford a ticket huddled close to the radio listening to the play-by-play details.

It was expected to be the best game of the year, with the air filled with footballs from Gene Keel of the Masons and Jim Jarrell of the Eagles. Both clubs had relied on their overhead games for a great deal of their gains so far.

"For one thing it will throw together two of the hottest aerial attacks in schoolboy circles," said one Fort Worth reporter.

Starting lineups: Masonic Home		Riverside
Moseley	L.E.	Hudspeth
Holmans	L.T.	Holliday
McHam	L.G.	Lewis
Torres	C.	Dearmore (co-c)
Bates	R.G.	Pool
Brown (co-c)	R.T.	Magers
Strange	R.E.	Hardin
Keel	Q.B.	Jarrell
Hudgins	R.H.	Millar
Bonds (co-c)	L.H.	Hollis
Stephens	F.B.	Johnson

Substitutes:
Earp, Roach, Webster, Bennett, Coulter

Coon (co-c), Conway, Snow, Rench, Stockton, Eudaley, Noah, Alken, Doyle, Rothrock

September 29, 1938, starting lineup, Masons vs. Amon Carter-Riverside.

The Masons and Eagles played a spectacular, scoreless first quarter. The Masons' ace champion fullback, Don Stephens, who could break through any line, limped off the field in the first quarter with a strained ligament. This allowed the big Eagle line to shut down the Mason's running game.

The Riverside Eagles found the fast, elusive Masons stubborn to bring down. Riverside was dumbfounded to see Stephens limp back into the game in the second quarter. Without wasting any time, he smashed off his right tackle for a first down on the two-yard line. The Eagles were determined to stop Stephens. When he glided around the Eagles' right flank, Riverside's center, Coon, threw him for a loss of a yard.

Later in the second-period, the Masons Frank Bonds threw a pass through the waving arms of a Riverside rusher, hitting Buster Roach in the end zone for a touchdown, the first of the game. Jeff Brown, the Masons' right tackle, kicked the extra point from placement.

During Riverside's next possession, Miller Moseley and A.P. Torres returned the favor and threw Coon as he attempted to punt on fourth down from the Eagle 21. In the second period, the Masons had Riverside and customers totally confused with mind-blowing trickery: Stephens plowed through the line and handed the ball to Gene Keel. Next, the little Eugene That Could lateralled behind the line of scrimmage to Buster Roach, who busted wide and fast around the Eagles left flank for 21 yards and the touchdown. Jeff Brown failed to make the extra point, his first miss of the season. Brown had led the district in kicking extra points the prior year.

It was half and the Masons led 13-0.

The orange shirts were beautiful in motion, but it was their passing that had the crowd mesmerized. During the third quarter, Keel threw a perfect pass from the Riverside 30 to Bonds who was running in the left flat. Bonds caught the ball on the run at the 10 and ran for a touchdown with no opposition. Jeff Brown then redeemed himself by making good on the extra-point attempt. By the middle of the third quarter the Masons dominated 20-0.

The Eagles' one-and-only touchdown came late in the third quarter. Their scoring drive started after Al Hollis returned one of Keel's punts to the Masonic Home 39. Later, as Coon blocked like a savage, Hollis managed to run around the Masons' left end for a first down on the Masons' 5-yard line. Hollis had to work overtime for every inch he gained as he crossed the goal line, carrying two Mason tacklers and Keel with him. Coon's kick was good, but the single score was not enough to help Riverside. The game ended with the Masons upset, 20-7.

After this game, the Masons' reputation ticked up a notch from "little boys" to "bullet-blocking little boys."

Game At A Glance

Masonic Home		Riverside
6	First Downs	12
66	Yards Gained Rushing	139
7	Yards Lost Rushing	50
151	Yard Gained Passing	144
8	Passes Completed	9
5	Passes Incomplete	14
8 for 315	Punts, Yardage	7 for 252
3 for 20	Runback of Punts, Yardage	3 for 38
4 for 165	Kickoffs, Yardage	2 for 62
17	Runback of Kickoffs, Yardage	67
5 for 25	Penalties, Yardage	3 for 15
1	Fumbles	1

Scores by periods:

Masonic Home	0	13	7	0–20
Riverside	0	0	7	0–7

First downs by periods:

Masonic Home	0	4	1	1–6
Riverside	6	1	4	1–12

As district coaches left the stadium, sportswriter Frank Tolbert witnessed them as they shook their heads in amazement and said, "Whoever beats the Masons…If anyone beats the Masons…will win the district."

At that point, the Masons were considered the probable district champion, but they had yet to play their next Goliath, the fierce North Side Steers.

The nonchalant kids nonchalantly walked back to the bus to return home.

§

Frank Tolbert spent a lot more time around the Masonic Home, more than he ever had in the past. It wasn't his usual quick stopover. This story seemed a bit more personal to him as he studied the private side of these small footballers. No other high school team in the league would have their personal lives in print as much as these quiet little boys. Sportswriters were drawn to their respectability both on and off the gridiron, win or lose. It was their quiet demeanor that seemed to draw more attention than the antics of any misbehaving footballer from any other team. A section from one of Tolbert's articles read:

> *The Masonic Home boys, like young fighters in their brown or blue dressing gowns, padded out of the dormitory, squinting their eyes in the sunshine. They walked along a sidewalk, a long line of them, some of them carrying shoulder pads, and disappeared into the football locker room. Rusty Russell the Mason coach, was sitting in the cool shade of the Home powerhouse, watching the boys file by. That is a way of Rusty's. He studies his polite, poker faced athletes all of the time. Often when they don't know he's watching them. This was the day after the Masons' opening conference victory over Riverside. But the Masons did not show their excitement, if they felt any, over a surprisingly one-sided triumph. There was a sort of ceremonial solemnity about them to match their sore muscles. Maybe this was because they'd all just come from the Home hospital, where their fullback, Stephens, was lying with strained leg ligaments that might keep him out of football for weeks. Russell and I followed them down the stairs and into the locker room. Rusty weighed some of the kids. I'd been arguing a little with Russell about the poundage of his right halfback, Frank Bonds. With his well-muscled legs and wearing his pads, Bonds looks as if he weighs more than the 145 he's listed. But Frank threw the scales only to the 143-pound mark.*

The large boys' building housed the Athletic Room where the school stored the athletic equipment and where the boys dressed for football and track. The last boy to walk into the Athletic Room one afternoon was Gene Keel, the quarterback, "A short boy, his thickish shoulders drooping," Tolbert reported. No one had a locker, but they each had their own designated spot to climb into and out of their uniforms. Tom Posey walked around with a laundry basket for the boys to throw in their dirty uniforms.

After Stephens, who alternated with Keel as quarterback, got injured in the Riverside game, a great load was dumped on Keel. Tolbert watched Keel sit down with a groan. Then Norman Strange walked in, a thin boy whose platinum blond hair set him apart from the other darker-headed boys.

"Where do you hurt most Gene?" Strange asked, sober-faced, not laughing. "I just don't know", said Keel. "I'm just one big ache" and then he saw Russell watching him. And he added loudly in the quiet of the dressing room: "But it is nothing but sore muscles and I will be perfect by Monday. Are we going to scrimmage today, Mr. Russell?"

Tolbert watched the Home boys with delight. Tom Posey, the bespectacled Mason tackle from the prior year's team walked into the room carrying a huge load of pads in his big arms. Tom was a large young man with a booming voice, whom the boys once dubbed a squealer, but it seemed as if they had all turned a corner.

Tolbert's eyes continued to comb the room from Posey to Russell's desk. Over in the corner, on his desk, sat a dog-eared old notebook. Russell's book containing his hocus-pocus plays. On the front, a proud and appreciative boy had carved:

"Mr. Russell, our coach, the best coach in the world."

Tolbert continued to watch the Masons taking care of their responsibilities. Now that Stephens was out due to injuries, he observed that seven of the starting athletes weighed 145 pounds or less.

There they were, along the wall: Amarate (A.P.) Torres, the wide-faced, truculent Mexican center; next to him the vividly blond Strange; Phillip Earp, Buster Roach, Buford Hudgins and Bonds, the backs.

His eyes kept studying the boys.

Miller Moseley, 132-pound regular at an end; Jack Bates, 137 pound guard.

Tolbert never enjoyed his work as much as he did that day. He could not wipe the smile from his face as he sat and observed.

And then there were the "bigger" boys: Jeff Brown, silent 165 pound tackle, lacing his shoulder pads around his thick neck; grinning James Holmans, the other tackle (he weighs 155 pounds), Keel, who weighs 150 pounds and Horace (Fats) Mc Ham, the great guard.
This is the smallest team the Masons have ever had. The Masons have a bigger following over the State than many a big college team. There are 87 boys in Masonic Home's high School this year. Forty-nine are out for the "varsity." Most of the others play on the lighter weight teams. We were thinking of this as the Masons still with that solemn, ceremonial air, padded silently out of the dressing room.

Little Keel's shoulder pads must have been a bit cumbersome, rising almost to his ears as he walked over to Russell, who was sitting in his chair behind his desk in the corner. "Are we going to scrimmage today?" he repeated. He moved painfully, with stiff motions, and added, "Jeff and Fats and Strange and Torres and everybody is ready to scrimmage if you want us to."

"Before we do," Professor Russell answered, "we need to have skull practice." "Skull practice" was the time spent preparing mentally for the game, such as discussing a scouting report and strategy. The boys put their heads together and listened to their coach with rapt attention.

Tolbert watched and smiled.

thirteen

Significant Injuries

North Side, Poly and the Masons were currently in a three-way tie for the district leadership, so the upcoming game against the North Side Steers was equally important to both teams; the consensus was that the winner would slide through to win district.

Meanwhile, Athletic Director Norman Earl and Assistant Director Herman Clark were eagerly getting LaGrave Field ready for another large crowd of 10,000 to 15,000.

"The high school block and tackle industry is going very good," Earl said. He wanted every paying customer to have a seat.

On October 4, 1938, the city of Fort Worth and points beyond knew the dramatic circumstances surrounding this game-of-the-year. The determined little boys in orange and white were accustomed to being rated the underdogs. Pound-for-pound, Rusty Russell's team ranked as the top contender in the state of Texas. The North Side Steers weight advantage of 27 pounds for each footballer was a significant variance, but the Masons had overcome large obstacles their entire lives.

On one side of the gridiron would stand the defending champion Steers. They were a large, resilient team, going for their third conference title in a row, with no thoughts of handing their crown off to any other team, especially a lightweight team like the Masons. On the other side, the undefeated Masons, possibly the greatest small team to come together in the Interscholastic League, were ready to take their first victory over the North Siders in three seasons.

Historically the North Siders and the Masons were intense competitors and had been since 1932 when the Masonic Home was voted into Class A football. From 1932 until 1936 the Masons whipped the Steers. Then coach Herman Clark came along and the big guys from the 1936 North Side team mauled Rusty Russell's boys 26-0.

No one figured the small 1938 team could win any of the games that season, let alone this one. But for the first time in these boys' lives, they were winning, and winning big.

Because of significant injuries to several of the major Masons players, Mr. Russell had no choice but to radically revise his backfield, which included Frank Bonds, Gene Keel, Buster Roach, and Phillip Earp. Several sports writers stood on the sidelines at the practice field with pencil, paper and cameras ready, taking notes and waiting for a chance to interview Mr. Russell. At the end of practice, and with Mr. Russell's permission, cameras flashed from every direction. No reporter was ever allowed to speak directly to the players

The team circled Rusty Russell and studied his every word. "We got by on passes against Riverside," he told them, "but we will need a lot of power to convince those North Side boys that without Stephens we've still got it." Stephens stood listening, leaning on his crutches and wishing he could play.

Because of their multiple injuries, the Masons would fight North Side with an average team weight of 140 pounds. "Don't let their small size compromise your thoughts as to how tough this team can play," said one Fort Worth editor.

The Masons had measured up to the powerful Wichita Falls Coyotes, 7-7. They had upset Highland Park, one of North Texas' favored teams, 14-13. And they met stubborn opposition against a veteran Amon Carter-Riverside team who outweighed the Masons 20 pounds to the man, and they won that game 20-7. And they did it without Stephens.

"Due to injuries, I have been forced to make unplanned, significant changes in the starting lineup," Mr. Russell announced.

"Frank," Mr. Russell said, looking Bonds straight in the eyes. "I realize you have never played fullback nor have had any amount of time getting acquainted with this new position, but due to injuries, we are counting on you to jump in and do the best you can as our new fullback. Gene!" he called to Keel. "The game is in your hands." These changes dominoed into additional significant changes: Philip Earp and Buster Roach were moved to halfbacks. These were major position changes which normally required many, many weeks of training to perfect. The Masons had a few days. The boys practiced hard to learn their new positions.

Missing key players and changing key positions at the last minute should have had an enormous impact on the outcome of the game.

The Steers probably ran through the Mason role call ahead of time and came prepared: Gene Keel, one of the most intimidating quarterbacks in the state of Texas; Buster Roach, a boy who could run so fast artists for the *Fort Worth Star-Telegram* drew cartoons in his honor; A.P. Torres, the hard-hitting center; and the smallest Mason of all, the sticky-fingered Miller Moseley, who rarely made a mistake.

Stephens had suffered torn ligaments in his knee during the second play in the Riverside game, and Hudgins, who had developed a painful charley horse over the weekend, lay on a cot in the Home hospital. Because Russell could not afford to lose another player before the game, he had no choice but to coach a rather mild workout consisting of "dummy" signal drills and new assignments.

On the other hand, North Side scrimmaged harder and more intensely than customary, staying on the field until dusk or when they could no longer see the ball. To insure the Steers knew what to expect when they stood face-to-face with the Masons, North Side's coach, Blanard Spearman, stepped in and played the role of Gene Keel, the Masons' quarterback. His performance on the practice field that day would have landed him a position on any pro team. He ran and threw passes all over the field, perfectly imitating Keel's style, including dropping occasional completions through the first string backfield's defense. The shock of seeing Spearman with a team of boys breathing down his neck was compared to the unbelievable chances of catching Mr. Dutch Meyer of the T.C.U. Horned Frogs behind the stadium at the half taking a bagpipe lesson.

After Coach Spearman had had enough practice as quarterback, he stepped to the side and let the Steers take over.

Meanwhile, behind the red brick Masonic Home buildings, the tough little Masons received additional assistance from William Mercer, the Masons' center from last season, a young man well-schooled regarding North Side maneuvers. Mr. Russell gave Armando "Jack" Torres most of the running and passing duties for the reserves, and he was taking a fearful load of punishment, particularly from his big brother, center A.P. Torres.

If it was possible, Mr. Russell's team had gotten lighter. "You have a tough battle ahead of you tonight against the North Side Steers," Mr. Russell told them just before they walked onto the field. "You will be going up against an intense, strong, persistent team. But I know if anyone can do it, the Masons can! Let's walk out on that gridiron calmly and stay entirely focused on your job." *The Fort Worth Star-Telegram's* headline read, "North Side and Masonic Home tonight." Those six words alone drew a huge crowd clamoring to get inside the gate at LaGrave Field.

The little underdogs had become the State's most popular eleven and an invasion of sportswriters and fans from across the country and as far away as New York stood in line at the ticket office. Wilbur Wood, editor of the *New York Sun*, requested an article regarding the David and Goliath teams of both the Masonic Home and Texas Christian University.

"The North Side Steers will be playing at full strength," Mr. Russell told the boys as they prepared for kick off. "They will have every regular in the game with no injuries, not to mention they have numerous players on the bench ready to run on the field. Play your best."

It appeared Blanard Spearman, North Side's head coach, had learned a little bit about psychological warfare from Russell. The rival coaches worked overtime going back and forth, trying to convince the other that their team was in the saddest state of health because they each had "bear" stories too sad to believe. H.N. Russell, the Masonic Home trickster, sadly reported, "All our plays, offense and defense were built around Stephens. Now he can't play. Neither can Buford Hudgins, a starting back. Even if we were at top strength, the North Side boys are too big, too strong and just plain too good for us."

Blanard Spearman, director of those "too good" boys, wasn't going to let Russell get the best of him. He was not going to rely on the fact that he had a large, powerful, skilled team to win this game; he was going to cover every single base there was to cover. He did not get beat up on the practice field for nothing, and he was not going to sit out of the moaning game. He quickly retorted with, "It's a good thing Masonic's crippled. It may be that now we have a bare, outside chance of winning, but I don't think so. Those boys are too well schooled, too fast, and they're in such superior condition. We'll just have to do the best we can."

Could it be that both coaches were worried? Absolutely. Each coach was taking atypical steps to put their best foot forward for this big game. It seemed the little non-threatening boys from the Home were causing the big boys to run scared.

The enthusiasm of the crowd was invigorating and continually expanding. The excitement increased as the crowd rose to its feet to cheer the teams as they took the field. Don Stephens could be seen easing onto the Mason bench with the aid of his crutches. The crowd silenced for the prayer and Pledge of Allegiance, followed by cheering that could be heard for miles. The cheers seemed slightly louder when the Masons took the field.

The Masons were known for having an abundance of courage, but this would push the envelope.

North Side		Masonic Home
Blackmon	LE	Moseley
Addington	LT	Holmans
Harris	LG	McHam
Roberts	C	Torres
Strittmater	RG	Bates
Tulls	RT	Brown
Wofford	RE	Strange
Conway	QB	Keel
Burklow	LH	N. Roach
Casteel	RH	Earp
Few	FB	Bonds

October 4, 1938, starting lineup, Masons vs North Side Steers.

The Masons began impressing the crowd on their fourth play of the game when Keel "*whooshed*" a 50-yard pass which Miller caught on the Steer 5-yard line. "And there is a mighty hornet hum of excitement from the 11,000 customers that press around LaGrave's ball yard," reported Frank Tolbert.

In the fourth quarter, minutes from the end of the game, Home quarterback Gene Keel tossed an unbelievably beautiful 27 yard throw to end Norman Strange, down in the right-hand corner of the field, for the touchdown. The crowd jumped to its feet. Jeff Brown, the Masons' all-district tackle, failed to successfully kick a field goal. The crowd sat down, only to quickly return to their feet when the officials made an off sides call against the North Siders and Brown was given a second shot from placement. As he lined up to kick the second extra point attempt, a hush settled over the crowd. Jeff missed his second attempt and the spectators slowly sat back down. The score was now 6-0 Masons.

The crowd was hoarse and the tension thick.

With two minutes left in the game, Stovall reached for his pistol and the crowd began to exit the stands.

"The Steers are going to town!" The crowd yelled and pointed to the field. Frank Tolbert later wrote:

With Stovall's pistol poised in the air, the North Siders lay down a breathless barrage of passes that ferry them right up to the Masons' 11-yard line. Casteel's 30-yard return of the kickoff, Charlie Conway passes, Pug Few and Jimmy Boswell figure in this drive. Then the Masons proved their intrinsic greatness. On Fourth down, the Steers' big quarterback, Charley Conway, attempts to pass. He is looking for his huge end, Floppy Blackmon. But Floppy is lost in a swarm of Rusty Russell's kids. Jeff Brown, the Masons' all-district tackle, breaks through and throws Conway heavily as the final gun booms.

To chart the reel and riot of this game from the first down to that Whisker-curling fourth quarter you need more space than they have in volume 8 of the Congressional Record. A.P. Torres, the courageous Mexican Center for the Masons, is at the bottom of half the tackles. Tackle Brown plays with that same quiet and workmanlike fury.

The Steers' captain-for-the-game, Pug Few, had a great defensive game for North Side. "The frequent pass interceptions kept the crowd in a constant dither. It was the best aerial circus in Texas."

And the Masons win the game, 6-0, which everyone agrees is, to all intents and purposes, for the District 7 football championship. Spaced between those two gigantic passes of Keel's are 60 minutes of throbbing suspense. This Mason-Steer game is a true life drama. Put it in the movies and the theatrical critics will rasp: "Overdone; Unbelievable!"

Frank Tolbert had witnessed hundreds of games in his career, but never had he witnessed a game like this one.

The Sonics walked off the gridiron with their splendid nonchalance, District 7 seemingly in their back pockets. And they won playing positions hardly rehearsed.

Sportswriter Lorin McMullen of the *Fort Worth Star-Telegram* wrote later:

But in twenty years we have never seen a high school football team pound for pound so talented as Coach Rusty Russell's little squad. It seemed ridiculous at the time to pick Masonic over North Side. The Steers, almost as big as Highland Park, had one of the most powerful defensive teams in the state. A fact that is borne by the fact of their record. The Masons did not do much to the North Side line, but the eleven little blockers managed to check those forward long enough for Keel, Hudgins, Bonds and Earp to start their monkey business.

"Now the field lights are being dimmed and the game is over between the North Side Steers and Masonic Home Masons, fiercest Welterweight footballers in all the world," reported Tolbert. "And I am playing my typewriter with shaking hands…."

District 7 Standing

Team	W	L	P. CT.
Masonic Home	2	0	1.000
Polytechnic	1	0	1.000
North Side	1	1	.500
Arlington Heights	1	1	.500
Paschal	0	0	.000
Riverside	0	1	.000
Technical	0	2	.000

Game At A Glance

North Side		Masonic Home
10	First Downs	11
163	Yards Gained Rushing	55
19	Yards Lost Rushing	20
39	Yard Gained Passing	119
8	Passes Completed	6
10	Passes Incomplete	29
6	Passes Intercepted By	3
86	Runback of Pass Interceptions, Yds.	15
11	Punts, Yardage	9 for 271
7	Runback of Punts, Yardage	45
30	Kickoffs, Yardage	95
42	Runback of Kickoffs, Yardage	0
3 for 25	Penalties, Yardage	3 for 15
3	Fumbles	1

Score by periods:

North Side	0	0	0	0–0
Masonic Home	0	0	0	6–6

First downs by periods:

North Side	2	0	4	4–10
Masonic Home	2	3	2	4–11

Scoring Summary
Masonic Home–
Keel passed to Strange for touchdown in fourth quarter (Brown failed to kick goal from placement).

Substitutions
North Side
Boswell, Henson, Hotchkiss, Keller

Masonic Home
Hudgins, Webster, A. Roach, Carter

The Sonics loaded the bus and headed home. Fifteen minutes later, as they turned onto the Pike, the little kids seemed to scream and clap louder than usual.

Eight-year-old Richard Opperman idolized Miller and the entire '38 team. They were his heroes. When the boys returned to the locker room, Richard asked the players, "Can we have your ankle tape?" He and the other boys then rolled the tape into a little white football to play with as a memento.

The Interscholastic League may have lacked compassion for the kids from the Home, but the Masons were tugging at the heartstrings of many higher-ups in the community and beyond. According to the *Star-Telegram*, Miller and the rest of the team had received a personal invitation to join Bob O'Donohue at the Worth Theater the following night as his personal guests. However, the *Fort Worth Star-Telegram* may have misspelled the man's name, as the record shows that Bob O'Donnell was a prominent businessman and philanthropist to whom both Bob Hope and Audie Murphy gave credit as the person who gave them their break into show business. He was the general manager for Majestic Theaters in Fort Worth, Dallas, San Antonio, and Houston, and he presided over 200 theaters. The Worth featured both film and live performances. Hollywood movie producers called him "the #1 exhibitor in the U.S." Broadway producers called him an "outside sizzler," organized charities called him a "port in any storm," and his employees called him "The Boss with a heart of Irish gold."

Bob O' Donnell made Miller and the rest of the boys feel very special that night. The grandness of the theater itself made any patron feel special the instant they walked through the door and saw the larger-than-life statues on the wall, a rose window on the elaborate ceiling and a grand balcony floating over the lower seating area.

After the Masons defeated North Side, they got a "breather," an extra week to prepare for the non-district game with the Sherman Bearcats on Friday, October 14, 1938. After that, they did not play again until Thursday, October 27, against the Bulldogs of Technical. Russell counted on taking advantage of the time between games for the injured players to fully recover and bring their team back up to full strength.

Thankfully, the Masons had made it through the stirring 6-0 conquest of the North Side Steers without any additional game-ending injuries. The lack of additional injuries was a win in itself, since many of the boys had played out of their element in their new positions.

The Masons had now defeated four of the most powerful teams in the state. And now they began to prepare for their non-district matchup with the Sherman Bearcats.

At the Home, Gene Keel's job would prove to carry a lot more significance than one would think—he rang the school bells between classes. But the day before the Sherman game, Keel had a lot of studying to do and a fellow student agreed to ring the bells in his place.

§

During the days of Indian summer, Russell's savage little eleven had conquered their toughest opposition, proving once again that the Masons were the best at taking advantage of every opportunity. This lightweight team was undefeated after walking off the gridiron against four of the most powerful teams in the State: the Wichita Falls Coyotes, the Dallas Highland Park Scots, the Amon Carter-Riverside Eagles, and the North Side Steers.

fourteen

Stay Calm

Although a hot battle with the team from Sherman was expected, the Masons had suddenly become the heavy favorite going into the game. The Masons were the only team in the district that week playing a "foreign foe," a term used to describe non-district games.

As they pulled into Bearcat territory, the customers were already seated and waiting. Arriving just in time for the game, the Masonic Home Masons filed off the bus, but instead of their usual nonchalant style, they sprinted to the dressing room. The customers would never know the nightmare they had experienced moments before walking onto the field.

During the bus trip to Sherman's Fair Park Stadium, the bus driver had an accident. No one was quite sure why it happened, or why the driver thought the bus could clear the railroad bridge, but it did not. The bus was clearly taller than the bridge. Everything on the roof, and part of the roof itself, was torn off upon impact.

The boys instantly covered their ears as a horrific screeching noise exploded above them. Sparks flew as pieces of the roof curled back. Boys ducked to protect themselves from debris.

The driver pulled the bus to the side of the road and Mr. Russell immediately ordered every boy to step off so he could personally ensure no one had been injured. Thankfully, no one had been seriously hurt; a little rattled, but no serious injuries.

Russell, the bus driver and the boys searched the area for supplies thrown from the vehicle and found enough space inside the bus to accommodate everything. After gathering up what they could find, they tried to settle back in their seats for the rest of the trip to Sherman. Russell wiped his forehead, relieved the boys had not sustained any injuries.

The boys held their breath during the driver's next attempt at passing under a bridge, but it turned out to be a snap since part of the bus was now missing.

Despite the dramatic trip, the Sonics walked onto the field without asking any favors or offering any excuses and played ball.

Leon Pelly, the Bearcat's ace halfback, scored two touchdowns against the Masons in the second period.

During the half, the little boys walked off the field and into the dressing room. Mr. Russell let them know they needed to improve during the second half and they discussed strategy. "We never heard Mr. Russell curse," remembered both Tom Brady and Miller Moseley.

The team left the dressing room and walked onto the field ready to face their opponent. Leon Pelly made a third touchdown in the third period.

An opportunity for the Masons came when Pelly received the ball from the center on the 10-yard mark and punted. Jeff Brown jumped high in the air and successfully blocked the kick, and Manson recovered the ball for a touchdown. Jeff Brown kicked the extra point. The Masons continued to push through the fourth quarter as they drove down to the 10-yard line. But they simply weren't their usual spectacular club and just could not get it together. They lost on downs after the team had taken the ball on a punt exchange on the Masons' 45.

No matter how high the score mounted, the Home forces would prove their greatness with an exhibition of determination and enthusiasm until the game ended. Sherman won. The final score was 20 to 7.

After the Sonics were back on the bus, Mr. Russell told them, "You played a good game. We must move on and get ready for our next game against Technical. This game is water under the bridge."

The boys leaned back in their seats. Back at the Home the kids had heard the outcome on the radio with disappointment and would not learn about the accident until the players stepped off the bus.

Starting Lineups:

Masonic Home		Sherman
Moseley	L.E.	O. Robnett
Holmans	L.T.	Livingston
McHam	L.G.	Carruth
Torres	C.	Baxter
Bates	R.G.	Meredith
Brown (co-c)	R.T.	Tolbert
Strange	R.E.	Crosby
Keel	Q.B.	Bean
Earp	R.H.	Petty
Bonds (co-c)	L.H.	Hatfield
Roach	F.B.	Reid

Substitutes:

Masonic Home	Sherman
Manson, A. Roach	McCall,
Hoskins, Coulter	Petty, Brown,
B. Bennett,	J. Robnett,
Webster, Ferguson	Huggins,
Carter, G. Brown	O'Hara,
M Torres, Lowrie	Willis, Stout

October 14, 1938, starting lineup, Masons vs Sherman Bearcats.

Score by periods

Sherman	0	13	7	0-20
Masonic Home	0	0	0	7-7

Game At A Glance

Sherman		Masonic Home
9	First Downs	8
165	Yards Gained Rushing	61
15	Yards Gained Passing	113
1 of 7	Passes Completed	15 of 38
12 for 349	Punts	7 for 200

The *Master Builder*, the perfect source for words of encouragement, read:

Don't Give Up
If the road is rough and the journey steep;
If you find it hard the pace to keep
Don't Give Up
If you seem to lose when you ought to win
If the feeling comes that you must give in
Don't Give Up
If reverses smite and lay you low
If the prompting comes that you must let go
Don't Give Up
If all the world seems hard and unjust
Keep close to God and in him trust
Don't Give Up

Back at the Masonic Home, inside the warm, dry, red brick building, the lights had been turned off. Spoken in a low tone, the boys discussed the strange accident and the disappointing loss that evening and they decided the loss might have had something to do with the fact that Gene Keel did not ring the school bells, which was most unusual. From that day forward, Keel's ringing of the bells was considered serious business.

The much-anticipated and much-needed rest between games was a welcomed relief far greater than had been anticipated, especially because of the unexpected bus theatrics. The coaches and the team regrouped, settled down, put the past behind them, and focused on the upcoming game against Tech. On Thursday night, October 27, 1938, Rusty Russell's pint-sized team would be ready to tangle with the Tech Bulldogs at LaGrave Field.

§

There were no other activities scheduled for the football team during football season other than practicing, scrimmaging and playing games. All dances were scheduled during the off season, and during that time the junior and senior dances were held in the gym with the music blaring from the Home's record player. Miss McGee, the girls' chaperone, generally held the dances, which lasted an hour or two. The boys wanted the dances to last longer, so they developed a system where one boy after the other would start dancing with Miss McGee, keeping her preoccupied so that she lost track of time. It worked. Whether she ever realized what the boys were doing or not was beside the point.

Upon entering their junior year, the Home allowed the boys a social hour date with their girlfriends. This took place on Sunday afternoon on a particular bench located in the circle in front of the large girls' building. It was understood that the kids had to maintain a distance of at least six inches between them. The girls' buildings were located on the south end of the campus, and the boys' buildings were on the north end. "We were never allowed to hold hands, and putting your arm around your girlfriend was a no-no, except at the dances," said Tom Brady.

During football season, if the boys were not studying, they spent their time on football. They had a set routine. When the school bell rang at 3:45 p.m., the boys walked swiftly to the athletic room where Tom Posey provided clean practice uniforms. The Sonics quickly dressed and they practiced until dark. Once it was too dark to see the flying football, they showered, dressed and arrived at the dining hall for dinner. In the dining hall the team sat together at tables set up specifically for the squad. After dinner they went off to study hall, that is, unless a boy was on the honor roll, as Miller always was. The boys who made the honor roll had additional freedom to decide how to spend their time. But in order to keep top honors on the honor roll, Miller continued to study hard. At 9:30 p.m. each night the lights flashed and all the boys returned to their dorms. Shortly after crawling into bed, the lights were turned off in every dorm room in the building. For boys who struggled to finish their homework, the Home allowed them to study in the restroom where the lights remained on at all times.

§

This would be the first time the Masons had ever played against Tech. By this time, the Masons had convinced the throng of fans to choose them for the unaccustomed role as favorite going into the game. However, the struggling Tech team had only won one game so far this season, against Eastland. The stats for Tech were lopsided; they had been outscored 72 to 19 in the five games they had played, so from the fans' perspective, the Masons were a shoe-in.

Tech's Lopsided Losses for the 1938 Season

Tech		Opponents
6	Sweetwater	25
0	Arlington Heights	7
0	North Side	14
13	Eastland	0
0	Poly	26
19	Total	72

Mr. Russell reported his disabled list was improving. Fullback Don Stephens would be ready to play a little football against Tech. Hudgins and the other Masons who'd had disabling injuries would be ready as well.

"Frankly, I'm afraid of the Tech game," Rusty reported. "They have a good team with lots of spirit and unless we're ready for a tough one, we may be surprised."

The Masons had a promising start when Horace McHam caught a Bulldogs' fumble in midfield. As the game progressed, Russell started sending in the substitutes. When the game ended, the only Mason on the field who was not a reserve was Don Stephens, and he was not put in the game until it was almost over, and that was to test his knee.

The Masons defeated the Tech Bulldogs 15-0.

§

The Texas Interscholastic Football League officially announced the proposed realignment for the 1939 state championship on Tuesday evening, November 1, 1938. The executive committee at Austin officially announced it would disqualify the Masonic Home's gridmen from future state championship competition due to enrollment. The league director, R.J. Kidd, stated that only schools with enrollments of 500 or more would be allowed into Class AA. Those with an enrollment falling between 450-499 would play Class A and schools with an enrollment which fell between 159-199 might be allowed to play in Class A by special vote. Since the Masonic Home and School only had 19 senior boys enrolled that year, this proposal dropped one of the State's finest football clubs with a winning record from Class A. They would not be allowed to compete in Class AA, Class A or Class B. The Fort Worth school system was prepared to protest this action which had been decided upon by a handful of members on the Texas Interscholastic Football League.

Mr. Russell was at home, sick, when the announcement was made and he could not be reached by the press. Reporters found his assistant, Otha Tiner, on the practice field preparing the Masons for their Friday night game. To answer the sympathetic news reporters, Tiner said, "It would break our hearts to get out of the top competition." The league never contacted Russell; he heard of the proposed changes through the *Fort Worth Star-Telegram*.

Russell said later, "It seems to me they do things without due consideration. We've had trouble all along over rules. It seems to me that somebody is exerting undue influence on the league heads. You can tell the world we'll fight this new thing. We appreciate the fact that the Class A division is becoming unwieldy but I don't think they will help any by dropping such teams as Vernon, Kerrville and Masonic Home."

Star-Telegram reporter Amos Melton wrote, "No advance notices of the proposed changes were received by say schoolmen here. This was unusual in itself. As have most of the recently proposed rules changes, it is believed the new districting plan is advocated by 'big city' schools such as Dallas, San Antonio and Houston. Fort Worth has almost always opposed and certainly does in this instance."

Norman Earl, Athletic Director for Fort Worth schools, promised to back the Masons and do whatever he could to fight the committee's decision. The Masons drew big crowds and much needed income for the school district. The huge, highly advertised new stadium, Farrington Field, would open its gates next year and it would be sad for the customers of Fort Worth to have this new, large, beautiful stadium without the little boys from the Masonic Home being able to play in it. Norman Earl said, "Masonic Home will stay in if we have anything to say. After all, it's really one of our city schools. The Mason games are always big drawing cards. Financially speaking, it's worth more to us to have the Masons in our district even if a city team never won the sector title and got into the state playoff. They're that valuable. But there's more to it than money. They belong in our district and should be there." Herbert Joseph, official of the Mosiah Temple Drum and Bugle Corps, met with Russell to discuss the matter at Russell's home where he remained confined by illness. Later, as he continued to battle his illness, Russell watched the Masons practice from his car parked on the sidelines.

§

If the Paschal Panthers could pull off a win against the Masonic Home Masons' tricks, they would cause an upset and move to the top of the district's standings.

At 8 o'clock on Friday, November 4, 1938, a full-capacity crowd lined up at the LaGrave Field ticket office, many of whom supported the Masons as they continued to edge closer towards their bid for the District 7 championship in what may very well have been their last contest in that district.

All the uproar and disbelief over the Masonic Home's demotion from the state championship football competition in 1939 may have hurt Paschal's shot at succeeding against the Sonics. Paschal's football team had improved and were looking as if they had a good chance of beating the Masons. They'd had a slow start, but had turned the team around. But now that the Interscholastic Leage had gone through great pain to shut out the Masonic Home, the Sonics' desire to win the game went much deeper than a simple "W" in the win/loss column. The Sonics were a superb team which had been denied by League members. The Sonics had incentive to show the League what they were made of, and if Russell was still too sick to attend Friday's game, the Sonics had another deep-rooted motive to exert every ounce of their strength to blast through the purple shirts: a win would be the perfect "get well" card for Russell. All the improvement in the world may not have been strong enough to beat the Sonics' physiological game.

It had been a wet week with constant rain. If the rain let up, Rusty Russell planned to be on the bench with his team that night, otherwise Tiner would take full coaching duties. For the first time in a while, the Masonic Home Masons would be at full strength on the field. Don Stephens would be in his old spot after the long layoff due to his leg injury. Co-captain Frank Bonds, Gene Keel and Buford Hudgins would fill out the backfield with a regular line that had played all of nearly every game that year. Moseley, Holmans, Bates, Torres, McHam, Brown and Strange would be on duty as usual. With a healthy team came hard workouts.

A muddy infield could play havoc with players. Due to the soggy field and the slim chance of any kind of effective ground game, fans and reporters alike expected the air show to be a spectacular competition. Both Paschal's Harmon Hightower and the Home's Gene Keel were considered the top two aerialists in the league, and this game could determine the king aerialists of District 7.

The Masons lagged 0-13 early on, but in the second quarter they came back and tied the game 13-13. After rallying from the 13-point deficit, the Home boys continued to push with undeniable energy all the way through the fourth to win the game 20-13. The officials got a kick out of listening to the crowd: the fans yelled, screamed and stomped their feet at the beginning of the game, but as the Masons began to dominate the Panthers, the roar of the crowd grew silent. Paschal's Hightower may have wowed the audience, but the Masonic Home's tempestuous little aerialists came out the winner in the end.

"It is a game to bring a lump to your throat and keep it there," reported Frank Tolbert of the *Fort Worth Star-Telegram,* "maybe in admiration for a Paschal passing attack that is as beautiful as anything you will ever see, or maybe in admiration for a Mason team that gets up off the floor from a two-touchdown count in the first quarter and goes on to win."

The night did not disappoint the fans; it was indeed a dazzling show of passing. However, it did come as a bit of a shock to Fort Worth fans when critics chose Harmon Hightower as the most excellent passer in the Interscholastic Football League over Gene Keel. Hightower was crowned king aerialist. Don Stephens gave a star studded appearance when he limped into the game and hobbled for eight yards through the middle. Several plays later, Keel charged in for a touchdown. Jeff Brown's kick was good. Later, Paschal sent the crowd to their feet with wild cheers and another touchdown. But the crowd sat down in silence when the announcer called back the touchdown due to a backfield-in-motion penalty.

Game At A Glance

Masonic Home		Paschal
16	First Downs	18
191	Yards Gained Rushing	138
8	Yard Lost Rushing	14
135	Yard Gained Passing	164
10	Passes Completed	17
10	Passes Incomplete	16
2	Passes Intercepted By	2
29	Runback of Pass Interceptions, Yds.	13
3 for 109	Punts, Yardage	3 for 135
15	Runback of Punts, Yardage	10
4 for 182	Kickoffs, Yardage	3 for 150
80	Runback of Kickoffs, Yardage	78
4 for 20	Penalties, Yardage	2 for 10
1	Fumbles	2

§

It had been a rainy fall in 1938 and if the weather permitted, the Masons would meet the Arlington Heights Yellow Jackets at 8 o'clock, Friday evening, November 11, 1938. Heights was still in the race for the District 7 title despite numerous injuries plaguing the team all season. The stakes were high for both teams going into the game. If the Masons lost they would wind up in a tie with the Poly Parrots. Fighting both Mother Nature and a tough competitor would be tricky on the slippery LaGrange baseball field.

Fans loved the hustle, hard work and positive attitude the Masons displayed on the field. This game would bring the "orphans" of the Masonic Home face-to-face against the wealthy students of Arlington Heights, who were referred to as "tea sippers." "Tea sippers" was a nickname Texas A & M called the Texas Longhorns because the University of Texas students were more likely to become doctors and lawyers; the label was passed on to the privileged students at Heights. A throng of 5,500 customers, including many of Fort Worth's wealthiest families, would be in attendance.

Heights had experienced a season riddled with injuries, but they had fought in a few impressive battles which had kept them in the race. Coach Mack Flenniken had a near full-strength team for the first time that season, and he felt very optimistic they could win against the Masons. Frank Bonds surprised Russell with a swollen knee that evening, but Russell was not quick to write him out of the game just yet. Other than Bonds, Miller, Stephens, Keel and the other Masons were ready to hit the wet, unstable gridiron.

The game had just started when Don Stephens smashed into Dewees on an off-tackle, reinjuring his knee. Don did his familiar hobble back to his familiar spot on the bench. Russell leaned over to make sure Don was okay or if he needed to return to the Home to let Dr. Hall look at it. Later, Gene Keel kicked a high 40-yard punt, but Yellow Jacket safety, Wood, caught the ball on his own 10 and took off running thinking he was in the clear. But when Wood hit the 20, Miller Moseley, A.P. Torres and Norman Strange appeared out of nowhere and he lost control of the ball. Jeff Brown recovered it for the Masons and scored a touchdown. The Masons blended colorful showmanship with fearless running and passes on the rain-soaked mud and turf. Jackets quarterback Scotty Finks and guards Mike Harter and Louis Heath played exceedingly well against the strong Masons team, but after Keel received some hard knocks, he ran the ball to the Jackets' 10. Later, on the fourth down, Keel flipped a perfect pass to Moseley in the end zone for a touchdown. Jeff Brown's kick was high enough, but slightly to the right of the crossbars, so it didn't count.

The Masons maintained their 6-0 lead fairly easily despite the elements. Suddenly, the game became a spectacular show. During the last few minutes of the second period, Keel blasted the Jackets with an assortment of laterals, spinners and plays that would make the pros queasy. Those stomach-churning plays carried the team almost the length of the football field. The Sonics were just short of another touchdown, when *bang!* Field Judge P.C. Stanley shot the gun ending the first half. As the teams exited the field, Heights fans were mentally exhausted.

As the teams walked back onto the field after the halftime break, Dewees of the Yellow Jackets fumbled a pass and the Home's Horace McHam gained possession of the ball. The clever Masons then tricked their opponent when Keel rammed into the line with a fierce punch, slipping the ball to Buford Hudgins who followed blocker Bonds down the sidelines and scored another touchdown. The Masonic Home eleven dominated the game at LaGrave Field, leaving the Arlington Heights Yellow Jackets empty-handed, 13-0, and the baseball field a mess. The Jackets congratulated the Masons and said they had never seen such an intellectually-played football game. The Masons were now caught in a tie for the District 7 football championship.

Game At A Glance

Masonic Home		Arlington Heights
10	First Downs	7
149	Yards Gained Rushing	123
32	Yard Lost Rushing	30
53	Yard Gained Passing	22
6 of 15	Passes Completed	5 of 15
2	Passes Intercepted	1
12 for 427	Punts (Yards)	10 for 327
3 for 15	Penalties	2 for 20
0	Fumbles	3

A warm shower always felt good after a hard-fought football game on LaGrange Field, especially when the red dirt from the pitcher's mound was caked on their skin. And at this age the boys were on their own, that is, they were no longer required to sit on stools to wait for their tad of toothpaste and time in the shower. They had earned their independence from the housemother's regimen.

§

Norman opened the paper and smiled a wide toothy grin when he saw the picture and caption in the *Fort Worth Star-Telegram*. He elbowed Miller and said, "Miller, there has been a lot of news about this Morris guy. Word is he is a pretty good football player. Will he be taking your place?" The boys laughed.

As the boys practiced for the upcoming contest between them and the Polytechnic High School Parrots on Friday, November 18, 1938, they knew it would be another grandstand show. The Parrot-Mason rivalry had had a strong influence on the District 7 title for many years.

The contest had begun in 1935 when the two teams fought bitterly for the District 7 championship. The first game was played at LaGrave Field and ended in a tie when Durwood Horner tripped over the pitcher's mound, losing a chance to score. They met once more on the gridiron at T.C.U, which resulted in another tie. However, the Masons ended up taking the title on 20-yard penetrations and played in the state playoff. Both teams intended to walk away from this game with a win, but even if the Masons lost this last game of the regular season, they were still guaranteed a tied standing for the District 7 championship.

1938 Records

Masonic Home	Opponent		Poly	Opponent	
7	Wichita Falls	7	0	Vernon	26
20	Riverside	6	25	Borger	13
14	Highland Park	13	7	Arlington Heights	0
6	North Side	0	25	Technical	0
7	Sherman	20	13	Paschal	13
15	Technical	0	0	North Side	0
20	Paschal	13	20	Bryan	21
13	Arlington Heights	0			

Once again, Athletic Director Norman Earl had to make adjustments to accommodate the more than 10,000 fans expected to attend the game before the 8 o'clock kickoff. But he was delighted to have such a dilemma.

Both coaches, Rusty Russell of Masonic Home and Luther Scarborough of Poly, expressed a pessimistic view Thursday afternoon to the sportswriters on hand.

Rusty Russell continued his pregame moaning ritual. Minor injuries pervaded the team, and he indicated he didn't know just how long those players would be able to play. Russell lamented about the injuries his first string backfield had experienced throughout the season, but the reality of the situation was the Parrots were in worse shape. Poly's bruising guard, Dutch Alford, was injured as well as their ferocious running back, Fred Smith. Coach Luther Scarborough pushed hard to groom his substitutes but he was not optimistic about their performance or the team's chance of winning the game.

"We'll do the best we can," coach Scarborough declared. "Nobody has stopped the Masons yet and I don't see how we can keep them from scoring. I hope we can score, too, but I don't know if we can tally enough."

Russell started a backfield comprised of Frank Bonds at fullback, Phillip Earp and Buford Hudgins at halfbacks and Gene Keel at quarterback. On offense, Scarborough's secondary would consist of team captain Johnny Hunter and Fred Smerke at halfbacks, Bert Moody at fullback and Bob Henderson in the quarterback slot. Fred Smith, one of the district's hardest-running backs was out with a shoulder injury.

On Poly's forward wall, Luther Scarborough installed Marshall McMahan and R.O Woodall as starting ends, Harold Brown and Bob Fannin as tackles, H.L. Nicholson and Chesley Lewis as guards, and Jack Garrett as center. The Mason linesmen, as usual, would be Norman Strange and Miller Moseley as wings, Jeff Brown and James Holmans as tackles, Jack Bates and Horace McHam as guards, and A.P. Torres as pivot.

Friday night, under the lights at LaGrave field, Scarborough's injury-plagued team succumbed to the powerful little Masons, who crushed the Polytechnic's Parrots 39-0.

Masonic Home	Game At A Glance	Polytechnic
23	First Downs	9
372	Yards Gained Rushing	49
13	Yard Lost Rushing	20
194	Yard Gained Passing	119
10	Passes Completed	10
11	Passes Incomplete	16
4	Passes Intercepted By	0
26	Runback of Pass Interceoptions, Yds.	0
7 for 264	Punts, Yardage	9 for 346
4	Runback of Punts, Yardage	19
6 for 444	Kickoffs, Yardage	2 for 105
20	Runback of Kickoffs, Yardage	63
4 for 20	Penalties, Yardage	1 for 5
4	Fumbles	5

The Parrots had won every district game that season and walked off the field sorely disappointed.

fifteen

Plenty of Room

Saturday, December 3, 1938, "Sunset will face a team Saturday which is to Texas schoolboy football what Notre Dame is to the national football picture," said Frank Tolbert, reporter for the *Fort Worth Star-Telegram*.

Ticket sales for the District 7 championship were estimated to be over 30,000, and to accommodate the fans, tickets were made available at numerous locations throughout Fort Worth and Dallas. This time, however, there was no need for Norman Earl to fuss over seating all of the fans; he knew there would be plenty of room for everyone at the Cotton Bowl in Dallas. For once, he could relax and enjoy the game.

In Fort Worth, customers flocked to the Masonic Home, Stripling's Travel Bureau, Renfro's at Sixth and Main, and at Greines Department Store on the North Side to purchase tickets before they sold out. In Dallas, the tickets sold out quickly, but Masonic Home officials promised to print as many tickets as needed.

Mason-Sunset
Starting Lineups

Masonic Home					Sunset High	
(Fort Worth Champions)			vs		**(Dallas Champions)**	
Number	Player	Weight	Position	Weight	Player	Number
6	Morris Moseley	128	L.E.	155	Hugh DeVoss	51
43	Jeff Brown (Co-C)	165	L.T.	167	Charles Henderson	66
23	Jack Bates	135	L.G.	150	Johnny Whilden	55
22	A.P. Torres	144	C.	145	Clay Stephenson	64
37	Horace McHam	157	R.G.	160	Billy Cobb	63
40	James Holmans	155	R.T.	176	T.C. Morgan	62
33	Norman Strange	137	R.E.	160	Garnett Terry	61
24	Gene Keel	150	Q.B.	152	Sonny Grost	54
35	Buford Hudgins	135	L.H.	165	Bryan Lloyd	68
28	Phillip Earp	131	R.H.	139	Duane Utgard	49
25	Frank Ronds (Co-C)	145	L.H.	175	Kenneth Robbins	70

Dallas Sunset Reserves

Number	Player	Number	Player	Number	Player
3	Lowery	23	Blagg	58	Simmons
4	Compton	24	Coffey	60	Mack
8	Hamman	50	Crisp	67	E.Smith
9	Reitz	52	Bender	69	Donald
15	Rawlings	53	Blaylock	71	Kockas
		57	Carroll	72	D. Smith

Masons Reserves

Number	Player	Number	Player	Number	Player
1	Manson	21	Finnigen	24	Lowrie
3	Crocker	26	A.Roach	36	Carter
4	Coulter	27	Bennett	38	Ferguson
5	J. Torres	29	Land	39	Crumbley
20	Webster N.	31	Hoskins	41	Stephens
		32	B.Roach	42	G. Brown

December 3, 1938, starting lineup,
Masons vs Sunset Bisons, District 7 Championship.

Sunset's coach, Herman Cowley, made sure his Assistant, Byron Rhome, had attended every Mason game that season, and what he reported back was an amazement that went beyond talent. The Masons never gave up. They never tired. They pushed and pushed until they had accomplished what they had set out to do even if it took them the last five minutes of the game to accomplish. He warned Cowley not to let the comparatively small Masons lull the Bisons into a free and easy state. The Masonic line was tough and agile, coupled with fine blocking ability and great speed. But the Bisons had two advantages. They blistered Sherman, 20-0, and they had a full month to prepare for the Mason-Bison playoff game.

Out on the Masons' practice field a throng of sportswriters tried to figure how to describe what fans could expect from the Masons. They watched the kids practice from the time they walked out of the dressing room until they returned to the dressing room for the evening, and the best they could come up with was, "The Masonic Home's opponents from now on may find the Masons' aerial offensive arrangements simply too annoying for words." But the Masons had more than their smoke and mirror plays to depend on. Don Stephens was one of the hardest-hitting fullbacks, and Gene Keel rattled opponents when it came to running a broken field.

On Saturday, December 3, 1938, at 2:30 in the afternoon, on a cloudy day and on a muddy field, the Masons walked onto the gridiron at the Cotton Bowl. The Dallas champion Sunset Bisons were already on the field warming up. The game was played exceptionally clean, without any penalties for roughness. The only two penalties were for off sides and backfield in motion. Frank Bonds switched with Keel a few times during the game, and when he did his target was Gene Keel. However, when Keel threw the ball, he showed no favorites, hitting Miller Moseley, Frank Bonds, Buford Hudgins, Norman Strange, Phillip Earp, Don Stephens, and Buster Roach with his heaves.

Norman Strange pushed the Masons toward the first touchdown in the second quarter when he intercepted a pass thrown by the Sunset center on the Masons' 39. Keel passed to left-end Miller Moseley for the first down on the Sunset 33. Then Keel threw to the right to Frank Bonds, who ran to the 11-yard line, then to Buford Hudgins on the 2-yard line. Hudgins dodged Sunset's Sonny Grost with a goat-like jump and crossed into the end zone for a touchdown. Keel's kick was no good. The Masons led 6-0 at the half. P.C. Cobb, the Dallas City Athletic Director, watched with a personal conviction. His son, Bill Cobb, was a Bison guard.

Frank Tolbert later wrote, "There is nothing more beautiful in motion than the orange-shirted Masonic Home boys when their offense is moving." It was like looking into a kaleidoscope as the orange moved superbly through the purple. Several plays into the second half Keel ran for a touchdown and Jeff Brown kicked the extra point. It wasn't long until the Masons led 20-0, at which time Russell sent in the substitutes, early in the fourth quarter. The fans did not leave disappointed. The savvy ball handling by the Sonics flabbergasted those who had never seen the orange shirts before. The game ended with the Masons eliminating Sunset 20-0. The little boys from the Masonic Home and School had run away with the District 7 championship.

"The common reaction of sportswriters, scouts and fans alike was, 'How can those little boys do any good against that Sunset team?' But a little over a couple of hours later when the crowd was filing out of the big stadium, the question had changed to 'How can those little boys do it?'" said Breezy Carroll, sportswriter for the *Fort Worth Star-Telegram*.

"The victory was a ringing rebuttal to the Masons' critics on the league executive committee who had already demoted Rusty Russell's bitter blocking little boys to a lower division of competition," wrote Frank Tolbert.

Miller had little time to rest between studies, chores, printing responsibilities, football practice and games, but he did manage to sit down for a minute one evening on the cold ground beside the practice field. Norman Strange plopped down beside him eager to relay the latest updates according to the *Star-Telegram*. "And it states this Morris Moseley guy is a pretty good football player and will be playing in your position for the Highland Park game." Miller flashed a smile.

§

Movie star Mary Pickford, known as "America's Sweetheart," was staying at the Adolphus Hotel in Dallas the week after the Masons trounced Sunset. Co-founder of both United Artists and the Motion Picture Academy of Arts and Sciences, she was in town as a political supporter. Excited fans sat through a dull, two-hour political yawn fest for the chance to see Pickford from across the room. Crowds formed in the lobby in hopes of a glimpse, but as she walked through she expressed more interest in the Fort Worth Masonic Home Masons and sent the boys a special invitation.

Prior to the quarter-final Mason versus Highland Park game, the Masons stayed at the same hotel as Mary Pickford. As wealthy socialites clamored for a glimpse of Miss Pickford, she wanted nothing more than to meet the famous high school football team and invited them to her suite for a visit. The Masons quietly filed into her room. Miller said, "I thought it was strange she was in bed."

After she was introduced to each player, she wished each boy good luck on their game against Dallas. "She kissed our cheek and gave everyone a personal autograph," said Jack Bates.

"I do not remember much about it, except someone told us to go in there and say 'howdy,'" Miller recalled.

Friday evening, December 9, 1938, Rusty Russell started his usual moaning and groaning to the sportswriters. The writers across Dallas and Fort Worth had caught on to his psychological warfare. In fact, he taught his very enthusiastic assistant, Otha Tiner, very well, for he too was feeling mighty sorry for himself as he stated, "There's not a way in the world we can win. At the best, it's a 100-to-1 chance." However, Tiner needed a little more coaching as Russell would never have stated such odds as 100-to-1; he would have weighed in at 200-to-1 at best. Russell had expressed deep self-pity and no confidence in his team on two previous occasions. On both occasions the Masons returned to the Home game winners, scoring 6-0 against North Side and 20-13 against Paschal. As Mr. Russell fretted, the reporters came away feeling the Masons just might win.

It was a tough decision, but Russell chose to skip Tuesday's scrimmage practice. It was definite: Philip Earp's knee injury would keep him out of the game and it wasn't looking good for Jack Bates either. He had become ill and had made a trip to the Home's hospital. Bates was beginning to feel better on Wednesday, but Russell felt all he could afford without losing additional assets was an incredibly long workout on defense. They went over and over their defensive maneuvers. All dummy work. Russell knew the Highlanders had a good passing game, but he was more concerned about their ground maneuvers. Both Keel and Bonds would be in good shape for the game and would alternate as quarterback.

The Sonics were pleasantly surprised to hear Sunset would be sitting on the Mason's side of the field on Saturday. The Masons were in high spirits when Don Stephens emerged out of the gates following the Sunset game uninjured.

Saturday afternoon at Ownby Stadium the Highlanders were the obvious pick to win the game, although one sports reporter said, "In 20 years we never have seen a high school football team, pound for pound, so talented as Coach Rusty Russell's little squad." All common sense pointed to Highland Park, a team which outweighed the Masons 26 pounds to the man. Plus Highland Park had the well-groomed star back, Dick Dwelle, who had been compared to Connie Sparks, Davey O'Brien and Earl Clark by sports enthusiast during that era, and he probably had a handful of scouts drooling over him.

Before the Masons took the field, Mr. Russell said, "You are going to have to play your best." When Russell used that line as a pre-game pep talk, the boys knew Russell thought they were in for a tough battle. Miller always played a smart ballgame and he always played a physical ballgame, but there would never be a scout in the stadium to offer him a much needed scholarship. The scouts were looking at the other teams, their opponents, the teams who were losing to the Masons. But the charisma of the small Masons enchanted the crowd into forgetting, if for only a moment, the lingering wounds of the Depression. Miller already knew he wanted to be an aeronautical engineer after he graduated, but how to pay for college was becoming a concern.

STARTING LINE-UPS

Highlanders Player	Position	Masonic Home Player
Seay	LE	Moseley
Swank	LT	Holmans
Waters	LG	McHam
R. Borgerson	C	Torres
Harkey	RG	Bates
C. Borgerson	RT	Brown
Germany	RE	Strange
Harris	QB	Keel
Dwelle	LH	Hudgins
Jordan	RH	Bonds
Munnell	FB	Stephens

December 9, 1938, starting lineup, Masons vs Highland Park Scots, Quarterfinals.

The two teams stood face-to-face again. At the beginning of the season, the Highlanders had an impressive record of fourteen wins and one defeat over the previous two years. Then the Sonics paid a visit to the Highlanders and muddied their statistics. Now they were standing eye-to-eye again. Highland was one of the most capable masters of the gridiron and they were ready for the elusive Sonics. The Highlanders came out strong. They had a near-perfect season and they worked hard to protect it. This was their chance to push some weight around and triumph in the quarterfinal Interscholastic League game. It was early in the game at S.M.U. Keel's kicks that night were as dangerous as his arm. He punted the ball and sent it fifty-three yards before it finally landed out of bounds on the Highland 13. Dick Dwelle, the 185-pound Highland halfback, went to work and quickly picked up four yards. On the next play the large halfback ran 87 yards for a touchdown. Dwelle was hot and the Dallas fans loved it.

Big Crowd Sees Plenty of Action in Schoolboy Grid Encounter Here

"In the top panel here, Dick Dwelle, ace ball lugger of the Highland Park Highlanders, is off on an eighty-two-yard run for the Scots' first touchdown Saturday on their second play from scrimmage. Grady Jordan is his teammate on the ground blocking out Jack Bates, Mason guard. Behind Bates are Miller Moseley then Virgil Harris and Jeff Brown. The inset in the large picture of the crowd is Grady Jordan of the Highlanders on a thirty-six-yard run for the Scots' second touchdown after catching a pass from Dwelle. Below the crowd picture Eugene Keel of the scrapping Masons is picking up eight yards on a wide sweep. Nearest to him in the picture is Johnny Seay. Back of the latter are Roger Borgeson (57) and Jack Swank (75)."

As Keel tried to stop Jordan on the five, three Scots ganged up on him. Dwelle missed the extra point after both touchdowns. The gun went off. Both teams exited the field for half.

Back in the dressing room, with the Masons down by 12, Russell looked at the boys as they sat quietly. They looked at him, eager to do whatever Russell instructed. The coach said, "You've had your break, now go play football." And that's what they did. Within a few minutes into the third quarter, the Masons took the ball on a punt at the Masons' 19 yard line and blasted down the field 81 yards on passes. Keel to Moseley, then Keel to Stephens, and again Keel to sticky-fingered Moseley for two first downs. They worked their way to the Highlander 12. Then Stephens moved the ball to the eight. Keel then shot one over the middle to Moseley for a touchdown. Unbelievable as it seemed, Brown missed the extra point again. Highland Park was leading, 12-6, but looked worn. The Masons on the other hand seemed to have endless energy. Following their touchdown, the Masons showed no emotion. They immediately got back to work. After they successfully stopped Highland Park from scoring, Dwelle kicked a beautiful punt that Buster Roach caught and ran with his famous speed back to the Highlander 39, from where the ball had been kicked.

After their first touchdown in the third, the Masons followed through beautifully, swarming the Scots with hornet-like zeal. At the start of the fourth, the clever Buster Roach ran back a punt 40 yards down the sidelines to the Scot 39 with Keel, Bonds and all the others blocking with determination. That was the run which beat the Scots: the Masons scored another touchdown. Again Bond's kick was no good.

The Scots then started a drive that ended on their 45 when the Masons indomitable guard, Fats McHam, broke through and tossed Dwelle for a five-yard loss. Dwelle kicked to the 23. From the 23, Stephens broke over his left guard and with power in every stride, he ran to the Dallas 26 before Dwelle took him down. Both Dwelle and Don got hurt on that play. Dick Dwelle, the 185-pound halfback and candidate for all-state was helped off the field after trying to tackle Don Stephens as the Mason fullback raced through the Dallas boys for 50 yards. Dwelle probably had family and scouts worried about how badly he was injured. Don stayed in. At this time penetrations favored the Masons 3 to 2. Two two-hundred-pound Highland Park tackles were then carried off the field groaning from the hard knocks received from 144-pound A.P. Torres, and 126-pound guard, Jack Bates.

Just before the game ended, Buddy Heminton, Scot back, fumbled on the Highland 47 when hit by Moseley, and Buster Roach recovered the ball. The game ended tied. "The score was 12-12. The Mason lightweights won on penetrations, 4 to 2. But Highland Park's most powerful team in history was beaten as thoroughly as if the score had been 59 to 2," said Frank Tolbert.

Game At A Glance

Scots		Masons
2	20-Yard Penetrations	4
12	First Downs	17
311	Total Yards Gained	398
246	Yards Gained Rushing	150
18	Yards Lost Rushing	17
88	Yards Gained Passing	245
0	Yards Lost Passing	0
3	Passes Completed	21
7	Passes Incompleted	19
0	Passes Intercepted By	0
8 for 205	Punts, Yardage	7 for 253
3 for 35	Penalties, Yardage	0 for 0
1	Fumbles Recovered By	1

With this triumph, the Fort Worth champions surged into the Interscholastic League's semifinals for the third time in seven seasons of Class A competition, most embarrassing for the elders in Austin who had already bounced Coach Rusty Russell's unconquerable kids from big-time competition next autumn.

Masons all over the state backed their boys. Every game the Sonics won was another argument in favor of convincing the Interscholastic League to reverse its decision. Weldon B. Chapman, the coach of the highly successful Westerners, whom the Masons would play in the semifinal Championship, had witnessed the sensational Highland Park-Masonic Home game from up in the stands. He had three words for Frank Tolbert: "Criminy, what passing!"

The Masons used three reserves. Miller played 100% of the entire game. "Highland Park failed to intercept a single one of Keel's 40 passes," said reporter Louis Cox. The Highlanders wished they could have kept the Masons off their schedule.

Park fans rose to their feet and burst into applause that continued until the Masons were out of sight.

As they loaded the bus, Jack Bates leaned over to Miller and said, "I hope Mary Pickford followed the game."

Sportswriters found it difficult to shine the spotlight on one specific Sonic. They had all equally contributed to a well-played ball game.

On December 10, 1938, Frank Tolbert wrote:

If my hands weren't shaking so, I might write a good story on how Masonic Home's little football-playing boys came from behind in the fourth quarter here Saturday afternoon with their undeniable passing magic and splattered Highland Park's cavemen Scots all over Ownby Stadium's gridiron.

Reporter Amos Melton said: "The countenances of certain officials of the Texas Interscholastic League must be a bright pink these December days. And it's not from cold either."

§

It's unclear why the Masons were in Longview, Texas, once in 1938, but they didn't go unnoticed. The Masons were respected for their clean plays and attitude, but a hotel staff learned their clean living went deeper than fans realized. As they left, the hotel guests watched the polite, quiet team pad through the lobby and out the door. The hotel manager alerted the cleaning crew. He then immediately called the local newspaper, which published the following story:

Order of Hotel Rooms Amazes Hotel Staff

It was too good to be true—but there it was, thought the hotel maid as she went to place in order the rooms which had just been deserted by the Masonic Home football squad here shortly after 7 a.m. Saturday. Could it be that anyone had used these rooms, she mused. She went to get the housekeeper. Sure enough, these were the right rooms. But not a single thing was out of place. The beds were made, the blankets folded, and the towels were all on their hangers. The floors were clean. The hotel manager was called. He inspected the rooms thoroughly. "That's the first time in all my experience as a hotel man that I have seen a football squad so orderly and well trained that they left their rooms in perfect order after departing," said Carl Kleppinger, the manager. He was high in praise of Coach H. N. Russell, who was in charge of the Masonic Home squad of 27 players. "That coach and his men certainly ought to be complimented," Mr. Kleppinger said.

sixteen

Lubbock

Every sportswriter wanted to win the Masonic Home as their assignment. What they would find when they dug deep into the lives of this team was they were a team on and off the field. Together they kept sadness away and together they stayed strong. As reporters followed the team with pencil and paper in hand as if they were royalty, the Masons continued on with their business, ignoring the reporters as if they were not there. And the sensational deluge of supporters continued to turn out in record numbers. All a newspaper had to print was "Masonic Home Tonight" and a standing-room-only crowd would faithfully attend. The scanty incomes earned during the Depression would not deter Mason followers from showing up wherever their team made an appearance. The Masons seemed to have the team effect on fans as well. As fans exited the stadium, they too felt encouraged.

When and where the semi-final championship game would be played was immensely critical to both the Lubbock Westerners and the Masonic Home Masons. The winner of a coin drop chose where and when the semi-final championship game would take place. If Russell won the coin drop, his pick was T.C.U. Stadium on Saturday, December 17, 1938. His tired boys would have a day of rest with no long trip and no threat of bad weather in Fort Worth. If Chapman won the coin drop, he wanted to play the game Friday afternoon at Texas Tech Stadium in Lubbock. The advantage: his boys would have over a week to practice, and he hoped to force Russell's boys back onto the gridiron in less than a week, leaving them little time to rest or prepare for the Westerners.

In addition to the time advantage, the Westerners were also accustomed to playing in the Texas Tech sand storms. Chapman desperately needed this game to be played in Lubbock. He needed to cripple the Masons in every way possible. If he won, the Masons would have no rest between games, they'd be forced to handle the trip to Lubbock, they'd have to play in less than desirable weather conditions and they would have little time to practice the Westerners' typical plays.

Due to the time crunch between now and the semi-final championship, the coin toss was performed after the quarterfinal game as the crowd exited Ownby Stadium.

Both Coaches stood motionless. Heads or tails? Rusty pushed his glasses up the bridge of his nose with one finger, looked at Chapman and said: "Heads." As the coin was thrown into the air, Rusty held his breath.

The coin fell. Due to Russell's poor eyesight, he could not tell how the coin had landed until he heard the official.

Tails!

He sighed heavily and stared at the ground. This was not good. Not good at all. The game Miller and every boy on the team had worked so hard for would be played in Lubbock at Texas Tech Stadium on Friday afternoon, December 17, 1938 at 2:30 p.m. Rusty Russell, the Home's bespectacled coach, said, "Both site and date were decided by the toss." Russell's wishes fell into chance's hands, and chance turned its face away from him and the boys.

The Masons had just played their heart out in a strenuous game against the Dallas Highland Park heavyweight Scots, and Masonic Home officials knew the boys could use a full week to recover and prepare for the semi-final championship against the Westerners. The Westerners had played their quarterfinal game the Friday before, giving them an extra day of rest. The Masons, at best, had time for two practices.

Record-wise, the two teams appeared evenly-matched: the Lubbock Westerners had scored 225 points to their opponents' 72 and had lost one game due to poor health. The Masons had scored 173 points to their opponents' 72 and had lost one game to Sherman. The semi-final championship contest would keep the nation glued to the radio, listening to the play-by-play action.

Masonic Home	1938 Records Opponent		Lubbock	Opponent	
7	Wichita Falls	7	7	North Side	6
14	Highland Park, Dallas	13	14	Abilene	0
20	Riverside	0	13	Capitol Hill, OK	14
6	North Side	0	7	Vernon	0
7	Sherman	20	67	Borger	13
15	Fort Worth Tech	0	6	Pampa	0
20	Paschal	13	6	Plainview	0
13	Arlington Heights	0	14	Lamesa	0
39	Poly	0	29	Amarillo	19
20	Sunset, Dallas	0	36	Breckenridge	14
12	Highland Park, Dallas	12			
===		===	===		===
173		72	225		72

Due to the publicity, officials also clamored for the opportunity to work this game. The officials who received the honor to officiate one of the most followed teams in the state of Texas were A.B. Curtis and Ray McCullough of Fort Worth, Jimmy Higgins of Dallas and R.H. Medley of Abilene.

As Russell studied his opponent he learned of an old legend. As the legend went, an invisible barbed wire fence served as a windbreak for Caprock country. If the fence was in good shape, it would keep the forecasted, chilly blast from sweeping over Texas Tech field and the semi-final championship game long enough, as sportswriter Amos Melton put it, "for the Masons to throw leather Friday afternoon." Tossing of leather would be very critical for the Masons.

Coach Russell grew sick with worry not knowing what to expect from the weather. He needed to find out how much the north wind would be blowing against the legendary barbed wire fence. "Even a five strand fence can't do much with snow," he stated.

If weatherman Paul Cook was pestered to death during the 24 hours leading up to the semi-final championship game, sportswriter Amos Melton suggested looking in the direction of a "tall, scholarly gent named H.N. Russell," as a result of his fretting over the weather forecast. "If the weather bureau phones keep gangling Tuesday and Tuesday night, it will only be Rusty trying to find out how much North wind will be blowing against that barbed wire fence," said Amos.

The Westerners outweighed the Masons by 23 pounds per man; the seven Westerner starters averaged 170 pounds whereas the seven Mason starters came in at a mere 147 pounds. Miller, the Masons' micro left end, weighed 132 pounds and was barely tall enough to sit at the adult table when he was awarded All District Player.

Lubbock Player	Weight	Position	Weight	Masons Player
Foster	145	L.E.	132	Moseley
Sewalt	230	L.T.	155	Holmans
Pytell	170	L.G.	158	McHam
Pipes	172	C.	144	Torres
Sanders	148	R.G.	137	Bates
Harris	166	R.T.	165	Brown
Winter	162	R.E.	137	Strange
Parsons	188	Q.B.	150	Keel
Joynston	162	R.H.	135	Hudgins
Jackon	160	L.H.	145	Bonds
Webster	185	F.B.	160	Stephens

December 17, 1938, starting lineup, Masons vs Lubbock Westerners.

The weather would play an unfair advantage in the semi-final championship. No amount of skill, agility, talent and perseverance could break through the savage winds promised at game time. The Masons' controlled overhead game could become out of control if Mother Nature took over. In addition to the biting wind, numbed receivers' hands and stiff quarterbacks' fingers, there was an additional new dynamic added to the forecast: a Lubbock sandstorm. It had been a long, hard season with injuries and illness, but the forces lined up against them for this game caused an unaccustomed concern.

On Monday, December 12, 1938, tickets for the Masonic Home versus Westerner game went on sale. In Lubbock, a long line had formed outside of the Red Raiders ticket office even before it opened for business. Within minutes 3,000 fans bought up all of the reserved seats. 15,000 more were expected to be sold regardless of the harsh economic times, and despite the frigid forecast.

In Fort Worth, Mr. Russell stood on the sideline and watched the Masons practice. Amos Melton from the *Fort Worth Star-Telegram* grabbed the opportunity and asked Russell if he was happy with the outcome of Saturday's game against Highland Park. "Happy? I was the happiest guy in the world," he said. "Those little lads really fought their hearts out in that last half Saturday. I was certainly proud of them, the way they came back against odds. But I don't see how it can happen again. You can't keep giving everything you have against teams that outweigh you 25 pounds to the player every Saturday. You're bound to get some injuries that may not be disabling but will handicap play. And we certainly know we'll be up against it in that game against a team like Lubbock."

"Those kids know football," said both Otha Tiner and Herman Clark, the assistant city Athletic Director. During their skull meeting on Monday, the Masons got an earful from the two scouts who had previously attended a Westerners game and watched them destroy Breckenridge.

On Tuesday, the assistant coach and assistant city Athletic Director put the boys through their most intensive physical workout of the week. Otha and Herman mimicked the Westerner's maneuvers and threw Westerner passes to get the Masons comfortable with their style of play.

"Get your longies!" yelled Tom Posey as the boys spilled off the field and into the dressing room. Tom scurried past the boys carrying a huge box on his back. As he walked into the dressing room he lowered the box packed with "long-handled" underwear with a thud onto the floor.

"Get your longies!" Tom yelled again. "It's going to be cold up on the South Plains." With Tom's booming voice everyone had heard him the first time, but he was caught up in the excitement.

While Miller, Horace and Buster thumbed through the box of brand new longies looking for their sizes, Russell's concern remained fixed on the weather.

In less than one week, a group of Dallas businessmen ordered, paid for and delivered approximately 30 complete uniforms—helmets, jerseys, shoes, socks, pants, undershirts, and shoulder pads—to the Masonic Home Masons football team. The grateful boys had never seen anything more beautiful. They fit perfectly. "Guess they thought we looked a little seedy," Russell grinned. "Our old uniforms are good but we'll certainly take some new ones if our friends want it that way."

The businessmen were overwhelmed with emotion from the gratitude the boys returned. Gifts were seldom seen during the Depression as most of the population had to be closed fisted. "Well, if we needed anything else, this sure ought to make us fight harder," said Jeff Brown.

The uniforms reflected the latest style. The pants were constructed of orange army whipcord and the jerseys were made of the new, shiny sateen fabric, orange with white shoulders, and each jersey sported each boy's number.

In Fort Worth, Russell watched dark clouds roll over the Masonic Home practice field earlier than had been forecasted. A bitter wind began to blow, giving the little boys an excuse to wear their new orange wind-breakers as Herman and Otha continued to drill the Masons in their mock scrimmage against the reserve team who did a fantastic job of mimicking Lubbock's tricky offense.

"This unusually cold weather is a break of a sort for us," Russell told reporter Frank Tolbert. "Maybe we'll be more accustomed to the cold by game time at Lubbock, Friday afternoon." But by the end of practice, Russell announced a change in plans due to the ominous clouds and wind. He decided to take his lightweights to Lubbock Wednesday morning, two days early. "We're going up Wednesday so we'll have a little time to get acquainted with the altitude and climate," Russell informed his team. No one complained. Frank Tolbert walked over to where Russell stood, and Russell expressed concern about the effect the intense cold in Lubbock would have on the Masons. Tolbert agreed. It would be an almost insurmountable handicap since the Masons' strong suit was their passing game. The receivers' cold hands would prevent good maneuvering and throwing. They were in for a long, long game. "And we're just praying for sunny, pass-catching weather," Russell said.

The Sonics spent long hours late into the evening working every possible angle and covering any drills on pass defense the Westerners might try. The Masons did not stop their intense practice until it became too dark to see the football. To add another layer of excitement to the upcoming game, there would be a competition between two cousins playing for the semi-final championship. Mason guard, Earl Webster, would come face-to-face with his cousin, Walter Webster, the Westerners strong fullback.

Russell's nerves over the weather got the best of him. At the last minute, Russell decided to cancel the train and take a bus.

"I just want them to get as used to the biting wind as much as possible," said Russell. "It would be tough on them to wait to the last minute and then go out on an icy field. They would shiver so hard they might shake the stands. Maybe we can get a bit used to it in two days."

"If it should be warm enough that Eugene Keel can cut loose with his whole string of overheads, there's reason to believe the Westerners will have a busy afternoon trying to knock down flying footballs," said Amos Melton.

The Masons faced a very serious dilemma: how could Keel be in Lubbock and ring the bells at the same time? The boys decided that to satisfy the football fates, Gene would have to ring the bells on Tuesday afternoon, the day before they loaded the bus for Lubbock. So that afternoon, after Keel and Bonds followed up on a mandatory visit to see Dr. Hall regarding minor leg hurts, they ran all the way to the school office so Keel would get there in time to ring the last bell. He rang the school bell several times to make sure it took.

Early on the morning of December 14, 1938, just five days after their tough brawl with Dallas, the Masons filed onto the bus and began their trip to Lubbock.

In the bus sat Rusty Russell, Masonic Home coach for the past twelve years, Otha Tiner, assistant coach for four years, Dr. E. P. Hall, Masonic Home Physician for 38 years, and, of course, none other than W.E. "Pete" Purnell, their trusted bus driver for the past ten years. And Moses, an elderly, African-American man who had climbed onto the Masons' bus for the first time in 1932. That was the first year the Home boys had won Class A state finals. No one had any idea who he was or where he had come from, but they welcomed him onto the bus nonetheless. Since that day in 1932, every year the Home boys played in the state playoffs, Moses showed up out of nowhere and accompanied the team to the big game. As he slowly stepped onto the bus, the boys shouted, "Moses!" He stopped by each seat so the boys could rub their fists on his thick, wild hair for good luck. The only "new kid" on the bus was said to be one of the reporters on board. Of all the "old kids," only one boy on the team would return the following year: Buster Roach. All the others were graduating and Russell would have a brand new crop of boys to coach the following year.

As the bus pulled out of the gate, the boys and girls lined up along the Pike and yelled their support. Don Stephens won the toss and received the honor of radio operator, which proved a challenging job as the boys had different views on which channel to listen to. However, the further they got from Fort Worth, the easier his job became as there was only one channel to choose from. When they reached Nolan County, Russell's childhood stomping ground, the boys continued to look wherever Russell pointed in hopes of glimpsing an object of interest. The boys studied the map as Russell reminisced and decided they must be in the city of Herndon. Russell pointed to the small house his family had lived in. The boys continued to stare out the bus windows hoping there might be something to see a bit more interesting than Mr. Russell's old house. He pointed out White Flat School where he attended in his youth, but declared the school building had been moved. The boys quickly lost interest. They sat back on their seats with little expression on their faces. After the bus rolled a few hundred more yards down the road, Russell spied an abandoned well and declared he was positive his old school used to sit next to that well. The boys hoped the sightseeing for the remainder of the trip might bring a little more excitement.

The bus pulled to a stop in the city of Sweetwater, where the local Masonic Lodge and the Board of City Development provided the Masons a nice lunch with all the fancy silverware and guest speakers. The first speaker was Mr. Russell, who was thankful for the nice lunch and admitted the Masons had had numerous invitations to additional lunches, dinners and training sites. "If he had accepted all the invitations extended to the team, the trip from Fort Worth to Lubbock would have required weeks," said one sports reporter.

The chairman of the Sweetwater Board of City Development, Carroll Conlee, cut the speeches short as everyone wanted to get the team to Lubbock as soon as possible so they could get onto the practice field. Despite the number of forks arranged next to their plates and the fancy food they had been served, their bellies still weren't completely full, but the boys were satisfied nonetheless as they loaded back onto the bus. They took their seats and continued to watch out the window and listen to the only channel Don Stephens could tune in on the radio.

At 4 o'clock on Wednesday, December 14, 1938, as the bus rolled into Lubbock, the boys pressed their faces to the windows and looked up at the clear sky. When the bus parked and Mr. Purnell opened the doors, the team stepped off to find the weather mild and non-threatening. In fact, it was a bright sunny day with temperatures around 45 degrees. As they walked into the hotel to check in, a large crowd of Westerner fans had been waiting in the lobby to get a look at the team who would come up against their boys on the gridiron. They shook their heads, comparing the Masons to their big Westerners in every way. They were not impressed with the little fellows. The lobby was eerily quiet as they stared. They asked which of the boys was Gene Keel or Buford Hudgins. The Masons spoke to no one and went straight to their room and got into their practice uniforms as Mr. Russell had instructed. As they filed back onto the bus and pulled out of the lot for Tech Stadium, a convoy of spectators followed even though it was widely advertised that fans would not be allowed in the area while the team practiced. Despite the warning, people lined up around the fence for a peek to see if the Masons looked any bigger in their uniforms.

Lorin McMullen, *Star-Telegram* sportswriter, reported, "A good little man can't beat a good big man, unless, the good little man's a lot better than the good big man thinks he is, and the good big man's not as good as he thinks he is."

The gawking continued as the Masons stepped off the bus and nonchalantly walked onto the Red Raiders' gridiron. To their amazement, the Red Raiders stopped practice and welcomed the Masons to Texas Tech stadium with a loud cheer. It was a heart-thumping moment for both teams. Tech officials quickly cleared out all the trespassers hanging around the fence. Following practice, the Masons returned for a skull meeting at which time Mr. Russell informed the boys that the Westerners would rely heavily on one specific trick play if they got down to the 40 yard line. Parsons, the quarterback, would typically fake a throw to the left and their running back would fake a ready stance at the same time, tricking their opponent's defense out of position. At that point Parsons would hand the ball off behind his back. The play was dubbed the Statue of Liberty. Miller knew if the Westerner's made it to the 40 yard line he could easily run in and grab the ball before the intended player could get to it.

The Masons were well-rehearsed mentally and physically, and ready for play.

Rusty Russell and Dr. E.P. Hall thought their only concern was the weather until several of the boys began complaining of upset stomachs. Earl Webster, who alternated with Jack Bates at guard, and tackle Bill Bennett both had high fevers. As Dr. Hall assessed the boys' health, he cautioned Russell that Earl Webster could be out. With so many children to care for at the home, Dr. Hall could not attend many games and they were glad to have him at this one.

Every hotel lobby in Lubbock bustled with sportswriters from all over the state. They followed Miller and the team as if they were royalty. To the boys, the crowds of fans, sportsmen and coaches all hustling around in preparation for the semi-final championship game was an electrifying experience. But Mr. Russell had instructed them not to speak to anyone— he did not want any negative talk to reach the boys. Superintendant Tom Fletcher and Rusty Russell stayed at the Texas Hotel. Joining them was Lubbock's Superintendant W.B. Irvin, high school principal R.W. Matthews, Coach Weldon B. Chapman, and the athletic business manager at Lubbock High, E.J. Lowrey.

A rumor had floated around that Buster Roach and Armando Torres had raised their weights so nobody would feel sorry for them being so small. Coach Russell backed the integrity of his boys and denied that neither his star back, Buster Roach, nor his center, Armando Torres, would ever "pad" their weight on the Masons' roster. "That is nothing but a rumor wanting to get started," he declared. "The roster is correct and let's put this rumor to sleep right now. Let's weigh the team, right now, right here. Buster is down for 142 pounds. Buster generally weighs between 135 and 140. My boys have integrity in the truth and there is no reason to feel sorry for these boys no matter what they weigh, and they feel the same way."

Russell's desk in the hotel room was piled high with over 80 telegrams from fans all over the state. One read,

"Entire Highland Park team pulling for you, win, lose or draw."
Signed by Dwelle, Munnell and Seay.

The critics grew apprehensive about the team weight disparity again. Though the Masons had beat the huge Highland Park Scots as well as the others, the fear of the Russellmen coming out ahead of a team with a weight differential of 23 pounds per man was once again discussed amongst the most devoted Mason follower. Win or lose, the Westerners and the Westerners' fans were unaware they were about to engage in the fight of their career.

Thursday morning, the day before the big game, Tolbert leaned on the side of the building and watched the Masons practice. After the boys finished, Mr. Russell ordered them to take the rest of the day off. "We'd rather work," chorused the Masons to their coach. Russell could see the anxiousness on each face. He also probably knew they would not be able to sleep, which was critical for the game, if they did not wear off some of their anxious energy, so he relented.

Later that afternoon the Masons, with Frank Tolbert tagging along, headed back to Texas Tech Stadium for another afternoon practice. The Big Texas Tech Raiders were delighted to host the little Fort Worth champions. They gave the Masons another rousing cheer when they appeared for their workout. The boys were relieved to see Moses walk onto the practice field and take a seat beside Russell and Tiner. They had been concerned he might not make it to the stadium. Pete Cawthon, head coach for the Raiders, watched the Masons practice and said, "Why, I believe they have been here all day and you can tell that they've enjoyed every minute of it."

"We've never received a sweller reception than these Lubbock people gave us," said Russell. "However, win, lose or draw, I know that they'll play 60 minutes of the best football of which they're capable, and that's all any coach could ask."

The morning of the game, the train in Fort Worth carrying Mason fans wasn't scheduled to leave until 4 a.m. However, approximately 200 loyal Mason supporters boarded the train and had taken their seats by 11:45 the night before. An additional car was almost added due to a last-minute flood of tickets sold.

A sportswriter walked amongst the throng of fans at 3 a.m. He thought he had arrived ahead of the crowd since the train wasn't scheduled to leave for another hour. He was amazed by the outpouring of dedication to the home team. The fans that had arrived the night before included Amon Carter-Riverside's left end, Bill Hudspeth, who lay stretched across two double seats trying to get a little bit of sleep. Masonic Home yell leader, Miss Ann Hargrove, and the yell leader sponsor, Miss Pauline Roberts, sat chatting. Kids from schools across Fort Worth were on the train to show their support for the Masons. James Rhodes from Technical High and Miss Elaine Montgomery, cheerleader at Arlington Heights High school, stood in the breakfast room, which was actually the baggage car converted for their convenience. The 45-piece All-City R.O.T.C. Band had also climbed aboard the night before. The entire band had been given an all-expense-paid trip as a surprise gift from four sports-minded Fort Worth businessmen. L.W. Kirchman showed up the night before wearing a white apron and chef's hat and busily prepared sandwiches for the next day.

A few of the early birds were determined to stay awake all night, and they found creative ways to do so. Norman Cardwell and the Masons' Physical Education teacher played a game of bridge. Still, there were a few passengers who actually wanted to sleep without a sportswriter walking around asking questions and taking notes. Shriner Bob King opened one eye as the reporter walked by his seat with a look that said, "Please go away and let me sleep."

The electrifying atmosphere on the train brought passengers together. Having the Masons as the common topic of conversation made people feel they had known each other for years. The stirring thrill of watching a pint-sized team who came from a meager life, none of whom had a mother to kiss them goodnight or a father in the stands pointing out his son to everyone around him, earned the respect and admiration from all walks of life.

The early-morning crowd of sleepy but enthusiastic fans soon arrived, fans who had waited until the last minute to crawl out from under their warm covers to brave the cold and board the train around 3 a.m. They came ready to relax and drink a cup of coffee and were surprised to find the six-car train already half-filled with customers who had spent most of the night on board.

On December 16th at 4 a.m., the Mason Special slowly rolled out of the T & P Station in Fort Worth. It stopped in Cisco to pick up fifteen additional Mason fans. As the train got closer to the stadium, hundreds of cars lined the streets in every direction.

When the train finally came to a stop in Lubbock and the doors opened, passengers poured into the freezing air, leaving behind pillows, blankets, books, and games as they made their way to their very cold stadium seats.

The night before the big game, sportswriter Frank Tolbert invited himself into the Masonic footballer's private world, as he usually did. After he knocked on Keel's door, Gene opened it a crack, immediately recognized Mr. Tolbert and let him in. Gene appeared a little beat up, but the team assured Tolbert that it was a regular occurrence and said they often threatened to bury Keel. Tolbert made himself comfortable in an extra chair and was humbled by what he saw.

"Don't sleep in that stuff, Buster," warned Gene. Buster Roach had crawled into bed wearing his new orange and white shirt and new orange pants. "It'll get all wrinkled and won't look nice."

"I wasn't really," replied Buster. "But I just like these things so much it almost hurts."

Dr. Hall decided that, due to their high fevers the day before, Philip Earp and Earl Webster would be out of the game.

§

At 2:30 on Friday afternoon, December 16, 1938, the gorilla-like Westerners stepped onto the field and a majority of the raucous customers went wild with support. Next, the Masons walked onto the gridiron in Texas Tech's horseshoe stadium with their usual nonchalant manner. The teams stopped and stood shoulder to shoulder as everyone rose for the Pledge of Allegiance, sang The Star-Spangled Banner and prayed. Standing on the same field as Sewalt, the Masons appeared as small as a chiggers, but like a chigger, their bite was annoying and had a tendency to linger. Back at the Home, every child and faculty member crowded around every radio, on every piece of furniture and across the floor. The cheerleaders sat in a circle and held hands and concentrated. The only sound came from the radio. The orange shirts looked good.

Vendors walked up and down the stadium steps selling Coca-Cola and peanuts.

Russell looked toward the west and could see an ominous haze barreling toward the field. If by chance the barbed fence could hold it back, he knew the Masons' chance of winning the semi-final championship could escalate from slim to probable. Sportswriter Lorin McMullen wrote:

"During the championship, Keel led his opposition to believe the Masons could gain only on passes. Then, when the chance came in the second period, Stephens' bullet plunges were a distinct surprise. Alternating the plan of attack as he did, Keel had the Westerners entirely confused and his quick kick on the first down at start of the period didn't help their peace of mind."

The invisible barbed wire fence did not hold. The cold winds roared in and the resulting sandstorm plowed into the stadium and pummeled the players and fans alike. The players could hear the sand as it pelted their helmets.

Suddenly, the Masons started breaking through the sandstorm as if the powerful winds were not blowing against them at all. Don Stephens suddenly dominated the massive Westerners defense line, allowing Keel time to make breathtaking passes to Miller Moseley and Buster Roach. The powerful wind should have taken all control away from Keel's bullets, but it didn't and the Masons drove the ball downfield to the Lubbock two-yard line where Stephens forced an opening for a touchdown. The score was 6-6.

The Masons walked off the field at the half with a tied score. Mr. Russell told the boys, "Now you have had your letdown, now play ball." As they walked out of the dressing room, they handed Posey their towels. And as they returned to the field, fans well beyond the state of Texas chanted MASONS! MASONS! MASONS! The stands rocked with wild enthusiasm. The Westerners' fans were starting to understand why this small group of boys from Fort Worth received so much respect. Within the first half of the game, the Sonics had gained new respect from the most inconceivable group: the Westerners' supporters.

"A cold wind came whistling out of the North Panhandle at the start of the fourth quarter here Friday afternoon and found Lubbock's

Westerners and the Masonic Home tied up in a 6-6 snarl," wrote Frank Tolbert.

The heart-pounding, thrill-a-minute game didn't disappoint the fans, with the light Masons holding the well-respected and exceptionally amassed Westerners to a tie score of 6-6 going all the way into the fourth quarter. At that point the fans' overwhelming enthusiasm seemed to have shifted over to the direction of the Masons. Sportswriters sitting in the press box asked if anyone in the stands were still supporting the Westerners. Every Mason fan from Fort Worth knew not to leave their seats because anything could happen up to the last second of the game when the Masons took the field. But the promised dust storm blasted everyone and everything with a solid sheet of brown, blanking out the sky with unbelievable power.

Dr. Hall looked over at Philip Earp and Earl Webster sitting on the bench in their beautiful new uniforms and he knew this would be their only opportunity to play in them. He walked over to Rusty Russell and said, "Let 'em play." Russell smiled with gratitude and sent the boys into the game. Moseley, Brown, Torres, Holmans, Strange, Keel and Bonds never left the game.

The most amazing thing about the mayhem on the gridiron was the mayhem surrounding the gridiron. Despite the biting cold wind mixed with the wild, thick sand, the fans enjoyed every minute of the game and had become hoarse from cheering and from the irritating dust swirling through the stadium and down their throats. On the sidelines, newsmen and others stood shoulder-to-shoulder to get a chance to watch the huge Westerners play the mightiest midget team ever to hit the grid. Everyone at the game swayed left and right as the players moved on the field, not wanting to miss anything. If one fan jumped up, everyone behind him immediately stood. The Masons gave the Westerners more work than they had been used to all season.

Neither team was able to break the tie until the beginning of the 4th quarter. With the aid of the strong wind, the Westerners got down to their 40 yard line. The fierce dust storm blew directly into the Masons' faces. Sand caked and smothered everything. It burned the Masons' eyes and stung their cheeks. It filled their shoes and covered everything and everybody with brown grit. The blowing sand made it hard to breathe. The large Westerners eased through the end of the game as the wind and dirt howled against their backs as if a cruel joke was being played against the Masons. However, the Westerners were exhausted. It grew even colder and the Masons would not give up.

Rested and strong, Coach Chapman sent in 230 pound Sewalt fresh off the bench in the fourth quarter. Sewalt was one of the highest-scoring tackles in the league. Just as Russell had warned, Sewalt took the ball from Webster and the ground shook as he ran in for a touchdown. The kick from placement was good. The 6-6 snarl had been broken. The Westerners' coach knew going into the game that the Masons could have whipped his oversized team, and he counted on the Masons fighting every inch of the way against the unaccustomed haze and freezing wind. With the wind's assistance, Lubbock scored their second touchdown in the fourth period. The score was now 20-6. Despite the Westerners' domination, the crowd seemed to have forgotten which team they had come to cheer for. In the Mason huddle, A.P. Torres gave animated speeches of encouragement to keep his team in the game, hands waving enthusiastically above the circle of helmets.

With the wind in their face and less than ten minutes to score 14 points, the Masons continued to toss the ball with unwavering determination. With blurred vision and with the strength of Sammy Baugh, the Masons burst through the driving sand and advanced against the Westerners. Keel began throwing first downs to Strange and Bonds and the Masons soon advanced to the Lubbock 45. Keel threw the football as if in slow motion and it dropped into the arms of Strange. Everyone in the stadium held their breath as they felt a dramatic ending was in sight. The Masons were not stopping. They kept going and going, until *boom!* The pistol went off. The sound seemed to linger in the air.

A loud sigh was heard across the stadium from the Westerner fans. The deafening sound of the pistol rang in the Masons' ears on the gridiron and through the radio. But it was a definitive drum beat to Westerners fans, because they knew that if the game had lasted one more minute the Masons would have scored in spite of the storm, in spite of the temperatures, in spite of being on foreign soil, and so did the Masons. Every touchdown made by the scoring team up to that moment had been made at the south goal, with the wind at their backs. Given one more minute that statistic could have been changed.

But the game was over. The score: 20-6. The fans quickly rose to their feet, not to run out of the freezing cold or from the annoying dust storm, or to beat the crowd out the gate, but rather to stand cheering, applauding and stomping for the most intellectually and physically polished football team they had ever seen walk across the gridiron in cleats. "The Lubbock players, officials and fans swarmed on the field to congratulate the little visitors for their astounding showing," reported Lorin McMullen.

The Sonics walked from the field in single file with all the class they were known for, but their heads hurt so badly from disappointment they could not hear the crowd's enormous admiration and their stomachs ached with a hollow, sickening feeling. They just knew that if it had not been for the dust storm they would have won. But they walked off the field calmly, without drama. No Mason affiliate ever made a critical remark. The Westerners team, as well as officials and fans, were still cheering when the boys loaded the bus. They cheered for the unbelievable talent no one ever saw coming. They rooted for their perseverance, courage and most of all, their character. The cheering continued as the smallest Mason team ever to take the football field loaded the bus.

Back at the Home, every child and faculty member did not move from the radio. The disappointment was so thick it was hard to stand up. Many wanted to cry. "It was a heartbreaker," said Tom Brady. Every inch of "win" in their lives had been won with an enormous outpouring of heart and effort. Every adult and child around the radio that evening understood what a win could have meant to this hard-scrapping group of good little boys.

The Westerners knew the Masons had played at a disadvantage, yet they had been whipped for the first time that season from one end of the field to the other by the extremely talented and extremely determined Masonic

Home Masons. The Masons had few family members in the stands that day, but the crowd swarmed the field to congratulate the visitors for their astounding strength and perseverance. Playing the game in Lubbock was a smart move made by the Westerners' coach. "They proved themselves to be gentlemen on the field as well as off and this spirit and attitude went over in a big way with the West Texans," noted sportswriter Breezy Carroll of the *Fort Worth Star-Telegram*.

Westerners' fans were proud of their team, but the brilliance of the small Mason athletes came as a shock to those witnessing their fight for the first time, and many left the stadium feeling that if the Westerners had to lose to someone, they would have wanted it to be to the Masons. The Sonics had generated admirers of many high-profile Lubbock businessmen who offered several Sonics jobs if they would return upon graduation. There seemed no end to the thoughtful gifts, which included tickets to see the Cotton Bowl Classic in Dallas on January 2, 1939.

"All the honors that were heaped on the Masonic Home team were accepted with a modesty that endeared them to all who came in contact with them," reported Breezy Carroll.

Game At A Glance

Lubbock		Masonic Home
19	First Downs	14
268	Yards Gained Rushing	83
28	Yards Lost Rushing	27
73	Yards Gained Passing	165
3	Passes Completed	18
5	Passes Incomplete	17
4	Passes Intercepted By	0
37	Runback of Pass Interceptions	0
6 for 222	Punts, Yardage	7 for 270
(3) 35	Runback of Punts, Yards	(2) 26
(5) 237	Kockoffs, Yards	(1) 48
1 for 23	Runback of Kickoffs	4 for 68
3 for 25	Penalties	1 for 5
5	Fumbles	2

After reporters halted Mr. Russell's exit from the field for headlines, he finally made his way toward the bus. When the door opened, a chill wind blew sand inside. The boys could see the top of his hat bobbing as he climbed the steps. Dead silence engulfed the bus. All eyes locked on Russell. They needed to hear him say something. Anything. He stopped at the front of the bus and looked at his disappointed team. The thickness in their chest needed release. He let the boys know how very proud he was and how honored he felt to be their coach. "This is just water under the bridge," Russell said.

During the trip back to the hotel, no one spoke a word. As the bus pulled up in front of the hotel and came to a stop, everyone on the bus was surprised when they stepped off the bus and found themselves surrounded by a large group of supporters and photographers in the parking lot. The throng poured into the lobby and waited for the team to file off the bus. To the Masons' surprise, the crowd cheered and requested autographs as photographers snapped pictures. The excitement was a little confusing to them; after all, they'd lost the game.

They returned to their rooms and sat down, tired, disappointed and covered in dirt from head to toe. Keel immediately lay on the bed too sore and disappointed to move. One-by-one they began to dig out from under the layers of sand, dropping their beautiful uniforms into a large laundry bag. Later that night they eased their sore bodies between the crisp clean sheets, but regardless of the tremendous exertion and physical abuse their bodies had battled, no one could fall asleep. They lay in silence, playing the game over and over in their minds. They had fought so hard for that win. Miller stared at the ceiling for hours, beating himself up. He had forgotten to put his plan into motion. If the Westerners got to the 40 yard line, he was to beat Sewalt to the ball. The Westerners got to the 40 yard line, and he forgot. He stared at the ceiling beating himself up mentally the entire night.

76 years later, Miller said, "I caught a few passes during my career, but the thing I remember most vividly are my mistakes."

The Sonics never comprehended that, despite the loss, they really had won that day. This special group of boys had proven to millions that hard work, heart, ethics, and good sportsmanship won the enormous respect of everyone they came in contact with and encouraged those with similar setbacks in life that they could win, too. Fans tend to crowd the winning team and walk away from the losing team. But for this team of boys, crowds actually increased around the Sonics after that game. The sports reporters had interviewed and followed many teams for many years, but never had they gained so much respect for any team as they did for the little Masonic Home boys and their stalwart coach.

seventeen

Home

Early Saturday morning they crawled back onto the bus to return home. At first, the team sat quietly. However, as the day progressed, the boys began to laugh and joke around. In fact, the conversation seemed to lean towards missing a good, hot meal from the Home followed by a game of touch football. Regardless of the love and devotion for the game, after several months of being beat up, they looked forward to a little rest.

The bus headed toward the town of Roby for lunch. Don Stephens was starving and was worried the town would not serve enough to fill him up. Dr. Hall had called in the order ahead of time and Don's reply upon arriving at the restaurant was, "They don't have as many forks here as they do in Lubbock. But boy, they give you something to eat. I believe the reason we lost is that we've been starved for the last three days." The boys laughed.

They were in for a treat. Hours later, when the team's bus turned onto the Pike, the Home kids who had waited so long and patiently for the team to return, stood up. As the bus, thickly covered with dirt, rolled down the brick lane, the boys gazed out the windows, and found every Home kid lining both sides of the Pike waving, clapping and jumping up and down for their team. This team consisted of their brothers. The orphans lived large through the success of the Masonic Home football team. Their team. Their brothers. When the bus came to a stop and the boys stepped onto home turf, the little kids swarmed them, as admired at that moment as when they had left. They were family. By this time, the dust had settled. Everything would be okay.

You would have thought the Masons had returned to Fort Worth victorious. Fans requested autographs and sent telegrams from across the state.

§

Looking as if they had played in a giant sandbox, the Masonic Home fans piled back onto the train bound for Fort Worth after the game finished. Many attempted to shake as much sand as they could out of their hair and from their shoes as they could before boarding the train, but it was no use; everything from shoes, hats, purses and eyeglasses were caked with dirt. One of the engineers walked down the aisle attempting to sweep up as much sand as he could. The R.O.T.C. band members' instruments were so filthy that some would never work the same again.

"It should be noted," Jack Bates said, "though we lost in that Lubbock game to a fierce West Texas sandstorm, we were very proud of our accomplishments. The state title was won by Corpus Christi High School.

They beat Lubbock in Dallas in the championship game. The District 7 championship game captured by the Masons' 1938 football team was a clear-cut title, with a record in district play of six wins, no defeats and no ties." Jack continued, "Miller was a sure-blocking, hard-tackling, sticky-fingered little competitor who was also an all-district performer for the Masons. He was exceptional each week, proving that he was well deserving of the all-district honors."

Miller had quietly walked onto the Texas gridirons, a meek and small 17-year-old boy facing lineup after lineup of outsized opponents. The same small boy who'd had his security compromised over and over years earlier had found the faith to face these giants, throw the stones and watch one after another topple under the fierceness of their controlled determination.

And there was Rusty Russell's faith: when he promised God to make a difference in a child's life if his sight was returned, the bespectacled mentor developed the ultra-modern passing attacks which were so impressive and bewildering that large-muscled professional football teams tried to copy them. Miller said, "It is nothing new. We played all those plays." By giving of himself, Russell received.

A sportswriter wrote, "A team well drilled in fundamentals, a team that takes any kind of chance when the chips are down, a team that fights every inch of the way—and a team that for passing is a miniature copy of another illustrious Fort Worth aggregation, the Texas Christian University Horned Frogs; there you have the Masonic Home Masons."

T.C.U. stars Bob Cook and Allie White enjoyed returning to the Masonic Home to encourage their team. The Masons were often included with T.C.U. as little teams slaying the giants. Both teams attracted huge crowds. On December 27, 1938, downtown Fort Worth was wall-to-wall with fans anticipating the T.C.U.–Baylor game.

Every high school coach in the city of Fort Worth was invited and every coach accepted their invitation to the 1939 Masonic Home football banquet. Miller Moseley, Jack Bates, Bill Bennett, Toy Crocker, Phillip

Earp, Harold Ferguson, Robert Lowrie, Alphonso Manson, Horace McHam, Arlos Roach, Buster Roach, Norman Strange, and Earl Webster each received a well-deserved award.

Russell called each boy one-by-one to the front of the banquet hall and handed every one of them a small, square jewelry box. After each boy took their seat, they immediately opened the box and found a gold football. Russell handed the box to each player without focusing on one particular person or on one particular play. He treated every boy equally, as he had the entire season. At no time did Mr. Russell or Mr. Fletcher ever call attention to one specific player for good or bad, and he continued that tradition at the banquet.

At the end of the banquet, the city coaches gave a rousing cheer to the Masons for their past accomplishments and future success. The direction in which their lives now headed had been successfully turned into an impressive future by Mr. Fletcher and Mr. Russell, two men who cared deeply for the welfare of these boys. Little did anyone know that soon the influence these men had on young Miller Moseley would help end a savage world war and save millions of lives.

eighteen

Graduation

Sometime in the spring of 1939, the girls planned a succession of dance lessons for the boys. Miller missed the first day. He had been sent to Lancaster to represent the Home in a speech competition. The next week he wanted to participate but feared he had missed too much and that would be a problem. He didn't participate and consequently never learned to dance. Had he joined in on the second class, no one would have known he'd missed a class because the Home kids danced so poorly; instead of the Jitterbug they called it the Masonic Home Stomp.

Spring was a busy time for the seniors. Miller and Harold Ferguson traveled to the Dallas Club of Printing House Craftsmen to represent the Home at the Graphics Arts Club. Miller and Harold represented all the boys in the print shop. They each gave a speech and presentation. The boys successfully brought back one of the highest honors. "The Graphic Arts Club was awarded the prize for the best work done by any club in the United States," Mr. Fletcher stated. "This was a signal honor and we are very proud of our Department of Printing. We also take pride in the fact that we have been able to train a large group of boys in the printing trades at no cost to the Grand Lodge. Up to date the Department has been self-supporting."

The Masonic Home Graduating Printers wanted to show their appreciation for the opportunity to participate in the printing course. Each senior expressed his thoughts in an edition of the *Master Builder*:

How My Printing Training Has Prepared Me to Face the World

by David Pillans

When I picked printing as my vocation four years ago. I did not know that I was about to take up a study of the world's third greatest industry; neither did I realize that I would be part of the great printing industry after I graduated from high school. But now, I comprehend some of the more important points of printing and life. I now realize that I have entered into an industry where there is a great future for the fellow with initiative and the backbone to put forth some study and labor. I now realize that the personnel of the printing industry receives better wages than the average working man in America. It is good to know that I am connected with a business where there is always work for the man who knows the trade and is willing to put forth his best.... But I could not have had this printing training had it not been for the Masonic Home Printing Department, one of the great contributions of the Masons of Texas to the Home. The Home is proud of its printing plant, which has the reputation of being the best school plant in the Southwest. I believe the training I received from the Masonic Home Printing Department will enable me to go out into the world and eventually make for myself a spot in society.

How My Printing Course Has Helped Me
by Frank Bonds

"Gosh! I'll bet this is an easy course. I don't have to do anything except stand up here and put type in a stick," I exclaimed in my first class as a printing student. But I was very dumb then and could not be blamed. Since that first period when I thought printing was a "snap" and there just wasn't anything to it, I've found that it is a highly skilled profession and one must really know his business to become a successful printer. Setting type is a very small part of printing. Press-work, bookbinding, linotype, embossography, stereotype and layout are a few of the other things that a printer must know and be able to do, not to mention the many other things he must know. My first years in printing taught me many things, namely; that to be a good printer requires work, time, and a love for the business. Immediately, I discarded the idea that this was a "snap" and "all I had to do was to put type in a stick." As a matter of fact, I learned that putting this type in a stick requires a skill. The stick must be held at just the right angle and the fingers must place each piece of type at exactly the right place or the job will be a flop. My, but I really did have a lot to learn. My next "snap" was feeding a press. I could hardly wait until I got to one of the presses. But, after I'd almost smashed a hand and ruined two or three hundred sheets of stock, I could hardly wait until I got away from it. However, I did master the art and am a fair feeder today. Another one of my first year "snaps" was the metal room. "Hotcha! I'm on the metal room today." Yes, it was easy until it

came to pouring that stuff; then I was ready for another job. I didn't think it ever got as hot as it did in that stuffy metal room. And with a good sized dipper of lead between your hands it was twice as hot. And when three or four drops of melted lead splashed on my hands, I was good and ready to call it quits. But I soon learned there was skill to that also. Now, as I look back over my years of printing, I cannot imagine how much I've really been taught in this course. I do know, however, that I've learned a lot and have a fair foundation for possibly the best profession in the world, second only to the great and everlasting medical profession, which I hope to follow.

What Printing Has Done For Me

by Philip Earp

Printing has taught me to rely on myself. I will be given a ticket and told, "Here, let's see what you can do with this." I'm on my own. I can ask for help—a certain amount is expected—but if I'm practically told how to do the job, then I admit defeat. It's the same way on the press side. "Here, make this job ready and run it." It makes you think for yourself.

And further into Earp's report he stated,
But, the most important thing I have gotten out of it is a trade at which I can make a living, and a good living too.

Working on the *Master Builder* inspired Bill Walraven to become a writer. He was a few years younger than Miller and went on to become a reporter and columnist for *The Corpus Christi Caller-Times* as well as the author of ten books. Years after graduating, Bill wrote a story about Ziggy, the Home's dog. Alfonso Manson played with Ziggy so much, the boys nicknamed Alfonzo, Ziggy. When the city added a street near the home, Ziggy—the dog, not the boy—was struck and killed. It was a rough time for all.

Ziggy—The Stray Dog That was Anything but Ordinary
by Bill Walraven

Ziggy, in my mind, has to be one of the great dogs of all times. He was the perfect dog to claim about 250 boys, from the first grade to high school seniors, as his masters. The school colors were orange and white. Ziggy was orange and white. The school symbol was a capital "M" on his forehead.

Those were only his surface credentials. He was of medium size and probably had a little pit bull in him. But he inherited his temperament from the other strains of dog in his ancestry. He never cringed or whined. Yet he wouldn't bite if somebody stepped on his foot or tail. He was tolerant to a fault, for even when he was tormented by some guy (unfortunately, there are always some people with a sadistic streak in them) he submitted without retaliating.

He was friendly. He loved to be petted, and there was someone around to pat his head and scratch his ears all day long. He could tell a home guy from a city guy on sight. So far as I know, he never attacked anyone, but he knew who his masters were. Strays were tolerated for a while. They were taken away and released. But if they persisted, they were executed. They were taken down to the dump by the big tree and shot. This would seem to be cruel punishment, but an animal seeking companionship, but for health reasons, a pack of dogs around a bunch of kids could not be tolerated. This was how Ziggy won his place as the home dog. From the start he chased other dogs off. Those who chose to fight rather than run made a terrible mistake, for the part of Ziggy I suspect of being part pit bull emerged and several times in fights he killed other dogs much larger than he. He was death on cats and no cat that valued its life ventured near the dormitories.

Ziggy's one weakness was the opposite sex. Instead of doing his job and chasing them away, he seemed to go out of his way to invite female dogs up to his place. He unwittingly caused the death of quite a few of his conquests which could not be persuaded to stay away. Once he pursued a lady love into a storm sewer and cost the city of Fort Worth a considerable sum to dig up the street and free him from the underground passage where he was trapped.

When he took off for the creek several miles over the prairie. He was ready to go. He caught rabbits, killed rats, and helped us explore the woods. I can still see him jumping straight up, appearing and disappearing in high grass, hot on the trail of a rabbit. He was particularly efficient when it snowed and the rabbits couldn't get traction on the slippery surface.

Ziggy was getting pretty old but he could still keep up with the guys on a long hike on a hot summer day. This way led through the pasture and over a broad rolling prairie to the wooded park area where he roamed. There was almost no automobile traffic the entire way. Then they built a road along the fence row. Ziggy was leading a bunch to the creek and paid no attention to the busy new road. He was hit by a car that badly injured him, but he was too tough to die. They took him down by the big tree and ended his life. He was nothing but a mongrel, but Ziggy, the only dog we ever had, was All-American in our book.

Graduation was around the corner and every boy who graduated received two suits; one for graduation and the other for business or leisure. The graduates did not wear caps and gowns. Few blood relatives attended the graduation, but plenty of family from the Home attended. The photographer required everyone to face the sun for a clear picture. With all the squinting and eyes burning from the glare, it was a miracle anyone was able to keep their eyes open.

As Valedictorian, Miller was expected to give the graduation speech in the high school auditorium. Miller's topic was titled, "The Challenge to Youth." There was no escaping it. This was always a boring time for the younger students and they dreaded this time of the year as much as "slimy oakrey" but attendance was a school requirement.

The graduates stood in a perfect line, with Miller leading the procession; Gene, Jack, Horace and the others stood close behind in great anticipation. They were excited and nervous at the same time. When they came to the Home, they weren't sure they wanted to stay, and now they weren't sure they wanted to leave. After receiving the signal to begin the ceremony, Miller began walking down the aisle and the others followed. Miller was introduced as the Valedictorian and all eyes fell on him as he took the podium and delivered the graduation speech. His Certificate of Award as Valedictorian of the Class of 1939 would end with the statement, "Anticipation of unusual achievement to come."

As everyone sat watching and listening, not one single person attending the commencement knew the extent of the truth of these words. Later, after the last graduate walked across the stage, the staff and fellow Sonics stood, clapping and cheering. The younger boys rose to their feet only because the commotion knocked them out of their deep trance. Miller could see Mr. Russell and Mr. Fletcher leaning on the wall with their arms across each other's shoulders, smiling with a satisfied look which seemed to say, "They made it." Through their love, devotion and hard work, these boys turned tragedy and emptiness into hope.

Outside on the lawn a cluster of kids sat in a crowded circle. Their laughter could be heard across the campus as the graduating class signed graduation cards and passed them back and forth to one another as they recalled their first day at the Home.

By this time, Miller had decided that, instead of fighting the press, he would sign his graduation cards as he was known to the outside world, "Morris Moseley." Sad as the memories were, many flashed back to their first week at the Home and how they had cried for days, and how others had run after their parent or neighbor as they drove down the Pike and out the gate. Others had lain on the ground, kicking and screaming while others stood in silence. This was the horrible, sickening, reality of being left. They each felt they had come into the Home as abandoned orphans, but they were now leaving as a large family. They were happy.

Soon it was time for everyone to say goodbye. They stood together while the girls wiped tears and the boys shook hands and promised to keep in touch. "Miller, be sure and give me a call," said Horace McHam. "Let me know how you are doing." They clung to their cards and left.

As a last sendoff, the *Master Builder* fellow editors and peers printed well wishes to all the Masonic Home graduates:

To the Graduates

Soon the class of '39 will break up and each one go his separate way. We have been together a long time and have grown close to each other. So as we each go our own way, the editor wishes to each graduate the most that life can offer, and that, as you go about making for yourself a place in the world, you will live—live not only for yourself, but for the pleasure and betterment of those around you.

One paragraph in the *Who's Who in the Masonic Home, Graphic Arts Club 1938-39* brochure, by David Pillans read:

Miller Moseley is one of the smallest regulars on the Masonic Home High School football team, but smallness doesn't count everything. He is an outstanding student and will be valedictorian of the 1939 graduating class. He likes to read sport, fiction and also good, hot, detective stories.

Transitioning to the outside world after living most of their lives under the protection, education and guidance of the Home was somewhat frightening as most did not have a family member to hold their hands if they turned the wrong corner. The graduates left the Home at different times over the course of the next two weeks. Some left immediately following the ceremony while others sifted out into the real world a few days later. Some had family while others did not. Miller left with his mother, but Cecil and Dot weren't the only family he left behind.

As Miller walked down the Pike for the last time, he dropped his suitcase to the ground, turned and gazed back at the Masonic Home. His home. What memories! He leaned down, picked his suitcase up, turned for one more glance, remembering the confused and scared little boy who stood on the other end of the Pike that frightful day watching his mother drive off. He had no idea that the excitement had just begun.

And as if in slow motion, Miller left the Masonic Home and School and walked onto the stage of the next unbelievable journey.

PART III

All pictures are courtesy of the Dr. Harrison Miller Moseley collection unless otherwise indicated.

September 1919.   Florence at mother and father's first home. A tent yet.

Papa Doc and Granny.

John Moseley on left.

John Harrison Moseley.

Harrison Miller Moseley and John Harrison Moseley.

John Harrison, Mildred, Miller, Cecil, and Dot Moseley.

Cecil, Dorothy, Mrs. Moseley, and Miller.

1935. Aerial view of Masonic Home and School Campus. *(Courtesy of Dr. Harrison Miller Moseley). Label (Courtesy of Tom Brady).*

1-Small Boys' Building, 2-Large Boys Building, 3-Cook Shack (next to cook shack is tank that contains oil), 4-Dining Hall, 5-Small Girls' Building, 6-Large Girls building, Between 6 and 7 is the Superintendent's Quarters. Not visible in picture. 7-Administration Bldg., 8-Hospital, 9-High School, 10-Pike, 11-Row of Hedges, 12-Road goes North and South and on out of the campus, 13-Road breaks off to small boys building.

Masonic Home and School, Small Boys' Building. October 1935.

Mr. Fletcher, Superintendent of the
Masonic Home and School, and his wife.

Ms. Cato, Matron of Dorm 2, Miller and Cecil Moseley.

Harrison Ferguson

Norman Strange

Buster Roach

J. W. Carter

Earl Webster

Dee Coolter

Seventy five pound team in practice, October, 1935.

Mr. H.N. "Rusty" Russell.

Otha Tiner and Mr. Russell.

Miller Moseley and David a working their plot on the Masonic football field.

Focused on polishing their offense
and their aerial attack.

June 1937-Bradley Bourland, Miller Moseley, Odell Goolsby, Edward
Cotton and Leo Tiberghien. "One name we did not appreciate was
'orphans.' The newspapers, neighbors and others would refer to us as
'orphans.' We were the 'Home kids.' The Masonic Home wasn't an
orphanage to us, it was our home."

Norman Strange and Harrison Miller Moseley on the practice field. Don Stephens on crutches in the background.

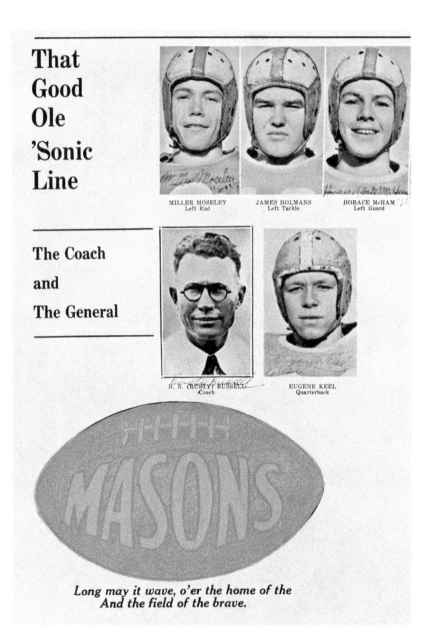

The 1938 Sonic lineup.

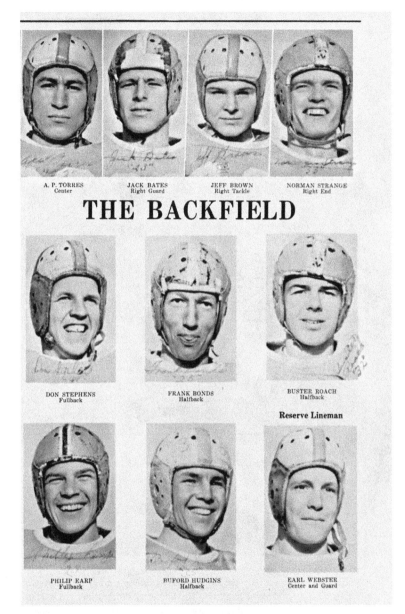

THE BACKFIELD

A. P. TORRES
Center

JACK BATES
Right Guard

JEFF BROWN
Right Tackle

NORMAN STRANGE
Right End

DON STEPHENS
Fullback

FRANK BONDS
Halfback

BUSTER ROACH
Halfback

Reserve Lineman

PHILIP EARP
Fullback

BUFORD HUDGINS
Halfback

EARL WEBSTER
Center and Guard

The 1938 Sonic lineup.

"Important Toe: With the Masonic Home gridmen going into the State playoff, the extra point kicking talent of Tackle Jeff Brown became increasingly important. Brown, extreme left, rested his educated foot on the knee of end Morris Moseley. Seated on the ground and massaging the tackle's foot was end Norman Strange. Behind Moseley stood guard Earl Webster, center, and back Buster Roach." *(Courtesy of the Fort Worth Star-Telegram)*

1938 Team.
Back row: Buster Roach, Buford Hudgins, Frank Bonds, Don Stephens, Phillip Earp, Eugene Keel.
Front row: Norman Strange, Horace McHam, James Holmans, Jeff Brown, A.P. Torres, Jack Bares, Miller Moseley.

1938 new uniforms--Bill Mercer, **5** Mondo (Jack) Torres (Back), **3** Toy Crocker (End), **1** Alphonso Manson (End), **6** Miller Moseley (Left End), **26** Arlos Roach (End), **42** Hardy Brown (Back), **35** Buford Hudgins (Left Half Back)

32 Granville (Buster) Roach (Back), **20** Earl Webster (Center), **21** Pat Finnigan (Guard), **41** Don Stephens (Full Back), **43** Jeff Brown (Right Tackle), **25** Frank Bonds (Right Half Back), **23** Jack Bates (Right Guard), Coach:Rusty Russell, Mascot-Rusty Russell, Jr., Assistant Coach:Otha Tiner

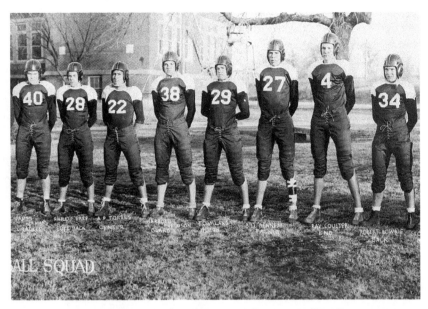

40 James (Freckels) Holmans (Left Tackle), **28** Phillip Earp (Full Back), **22** A.P. Torres (Center), **38** Harold Ferguson (Guard), **29** Tom Land (Guard), **27** Bill Bennett (Tackle), **4** Ray Coulter (End), **34** Robert Lowrie (Back)

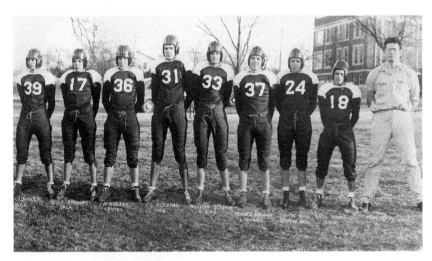

39 George Crumbley (Guard), **17** Bill Brigman (Back), **36** J. W. Carter (Center), **31** L. C. Hoskins (End), **33** Norman Strange (Right End), **37** Horace McHam (Right Guard), **24** Eugene Keel (Quarter Back), **18** Basil Smith (Back) Manager: Tom Posey

Mr. Russell and Mondo Torres discussing an offensive play in the opponent's athletic room. *(Courtesy of the Fort Worth Star-Telegram. Special Collections, The University of Texas at Arlington Library, Arlington, Texas).*

April 1938. Miller Moseley and others working on the practice field.

THEY ARE MASON WINGMEN

"Although comparatively light, these wingmen have been outstanding for Masonic Home this year. They are due to sparkle against the Poly Parrots tonight. Left is Norman Strange, lanky 137-pounder. Right is Morris Moseley, 132." *(Courtesy of the Fort Worth Star-Telegram).*

Unidentified boy and Coaly mowing the lawn.
(Courtesy of Bruce Riddle)

MASONS' FIRST TOUCHDOWN—The first Mason score in the game between Masonic Home and Highlan was tabulated in th

Clever end Miller Moseley pivoting into the end zone. Masonic Home versus

SPORTS

FORT WORTH STAR-TELEGRAM

A FORT WORTH OWNED NEWSPAPER
FORT WORTH, TEXAS ★ ★ ★ *Where the West Begins* ★ ★ ★ SUNDAY, DEC.11, 1938.

MOSELEY
MASONS

JORDAN
SCOTS

at Dallas Saturday
l quarter on a pass

from Quarterback Gene Keel to the clever
end MORRIS MOSELEY. Here he is pivoting
into the end zone after he'd taken the pass.

Highland Park. December 9, 1938. *(Courtesy of the Fort Worth Star-Telegram).*

SHOVE SAVES TOUCHDOWN: This Mason pass on fourth down into the end zones in the fourth quarter of the Masonic Home-Highland Park game at Dallas Saturday failed when the Scot quarterback, VIRGIL HARRIS, pushed MORRIS MOSELEY (front) just as the Mason receiver attempted to catch the ball. Had Moseley caught the pass it would have broken a 12-12 tie, the final score. The Masons won the quarterfinals championship game on penetrations. (Star-Telegram Photo by Tommy Dillard).

Miller Moseley pushed by Highland Park quarterback, Virgil Harris. *(Courtesy of the Fort Worth Star-Telegram).*

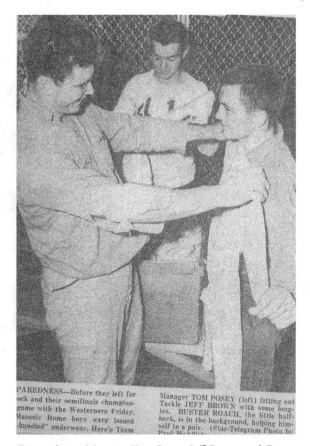

PAREDNESS—Before they left for
ock and their semifinals champion-
game with the Westerners Friday,
Masonic Home boys were issued
-handled" underwear. Here's Team

Manager TOM POSEY (left) fitting out
Tackle JEFF BROWN with some longies. BUSTER ROACH, the little halfback, is in the background, helping himself to a pair. (Star-Telegram Photo by
Paul McAllist—

Preparedness. Manager Tom Posey, Jeff Brown and Buster
Roach unpacking their long-handled underwear. *(Courtesy of
the Fort Worth Star-Telegram).*

Eager Masonic Home fans camped out on the train five-and-a-half hours before it would depart Fort Worth for Lubbock. *(Courtesy of the Fort Worth Star-Telegram).*

The Home's truck—Mr. Russell refrained from driving when accompanied by a child due to his poor eyesight.

Semi-final championship game. Rested and strong, Coach Chapman sent in 230 Sewalt fresh off the bench in the fourth quarter. Norman Strange on the ground won't let go of Sewalt's leg. (*Courtesy of the Fort Worth Star-Telegram*).

Field and clouds at half-time, Masons vs. Westerners, Dec. 16, 1938. Score tied 6-6.

The Masons walked off the gridiron "in style".

Mr. Russell signing his autograph on a football.

Masonic Home football vs. Polytechnic H.S at Farrington Field.: Hardy (Gordy) Brown with the ball; J. O. Strahan, Poly, being blocked by Basel Smith of Masonic Home (at left); DeWitt Coulter, Mason guard at Brown's right; Orville Lyles is Poly Parrot trying to push through, 11/21/1940. *(Courtesy of the Fort Worth Star-Telegram. Special Collections, The University of Texas at Arlington Library, Arlington, Texas).*

W.H. Remmert in the Supply Room of the large boys' building.

Miller and his friend, Horace McHam,
next to the hedges lining the Pike.

Miller Moseley at work in the pressroom.

A portion of the display of work of the three student clubs at the Masonic Home Printing Department, Fort Worth, Texas, at the meeting of Dallas Club of Printing House Craftsmen held there recently. Inset shows Miller Moseley, left, and Harold Ferguson, right, who were speakers.

The Graphic Arts Club was awarded the prize for the best work done by any club in the United States," Mr. Fletcher stated, "This was a signal honor and we are very proud of our Department of Printing. Inset shows Miller Moseley, left, and Harold Ferguson, right.

Miller Moseley.

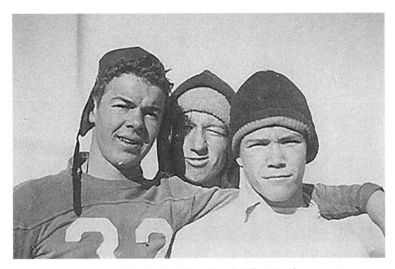

Buster Roach, Frank Bonds and Miller Moseley.

1936 snow fight.

Billy Jack Cook, John Knox Norman, David Pillans, Tom Hurst, Miller Moseley, Horace McHam, and Elmer Hudgins.

Early 1950's. John Jentry Miller.

Masonic Home and School.

April 1938 – Miller Moseley at the Masonic Home.

Unbelievable

MASONIC HOME GRADUATION CLASS
1939

The 1939 Masonic Home graduates.

Front Row—Eugene Keel, Tell Lodge No 1046, Mary Nell Reynolds, Pine Lodge No. 203, Robert Lowrie, Atoka Lodge No. 573, Alice Tempelmeyer, Billie Mosse Lodge No. 1152, Homer Hamilton, Gladewater Lodge No. 852, Charlcie Bransom, Tyre Lodge No. 198, William Mercer, Wiley Manning Lodge No. 702

Second Row—Horace McHam, Paris Lodge No. 27, Toy Crocker, Tyre Lodge No. 198, E. A. Mauzy, Lone Star Lodge No. 403, Joyce Thomas, Cleburne Lodge No. 315, Harold Ferguson, Fulbright Lodge No. 769, David Pillans, Winkler Lodge No. 826

Third Row—Alphonse Manson, Ennis Lodge No. 369, unidentified girl, Phillip Earp, Greenville Lodge No. 335, Ella Lou Thornton, Burleson Lodge No. 649, Woodrow Pittman, Woodland Lodge No. 1157, Miller Moseley, Dundee Lodge No. 994, unidentified girl, Norman Strange, Caddo Grove Lodge No. 352, Jimmy Ruth Alexander, Boggy Lodge No. 739

Back Row—James Holmans, League City Lodge No. 1053 Mary Martha Brice, Honey Grove Lodge No. 164, Buford Hudgins, Frank Sexton Lodge No. 206, Jeff Brown, Commerce Lodge No. 439, Frank Bonds, Belton Lodge No. 166, unidentified girl, Don Stephens, Commerce Lodge No. 439, June Mayo, Cotton Gin Lodge No. 154

Not pictured; Tom Posey, Harlandale Lodge No. 1213

Note: The three unidentified girls may be, Janice Anderson, George R. Reeves Lodge No. 396, Selma Belt, Canadian Lodge No. 855, and Bettie Morrill, Yoakum Lodge No. 662.

Leaving the Masonic Home, 1939.

T.C.U. yearbook photo.

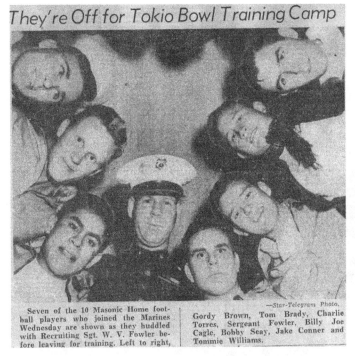

They're Off for Tokio Bowl Training Camp. Gordy Brown, Tom Brady, Charlie Torres, Billy Joe Cagle, Bobby Seay, Jake Conner, and Tommie Williams. *(Courtesy of the Fort Worth Star-Telegram).*

Harrison Miller Moseley's draft photo. Courtesy of National Personnel Records Center, National Archives.

Dr. Pollard. Episcopal priest, nuclear physicist, author, teacher, administrator—Oak Ridge Associated Universities (ORAU) founder and first president of the Oak Ridge Institute for Nuclear Studies. *(Courtesy of ORAU).*

Bud Miller, spring of 1943. Years later, Miller had planned to take Dene to see his cousin, Bud, participate in the rodeo at Will Rogers Coliseum.

Dr. and Mrs. Harrison Miller Moseley and family.

Dr. Moseley in 1971. *(Courtesy of Dr. C.A. Quarles, TCU Professor Emeritus).*

1970 Masonic Home reunion in Austin, Texas. Freckles Holmans, Dr. Harrison Miller Moseley, Mr. Rusty Russell, Gene Keel, and Jack Bates. *(Courtesy of Jack Bates and Claudia Bates Kravitz)*

The story of the Dr Pepper machine (It's not a "Coke" machine!) *(Courtesy of Dr. C.A. Quarles, TCU Professor Emeritus).*

The Castells, Roddy, Cristina, Cheryl, and Rod. *(Courtesy of Cheryl Castells)*.

Alan and Karen Messick, Dene Moseley, Andrew Messick, Miller Moseley, and Brian Messick. *(Courtesy of Karen Messick)*.

Richard Opperman, Horace McHam, Lacy Brady, Dr. Moseley, Tom Brady, and Bruce Riddle at the Masonic Temple, Fort Worth February 28, 2014. (*Courtesy of David Hughes*).

Dr. Moseley, Age 92. February 28, 2014. (*Courtesy of David Hughes*).

Tom Brady, Richard Opperman, Horace McHam, Dr. Moseley, Bruce Riddle, and Lacy Brady. (*Courtesy of David Hughes*).

Dr. Moseley and author Stella Brooks. (*Courtesy of David Hughes*).

Tom Brady and Dr. Moseley. (*Courtesy of David Hughes*).

Bruce Riddle, Dr. Moseley and Stella Brooks
(*Courtesy of Richard Opperman*).

nineteen

T.C.U.

Confusion and havoc broke out less than four months after Miller graduated from the Masonic Home. On September 1, 1939, Nazi Germany invaded Poland, including the capital, Warsaw, without any warning or any ultimatums of war. The terrifying roar of German planes seemed endless as squadrons of 50 aircraft flew over Poland every half-hour. The Poles had no time to stand in shock—they scrambled for their lives, taking cover under whatever they could find.

Only after the attack did a German radio broadcast a list of "demands" never submitted to the Polish government. 1,500 were reported killed or injured in the unwarranted, unexpected and unprovoked attack.

§

Miller worked long hours in a print shop bent on saving enough money to study Aeronautical Engineering at a university. In 1939, as the Depression's lingering damage was still being felt, Miller had not given up. One day, as he opened *The Fort Worth Press* newspaper, a small announcement in the far corner of a page caught his eye. The newspaper was sponsoring a scholarship for an Aeronautical School in Kansas for one lucky winner. Miller rushed home and worked late into the evening on his submission. When he felt confident, he neatly folded his entry, placed it in an envelope, walked down the street, and slid the envelope into a large mailbox. As he returned home, he could not help but to dream of the opportunities he would have if he was awarded the scholarship. It had to be fate.

A few days later, *The Fort Worth Press* announced the winner. Miller walked directly to the newspaper stand straight from work, handed the man some change and flipped quickly through the pages, skimming up and down each page for the announcement. There it was. In bold letters. The winner. It wasn't Miller. Once again Miller drew the second-longest straw; he had come in second place. He folded the paper, placed it under his arm and walked home.

Though disappointed, he wasn't going to stop working day and night until he had saved enough money for tuition. With his easygoing, quiet demeanor, he depended on accolades from hard work rather than chatting people down. A few days after receiving the disappointing news, Mr. Fletcher, the Masonic Home and School superintendent, stopped by Miller's place of employment.

"Miller, how is everything going?" he asked.

"Good," Miller replied.

Mr. Fletcher walked over to Miller and sat down. The machines were loud and Mr. Fletcher had to yell to be heard over the commotion of the press room. "I read about the scholarship in the paper and I know you must be disappointed," he said. "I may have something you might be interested in." He looked straight at Miller. "The York Rite Masonic Scholarship for T.C.U is yours if you want it," he announced. "It will provide full tuition plus laundry money. In return you would be required to work 15 hours a week at the University." He smiled. "What do you say?"

"Absolutely," Miller answered. "Absolutely."

Mr. Fletcher smiled, shook Miller's hand and said, "You deserve it."

Miller walked out of the loud, hot pressroom for the last time and headed straight to Texas Christian University. Within minutes he found himself walking across the lawn in disbelief. With the huge burden of trying to find ways to pay for college off his shoulders, his mind raced with thoughts of enrollment, classes and which building was where. Between the large buildings and old oaks scattered across the lawn, a feeling of relief overwhelmed him. It was a particularly hot day, but Miller didn't notice. He planned to make the most out of this opportunity.

A week later, Miller stood in T.C.U.'s Amon G. Carter stadium behind a long line of other students enrolling for classes. After running around the stadium enrolling for classes, some of which had been closed by the time he reached the professor sitting at a table, he headed to the bookstore. The stack of books he left with was cumbersome to carry, yet beautiful and exciting.

The next day, his work on campus began. His first job was answering incoming calls. The phone seemed to ring off the wall.

"Hello," Miller answered as he picked up the phone. "Texas Christian University."

"Yes, could you please connect me to Dean Hall?" the voice on the line requested.

"I'm sorry, we do not have a Dean Hall. We have a Clark Hall, Jarvis Hall and Goode Hall, but not a Dean Hall." The caller hung up. To Miller's embarrassment, he later realized the caller had wanted to speak to the Dean of the University, Colby Hall.

Later that night Miller walked across the lawn to his dorm. Upon reaching the entrance, he was informed he had received a phone call from the *The Fort Worth Press*. He immediately went inside and returned the call.

"Yes," the person on the other end of the line answered. "The winner of the scholarship has changed his mind and has decided to attend Texas Christian University instead, which means, as runner up, the full ride scholarship is yours."

Unbelievable, Miller thought. But he had already accepted the scholarship to T.C.U. and he was not about to make a phone call to Mr. Fletcher, the man who had cared for him as a child at the Masonic Home and had so generously offered him a scholarship, and turn his nose up at his generous offer.

"I am already fixed up," Miller replied.

The Fort Worth Press scholarship would be awarded to the third runner up.

The next morning, Miller eagerly walked into his first class at T.C.U. It was a freshman English class and the teacher decided it would be much easier on her if the students sat alphabetically. Miller stood near the door waiting for his name to be called.

Once seated, the students introduced themselves to those sitting around them and the fellow who had won first place in the *The Fort Worth Press* scholarship and later turned it down was sitting in front of Miller. The guy who'd won third place for the *Press* scholarship had also turned it down, and he, too, was sitting beside Miller. And a man by the name of Jim Moudy sat behind him. Jim Moudy would one day become chancellor of T.C.U. "It was a very odd coincidence, the whole group of us sitting next to each other," Miller said.

Jim Moudy had been an Aeronautical Engineer but decided to pursue the calling to preach. When Miller found out, he was too shocked to speak. He could not imagine anyone lucky enough to have the opportunity to be an Aeronautical Engineer leave the profession for any reason.

§

Around March of 1939, Dr. Ross Gunn, a highly respected and accomplished physicist who had been appointed as the technical adviser of the United States Naval Research Laboratory, convinced Naval authorities to develop a method of splitting atoms to obtain energy for use in submarine propulsion. As early as May 1939, the Naval Research Laboratory (NRL) successfully obtained funds and support for research projects to investigate the separation of uranium isotopes to provide atomic energy for this propulsion system. Gunn is credited with coining the term "atomic submarine."

> *The discovery of uranium fission opened up vast new possibilities for useful applications. Among these was the energy-yielding chain reaction. Since only one uranium isotope (U235) took part in this process, it was thought likely that it might be necessary to obtain some separation of the isotopes of uranium in order to liberate energy. Representatives of the Navy were interested in the possible application of atomic energy to submarine propulsion. To attain the small weights and small volume necessary for submarine installations, an energy source built up either of separated uranium or of uranium plus heavy water seemed essential.*

The problem was, of the three isotopes of uranium—uranium-238, 235 and 234—it would be the rarest isotope of the three that would prove to have the most value. Each isotope contains ninety-two protons in their nuclei as well as ninety-two electrons in orbit around each nucleus. However, uranium-238 has 146 neutrons in its nucleus, uranium-235 has 143 neutrons and uranium-234 has 142 neutrons. Uranium-235 is the rarest isotope at a 0.7 percent of natural uranium. And as with all aspects of life, it would be the uncommon isotope that would be needed to succeed.

§

In August 1939, just before the Nazis invaded Poland, Hungarian scientists Leo Szilard, Edward Teller and Eugene Wigner wanted to inform the American government that German scientists were equipped and motivated to put the power of nuclear fission to destructive use. They knew they had little influence in Washington so they convinced Albert Einstein to sign a letter they had written to President Franklin Delano Roosevelt. Due to the lasting effects of the Depression and the wars, Roosevelt did not have an opportunity to respond to the letter until October, almost three months later.

On October 19, 1939, Albert Einstein received the reply he had hoped for. He had successfully convinced Roosevelt that the United States could be in grave danger if Hitler built the most powerful bomb in the world first. The race to see which nation could produce the first atomic bomb had begun. But in order to produce the energy-yielding chain reaction needed for the bomb, American scientists first had to discover a successful method of separating uranium isotopes.

The scientists had to split the isotopes apart, but there were so many unknowns. It was as if the scientists were given a blank sheet of paper to work with. Any method known at that time wasn't understood to an acceptable degree to allow an immediate engineering development, so the U.S. government was forced to examine any method that showed any promise.

twenty

That '38 Team

On the evening of November 3, 1939 at 7:30 p.m., a 1,000 voice chorus sang patriotic songs during the dedication of the beautiful new football field on the west side of Fort Worth. The stadium was dedicated to E. S. Farrington for his devotion, efforts and dream to construct an all-purpose sports arena. He died shortly before it was completed. No longer would high school football teams trip over the pitcher's mound at LaGrave field, and no longer would large numbers of Masonic Home fans be turned away from an event due to lack of room.

To begin the ceremonies, Reverend J. N. R. Score, pastor of Fort Worth's

First Methodist Church, gave the invocation and dedicatory prayer. Amon G. Carter followed with introductions so sententious and windy that the speaker had no time remaining. Bands from local colleges and various organizations played. All local football teams sat in a special section of the stadium.

But for the Masons, the dedication of the new stadium was bittersweet: after years of being wooed by other high schools, their beloved Rusty Russell accepted Highland Park's offer midseason that year. The Masons had made Russell famous, and Russell had made the Masons famous. Together, the Masons could whip big teams, yet they had been demoted by the Interscholastic League. Russell had struck a deal with Highland Park agreeing to coach only if he could also continue to coach the Masons until the end of the 1942 season. Russell had probably looked forward to getting his hands on the 1942 group. They not only had the same appeal as the 1938 team, they had size. With DeWitt Coulter, Hardy (Gordy) Brown and Tom Brady, the Masons would be the big team. He could not leave such a one-time opportunity. Highland Park gladly accepted Mr. Russell's terms.

Sportswriters wanted the scoop, vying for Russell's plans and expectations with Highland Park. But one Sunday afternoon, shortly after the reporters arrived at Russell's home, they quickly realized he had his own agenda. He leaned back in his chair, stared at the ceiling, leaned forward, rubbed his hands together slowly, and said, "I guess that my best all around ball club was last year's team. Those boys were great defensively, and they could move on the ground and in the air."

"Absolutely," a sports editor replied, but what changes do you expect to make with Highland Park?" Mr. Russell took a deep breath and continued: "But my most phenomenal team was the 1938 eleven," he said with enthusiasm. "And the most exciting game that I ever witnessed was when the '38 team beat Highland Park."

"Yes sir," agreed the sports editor, "and speaking of Highland Park, when do you plan to move?" Smiling at the reporter, Russell continued with a slight laugh. "The biggest boy I had that year weighed only 160 pounds. Highland Park was out in front 12-0 at the half, but with Gene

Keel pitching and Moseley pulling them in, we tied the score and won the game on penetrations. Those boys won on heart and fight."

The editor then asked, "When do you plan to hold your first practice with Highland Park?"

"But the most polished ball club was the '38—"

Frustrated, the editor cut Russell off in mid-sentence and asked about his current Highland Park team, but Russell would not let the rude sportswriter deter him from the story he wanted to tell. "But back to the 1938 team—" At this point the writer jumped up and declared he had to leave to make a deadline.

The reporter's intended title had to be changed to read, "And about That 1938 Team. Rusty Recalls Some Thrills from Masons' Grid Games."

§

The Primary problem, other than finding circumstances under which a controlled chain reaction could be sustained, that faced scientists engaged in this country's atomic energy program in early 1940 was the development of methods for separating uranium isotopes on a large scale. Time would not permit a gradual development of individual separation processes, followed by the full exploitation of the best method. Consequently it was necessary to launch a number of separation projects simultaneously.

No experiments had been conducted employing heavy elements, and no tests had been made involving uranium in any form. No dependable theory had been evolved covering the phenomena. The dependence of separation on apparatus constants had not even been surveyed, and very little was known regarding behavior as a function of temperature conditions.

Philip Hauge Abelson, an American nuclear physicist at the Department of Terrestrial Magnetism of the Carnegie Institution of Washington, set out to liberate energy by examining the feasibility of large-scale separation of uranium isotopes with Liquid Thermal Diffusion under the general direction of M.A. Tuve and John A. Fleming, Director of the Department of Terrestrial Magnetism. In 1940, preliminary studies showed sufficient promise, so the Navy provided $2,500 to the Institution for further studies. Shortly after, Abelson achieved a small separation of uranium isotopes and became the first in the country to successfully produce uranium hexafluoride (UF6), the chemical form of uranium used during the enrichment process.

Ross Gunn immediately invited him to join the staff at the Naval Research Laboratory and his work was transferred to Washington D.C. Gunn and Abelson were both convinced an atomic (nuclear) submarine was possible. Conventional submarines were powered by batteries, which in turn were charged by electricity supplied by generators coupled to diesel engines. These required air, and as the submarines surfaced to recharge the batteries, they became vulnerable. Work on the Liquid Thermal Diffusion method was initiated after Phillip Abelson and Ross Gunn of the Naval Research Laboratory, and members of the federal government's S-1 Uranium Committee, recommended this process to committee chairman Lyman J. Briggs in September 1940.

§

Miller decided to change his major from Aeronautical Engineering to Chemistry, and his curriculum included a physics class. When he walked into the class, he had no idea what physics was—he thought it had something to do with the study of medicine. Within the first few weeks of his freshman physics class, taught by Dr. Newton Gaines, chairman of the department, Miller was intrigued. It did not take him long to change his major for the last time, to Physics and Chemistry.

Dr. Gaines also taught a course in photography, and he requested Miller's assistance. Miller walked to the Physics building to follow up with Dr. Gaines' request, but found his office empty. He walked outside and waited on the sidewalk. As he waited, he and another student struck up a conversation. As they stood in the sun, the boy pointed to a student who was walking up the library steps with a large pile of books, "See that boy going into the library? That's Miller Moseley. He played on the Masonic Home football team." Miller laughed because, unbeknownst to the student, he was talking to the actual Miller Moseley. Miller thanked the boy for letting him know he had gone into the library.

At that time, Gaines rode up on his bicycle somewhat out-of-control and Miller had to quickly step out of his way. Dr. Gaines tied his bike to the stand and they walked into the building to discuss the job. Miller accepted the task and took full control of the photography lab, including the chemicals and darkroom schedule. After he became acquainted with the workings of the photography lab, he called a mandatory meeting with those enrolled in the class. Once every seat was taken, Miller called roll as a way to get to know his fellow students. He called each student by their last name, unless two students shared the same last name, in that case he called both the first and last name.

"Brown!"

"Here."

"Martin!"

"Here."

Everything was going pretty well until he called the name Jordon.

"Jordon!"

No answer.

He looked on the sheet to make sure there was only one student with the last name Jordon. Confirming this, he looked back up at the class and called,

"Miss Eileen Jordon!"

A girl raised her hand, stood up and said, "You must mean me. However, you mispronounced my name. I am Miss JorDON."

Miller smiled and snickered, then called, *"Miss JorDON!"*

She stood up again and said, "I still have one objection. There are a lot of Miss JorDONs. But there is only one MISS EILEEN JorDON."

This time, Miller could not help but to keep laughing. The rest of the class joined in and said, "Hooray for Miss JorDON!"

That was the last time Miller saw that girl. She never came back.

The lab wasn't Miller's only responsibility; he also manned one of the gates at the T.C.U. football stadium. His supervisor had instructed Miller to handle any issue that might arise with whatever decision he felt would be in the best interest for T.C.U. Miller decided it would be in T.C.U.'s best interest to let any Masonic Home kid in for free.

Sonic Bob Cook, who had played for the T.C.U. football team, hobbled over to Miller with his cane and said, "Miller, the only reason I played football was because it was the only way I could afford school. But you don't have to play ball, and every time I see you working the ticket booth, I want to take this cane and whip you with it." Then he added, "If anyone gives you any trouble, just let me know."

Miller considered Dr. Gaines his immediate supervisor, and Miller's various part-time campus jobs netted him roughly $200.00 a year.

Miller appreciated and realized the importance of respecting and caring for the smallest of accommodations. He built, varnished and labeled a box perfectly suited for each and every tool used in the lab.

In addition to his physics and chemistry classes, Miller took a full load of mathematics. "The school of education was the power to be," Miller said. "And they had a rule: every student was required to take a course on the teaching of their major." To fulfill Miller's requirement, he enrolled in a class called The Teaching of Physics. But he had accumulated a lot of hours in mathematics and was told to enroll in The Teaching of Mathematics, too. He informed the counselor his major was not education, therefore there would be no value in taking an additional class on the subject.

§

In Miller's freshman Analytical Chemistry class, the professor frequently gave the students samples to analyze to determine and report on the percentage composition of each sample. Many times the report included information they had not studied. One day, the professor asked, "Which is the heaviest compound with the largest density?" The class had not studied anything on this subject. The answer was osmium, with a density of 22, the professor informed the class. Information that Miller found as an "oddity," such as this question, he never forgot.

twenty-one

The Column

In the frantic race to beat Hitler, the U.S. government shifted emphasis from developing the energy aspect of nuclear fission to the weapon aspect and the Manhattan Engineer District of the Corps of Engineers was created. The Uranium Committee chose to explore gaseous diffusion, centrifugation and diffusion by mass spectrometers to separate uranium isotopes. The U.S. government had spent numerous manhours and extensive budget to successfully develop each method. The Navy, however, chose to continue its research into Liquid Thermal Diffusion.

Liquid Thermal Diffusion required the use of a diffusion column which magnified the separation that occurred when a mixture of isotopes was subjected simultaneously to two different temperatures. In June 1941, at the United States Naval Research Laboratory in Washington, D.C., scientists determined the optimum spacing between the hot and cool chambers of the column to effect maximum separation of uranium-235 isotopes from the host material.

About this time, the Administration of Military Research was moved under the direction of a new civilian agency, the Office of Scientific Research and Development. Vannevar Bush, an engineer, wanted full control of the engineering development, which included all military research, and asked President Roosevelt to appoint Bush himself to the position. In addition, Bush wanted Roosevelt to exclude the Navy from nuclear research and instead give the work exclusively to the Army. Roosevelt agreed.

§

On December 7, 1941, many Americans were napping, lining up for the movies or lounging near the radio when a newsflash announced that Japanese forces had attacked Hawaii.

On the beautiful, peaceful Hawaiian island of Oahu, on that clear, sunny Sunday morning, sailors tossed the football or napped in the sun. Soldiers, sailors and Marines who had been out on the town the previous night were shocked when, without warning, Japanese planes began attacking. The sailors never had a chance to alert Pearl Harbor before it was hit. "The crash of bombs and the chatter of machine guns were burned into their consciousness and they were dying without knowing a war had started."

Even though bells were clanging, the boys thought it was a drill. Then suddenly they heard, "Man your battle stations! This is no drill! This is no drill!" Japanese Torpedo bombers aimed for Battleship Row, and the men watched the Japanese break the *U.S.S. Arizona* in two, sink the destroyer *Shaw* and roll the *U.S.S. Oklahoma* slowly onto its side.

At nearby Schofield Barracks, a U.S. Army installation, personnel could not see Pearl Harbor because a hill blocked their view, and many soldiers were annoyed that the Navy was conducting maneuvers on a Sunday, a day designated for rest. But they soon learned the horrific reality as 183 Japanese warplanes attacked the Naval base and killed hundreds.

Witnesses watched as a launch, the largest boat carried by a warship, burst through the raging fires in an effort to rescue those trapped in the *Oklahoma* and *Arizona*. Through the chaos, a light cruiser began backing down, which threw every rescued sailor into the water. Many of the wounded drowned.

Young sailors with little training fought for their lives and used equipment they knew little about. "The Japanese put all their airplanes up and threw everything they had at us," said Simon Gutierrez, a 19 year old kid who woke up that Sunday morning at Schofield Barracks to find bullets flying at him from an enemy he didn't even know he had. As they flew over Hickam Field, "The Japanese planes were so low we could see them waving goodbye to us," he said.

At Pearl Harbor, Chaplain Howell Forgy was on the dock patting the guys on the back, when he suddenly put his Bible down and began firing back, saying, "Praise the Lord and pass the ammunition!"

"Looks like they got us this time," Crewman Albert Johnson said to the chaplain.

The chaplain replied, "No, they haven't, God's on our side."

"And we made it, too," said Johnson.

§

President Franklin Roosevelt immediately announced that America was now at war with Japan. America's fears had been confirmed. He told Congress the Free World must act quickly and decisively against the enemy. "The forces endeavoring to enslave the entire world now are moving towards this hemisphere," he warned. "Delay invites danger. Rapid and united efforts by all peoples of the world who are determined to remain free will ensure world victory for the forces of justice and righteousness over the forces of savagery and barbarism."

Following the shock of Pearl Harbor, American citizens flocked to volunteer for military duty. A sense of urgency permeated the federal government's science enterprise. Both military and science worked together to win the race to build a powerful, chain-reaction weapon.

On December 11, 1941, Germany declared war on United States, and two hours later, the United States declared war on Germany.

§

Russell's 1941 team should have won the state high school football championship. Three years earlier, Miller's 1938 team was one of the most talented and respected teams in high school football. They did it all without weight. But Russell's 1941 team had all that *and* the weight and they were powerful. A *Dallas Morning News* reporter said, "The Masons used to be little and good—now they're big and good."

But not everyone wanted the orphans to succeed. During the 1941 game against Amon Carter-Riverside, the Sonics were losing 7-6 with 55 seconds to go, and they stood on their own 45 yard line. In the huddle Gordy Brown called for a screen pass. Louis Buress, the tailback, took the centered ball, faded back, then flipped the ball to Brown who was in the right flat behind the line of scrimmage. In the meantime, Tom Brady and J. L. Daniels ran straight down the field blocking as Brown caught the ball and ran down the right sideline untouched for a touchdown, and the Masons won 12-7. "This play was selected as the most exciting play in District 7 for 1941," said Tom Brady.

Previously, in the first game of the season, the Masons had beaten Wichita Falls with little effort and believed they could go on to win the state championship that year. But despite moving toward the championship game undefeated, the team they had so easily beaten earlier in the season, Wichita Falls, ended up winning state.

This time, it wasn't the Interscholastic League trying to take the game away from the kids, it was Tarrant County Judge Dave Miller and Amon Carter-Riverside's coach, W.C. O'Harris. The summer prior to the 1941 season, the Fort Worth judge pored through courthouse records pertaining to every player that would play on the 1941 Masonic Home team until he found one whose birthday was in August—not September as school records indicated. But instead of notifying the Home before the season started, Miller and O'Harris, ruthlessly withheld this information until the end of the season. Following Amon Carter-Riverside's loss to the Masons, Riverside's coach and Judge Miller announced their finding. They had the Sonics disqualified.

Mr. Russell was coaching both the Masonic Home and Highland Park at the time. He immediately made a special trip to Fort Worth after receiving the bad news. He wanted to be the one to break the news to the boys, and they were devastated.

The next week, Miller pulled into the parking lot at Farrington Field, located minutes from T.C.U. The line of customers wrapped around the building. As he climbed the stadium steps he looked up and saw several former Sonics waving their arms. They were there supporting the Sonics who had been savagely dumped on.

Russell fought hard in a last ditch effort to keep the Masons from being dropped from the highest classification. Mason supporters were able to convince The Interscholastic League to keep the Masons in Class A for a few more years, but this effort didn't make a difference on the outcome of the 1941 season.

The customers filed through the gates at Farrington Field in an almost reverent manner. An unusual silence permeated the stadium as fans took their seats.

Sportswriters hovered and cameras flashed all around the Masons. Miller watched from high in the stands. He could not imagine playing a home game without bases and a pitcher's mound. He could remember leaving a football game looking like he had slid in for a home run rather than a touchdown. But at Farrington Field, the turf was a nice bed of grass. On the field, the Masons looked great. The uniforms donated the year Miller played the emotional Lubbock game still looked as good as new, but he knew how devastated each boy standing down on the field felt at that time.

The cruel behavior of the judge and coach was unbelievable.

The Sonic's professional attitude glared at the adults who continued to trample on them. The Sonics stomped Poly and walked quietly off the field.

It is feasible to imagine Norman Earl, the Fort Worth Athletic Director, standing near the field with a cupped hand over his mouth and his eyes on the packed stands as he listened to the enthusiastic crowd cheering for the Masonic Home orphans in disbelief of the horrible treatment toward innocent children and the horrible damage a few caused for so many without remorse.

The Sonics played the last two games of that season with more style and sportsmanship than neither the judge nor Amon Carter-Riverside's coach could truly grasp and understand. The Masons never walked away. They played and won both games by high scores.

Miller and the other Sonics in the stands that evening waited until the stadium had emptied and the reporters had thinned out. Then they slowly and nonchalantly stood, walked down the stadium steps, out the gate and waved at the Sonics as they loaded the bus.

The winning season was forfeited. The judge had won the District 7 championship for his team, Amon Carter-Riverside.

§

In 1942, just before the Masons walked onto the gridiron to face Amon Carter-Riverside for the first time since the previous disappointing year, Mr. Russell said, "Boys, they beat us on paper last year, but this year the game is going to be played on the field, so go out there and give it all you have." This was Russell's last year with the Sonics. During practice, Mr. Russell stated, "T.C.U. ran our screen pass last Saturday, but we are going to show them how to run it."

Later that season, Rusty Russell sat on a bench in the bright lights of Farrington Field with his gaze fixed on his team as they battled the Polytechnic Parrots. This would be the last game he would ever coach with the Masons. The Sonics gave Russell the best going away present they could give: they beat Polytechnic 32-0 and clinched the tie for the District 7 title.

Mr. R.N. "Rusty" Russell landed at the Masonic Home, caring for small orphans and receiving blessings tenfold. He considered it a true delight to have been given the chance to mentor such an amazing group of children. No coach in the Fort Worth Independent School District would ever understand that leaving the boys was a violent uprooting of unusually strong connections.

Through God's grace, they entertained and impressed with Russell's short passing game and trick plays popular among today's NFL teams. It all started with Mr. H.N. Russell and the Masonic Home Masons, and the combination was explosive. Russell once said, "I played with the opposing team players by splitting two or three players out to the side some distance from the line of scrimmage and would run the ball to the opposite side." The offensive linemen could not cross the line of scrimmage on passing situations. He sometimes had only one or two players rushing the passer while his defensive players covered the receivers. Rusty Russell was inducted into the Texas High School Hall of Fame in 1971 and inducted into the Texas Sports Hall of Fame in 1987.

The era of watching a small band of orphans walk onto the field with Russell as their coach ended in 1942, leaving only memories for those who played the games, and for those who watched them.

§

Philippine President, Manuel Quezon, had a penthouse built for General Douglas MacArthur on the top floor of the majestic Manita Hotel. "Word was MacArthur had enough furniture to outfit a nice sized city," Miller said.

April 9, 1942 was the beginning of a horrific nightmare for the Americans in the Philippines. They surrendered.

The Japanese had intended to attack the Philippines, Pearl Harbor and other American and Allied destinations located in the Pacific simultaneously. But due to bad weather, the Japanese military command delayed the attack on the Philippine Islands.

The American forces in the Philippines worked night and day installing new 50-caliber machine guns and getting their aircraft ready to counter the anticipated Japanese offensive. They knew they were Japan's next target. "The planes were moving and the pilots were about to take off when suddenly everything came to a halt. General MacArthur commanded: 'All planes are grounded until further notice!' He said we could do nothing until war was declared," said Virgil Catchings, who was crew chief for a P-40 Warhawk, a fighter used by American forces in Southeast Asia. Then the bombs fell.

As the U.S. Army sat waiting for the nod to begin their offense in yet another battle, the Japanese air attack obliterated the U.S. Army aircraft, and the American and Filipino troops had no choice but to surrender. The following day, April 9, they were forced into the infamous Bataan Death March. 70,000 U.S. and Filipino prisoners captured in the Philippines were forced to march 63 miles from the southern end of the Bataan Peninsula to a prison camp. Guards were frequently replaced as they became tired. From San Fernando, additional prisoners were transported by rail to Capas. The prisoner's physical abuse was deplorable. Along the way, many were buried alive while others were burned alive. "Bodies were pushed off the side of the road," Catchings said. About a month later, Catchings was brought down the same road for prison duties. The sight sickened him. "Animals had dug up the remains and each side of the road was white with human bones."

Due to MacArthur's procrastination, ready and able men and equipment were lost.

It was rumored that MacArthur argued his orders were explicit not to initiate hostilities against the Japanese. However, Japan had obviously initiated hostilities at Pearl Harbor.

§

The Chaplain's plea, "Praise the Lord and Pass the Ammunition," was made famous when Frank Loesser put the quote to music in 1942. It was a huge hit and burned up the airwaves. Two million records were sold and a million copies of sheet music went out the door. Numerous recording artists wanted in on the act, creating several versions of the song. It became so popular that the government decided to limit radio coverage to once every four hours "to keep it from being played to death."

twenty-two

The Manhattan Project

In July 1942, despite Vannevar Bush's efforts to exclude the Navy from developing an effective method for separating uranium isotopes, the Navy received authorization to build a small 14-column pilot plant at the Philadelphia Naval Yard with Philip Abelson in charge. "For a time, the facility at the Naval Research Laboratory was the world's most successful separator of uranium isotopes," said Abelson. They developed the first practical method of producing uranium hexafluoride as well as other inventions and studies critical to obtaining the end product. In August 1942, Ross Gunn informed Lyman J. Briggs of the new developments regarding the success at the Naval Yard. Even though emphasis was shifted from energy to the weapons aspect of nuclear fission, and the Manhattan Engineering District of the U.S. Army Corps of Engineers had been created, the Naval Research Laboratory still continued their isotope studies. The Navy's goal was to obtain useful energy production as fast as possible.

Dr. Vannevar Bush was not happy with progress on the Manhattan Project, and he informed General Brehon Somervell he needed an aggressive leader. General Somervell suggested Major General Leslie Groves of the U.S. Army Corps of Engineers, who oversaw the colossal construction of the Pentagon.

But, unlike other engineering districts, this one did not have any geographic boundaries, only a mission: to develop an atomic bomb. As Groves stepped out of a hearing room where he had been testifying before the United States Congress committee on military housing and into the hallway, Somervell walked up to him and informed Groves that the Secretary of War had selected him for a very important assignment, and that the President of the United States had agreed. Upon learning of his new assignment, Groves replied, "Oh, that thing." He would have rather received a combat mission than be put in charge of the Manhattan Project.

On December 10, 1942, General Leslie Groves and representatives of the Army's Manhattan Engineering District visited the Naval Research Laboratory plant to inspect the setup even though Vannevar Bush had said it was "a mistake."

It was at this time that the NRL first learned the Army had been put in charge of isotope production by order of the President. Gunn was not happy with the situation.

Ross Gunn felt the rug had been pulled out from under him, as he was the one who had initiated the first research into atomic energy, only to have control placed in the hands of the S-1 Committee, with the limelight being given to the Army.

On December 28, 1942, President Roosevelt approved the Manhattan Project. It included full-scale gaseous diffusion and plutonium plants, an electromagnetic plant and heavy water production facilities. The President's approval could not guarantee that the United States could overtake Germany in the race to develop the bomb, but every effort would be made to stop Adolph Hitler from using his scientific might to succeed.

Gunn and Abelson continued isotope studies with hopes of producing useful energy at the Naval Research Laboratory despite the extreme efforts to take the research out of the Navy's hands.

As World War II dragged on, the scarcity of uranium began to critically impact the workload on the scientists. Usage in the commercial world was small—only 150 tons was used in the manufacture of ceramic colors and for photographic use—but the U.S. government had strategically consumed all of it, and companies which depended on this resource for their livelihoods suffered. But it still wasn't good enough. Scientists were forced to recycle and conserve. This conservation slowed results, but there was no choice. Conservation Order M-288 was issued by the War Production Board (WPB) in January 1943.

§

As Miller studied physics and chemistry at T.C.U., his brother, Cecil, played football at Southern Methodist University in Dallas. But in 1942, his education came to an end when Cecil suffered a car accident, missed finals and became discouraged.

Cecil enlisted in the Marines on December 10, 1942, and was later deployed to the South Pacific to fight against the Japanese.

§

On January 6, 1943, ten Home boys from the 1942 team began their military career together, including boot camp. Billy Joe Cagle, Bobby Seay, Jake Conner, Tommy Williams, Charlie Torres, Ted Crumbley, and Tom Brady signed up for the Marines. Brownie Lewis, Woodrow Wilson and Gordy Brown from the '41 team also joined the Marines. Louis Burrus, Wallace Graham and other teammates on the new Marines team had been in the Merchant Marine School in Brooklyn for several weeks. Cecil Moseley, Gordy Brown and Brownie Lewis had left Southern Methodist University where they played football to enlist. "Cecil, Gordy Brown and Brownie Lewis were about as tough as any guys you'll ever find," said Bill Walraven. Cecil left for training three weeks before the others did.

"He always did start getting in shape early," said Billy Joe Cagle.

At 17, John L. Daniels was told he was too young to enlist in the Marines, so he left a few days ahead of the group for a Navy training station along with the Masons' water boy, Jerry Crumbley. As Daniels left the recruiting office, he yelled back at his fellow Sonics, "I promise to send you guys a good scout report of the Nipponese plays if I see them first."

As the boys stood at the recruiting office in the United States Courthouse in Fort Worth watching Daniels and Crumbley leave, they turned to Staff Sgt. W.V. Fowler and asked, "When do we get our equipment?" He promised their equipment would be in their hands soon. A few minutes later, the boys were seen leaving for a Tokyo Bowl training camp. They said, "We are playing for keeps with no quarter or time out."

§

In 1943, Miller graduated from Texas Christian University with Distinction and a Bachelor's Degree in Physics and Chemistry. Soon after graduation, he left Texas for the first time in his life. He had received a fellowship to pursue graduate studies at the University of North Carolina at Chapel Hill and was eager to begin his advanced education there.

The Depression had ended, but 1943 was a year of firsts and rations. There would be a very significant new word used for the very first time: "antibiotics." The word was contrived by Selman Waksman, who had discovered streptomycin.

Campbell's Soup could no longer afford to sponsor a popular radio show, *Amos 'n' Andy:* due to the war effort, tin was in short supply and this affected Campbell's production. Other rations included gas, coffee, shoes, meat, and more. Radio was still a source of entertainment, but it had also become a constant reminder of the war.

Miller packed all his belongings, but before he left the state of Texas, he stopped by his mother's house and discovered that his mother's old childhood friend, Dr. John Rice, had stopped by for a visit. John was a Baptist preacher in Dallas who had launched the radio program, "The Sword of The Lord," which had become the largest independent religious weekly program in the world. Miller walked into his mother's house, grabbed a wooden chair from the dining room and brought it into the living room where the three visited.

Mildred and Pastor Rice laughed as they remembered four-year-old John preaching to the neighborhood kids down in the storm cellar. Miller could not stay long, as he was due to arrive at Chapel Hill, so after the visit Miller stood up, placed the chair back in the dining room, shook Pastor Rice's hand, and said goodbye.

During the 20-hour drive from Texas to North Carolina, sleep never entered into Miller's consciousness. He stayed alert from the excitement of the new opportunity to pursue a fellowship at North Carolina. As he left Texas and entered Louisiana, the humidity made it hard to breathe. Every window was rolled down, but even with the wind blowing through the car it was still as sticky as a steam bath. Miller continuously wiped the sweat off his forehead to prevent the sweat from trickling into his eyes and making the drive tortuous.

He crossed the Mississippi River on a narrow bridge with one lane in each direction. As Miller traveled through Mississippi the sky was clear blue and the massive trees were breathtaking. He passed magnificent plantation homes and decided Meridian, Mississippi, would be a good place to rest for the night. To stretch his legs, he slowly walked the uneven, red brick sidewalks with bricks poking out of the ground, pushed up by the roots of the enormous trees that provided a blanket of shade so thick the sun could not penetrate through. The uneven bricks represented the lives, generations and history of the state, not to mention the added charm pristine sidewalks could not offer. The homes were close to the sidewalk which added a connection of sorts between residents slowly rocking on their porches in the heat of the evening and those walking past. Each warmly waved and offered a "Hey there."

§

The next day, Miller smoked a cigarette, ate some warm grits with butter, climbed back into his car, and continued on through Alabama, Georgia and South Carolina, finally arriving at the University of North Carolina at Chapel Hill.

After Miller unloaded the car, he walked across the campus grounds to get an idea where the buildings were located ahead of time. He marveled at the Forest Theatre, an outdoor theatre built in 1916, Old East Residence Hall built in 1793 and the incredible library. He sat on the ground under a large tree, removed a cigarette from his front pocket and watched a yellow butterfly quietly land on a leaf, then flutter across the lawn. So free. But free was not the full picture. Many young men were fighting an ugly, inhumane battle for freedom. He finished the cigarette, stood up and busied himself with settling into his new home.

The immense beauty that the southern states offered, as well as their hospitality, made the transition easy. The following morning, Miller walked into his Theoretical Physics class and decided to sit near the back of the room. The sun was shining through the tall ceiling-to-floor windows. The beige shades were pulled halfway down the windows with the bottom pane pulled open for a breeze. A black fan oscillated in the corner of the room with a faint, hypnotizing sound of the air spinning through the blades. Miller leaned back in his chair, smoked a cigarette and watched his fellow students enter the classroom. One-by-one their eyes scanned the room for an empty desk, their arms heavy with books, a pencil clinched in their fingers. He watched their forms collapse slightly as they released their piles of books onto their desks.

After the classroom had practically filled, Professor Ruark, who was the chairman of the department, walked directly to the front of the class, printed his name on the chalkboard and immediately began lecturing. As he wrote the outline on the chalkboard with his back to the students, Professor Ruark suddenly asked the class the most surprising question. A question that seemed as if he had chosen it out of the blue:

"What is the density of osmium?"

Everyone in the class heard the question. No one answered. Ruark continued to write on the chalkboard. Students began opening their books, flipping through the pages hoping to find the answer while others looked as if they were lost at sea. Still no one answered.

Ruark stopped writing on the chalkboard and turned around with his arm still raised as if he were writing in mid-air. He began to repeat the question, "What is the—" He noticed one student had his hand raised.

"Yes," he said, looking straight at Miller.

"22," Miller answered. "The answer is 22."

Ruark looked at him curiously and asked, "How did you know that? No one ever knows the answer."

"It was just one of those oddities you happen to pick up," Miller replied.

This was only the beginning. The professors at the University of North Carolina would soon learn Miller would be a very impressive student.

Several students turned to take a quick look at their fellow student who had just made a name for himself with Dr. Ruark. He was very impressed with Miller. "Ruark thought I must be a pretty smart guy to know the answer to that question," remembered Miller.

Dr. Arthur E. Ruark was the Head of Physics Department and had been a high official at the Atomic Energy Commission. He had collaborated with Dr. H.C. Urey on *Atoms, Molecules and Quanta* in 1930, a work which had become a bible to thousands of physicists. His level of experience was nothing less than stellar, so for him to be impressed with this young kid from Texas was saying a lot. Dr. A.E. Ruark would become Miller's immediate supervisor from June 1943 to April 1944. Miller was a part-time Physics instructor at the University while working toward his Ph.D. In June of 1943, Miller's starting salary was $600 per year, and within the year it quickly jumped to $2,400 per year.

At the end of the day, Miller returned to his apartment mentally exhausted from the heavy class load and physically spent from lugging around the heavy books. As he slowly walked up the steps he could see a small package by the front door. With his hands full of books, he bent down carefully so the books wouldn't topple out of his arms and picked up the small brown package.

He let the books slide out of his arms and thump into a chair on the front porch. The package was from Cecil, who was now serving with the Marines in the South Pacific. Miller placed the package under his arm as he unlocked the front door. He put his cigarette out in the ashtray and cut the string with his pocket knife. Slowly he pulled out the gift his brother had sent him; a diffused hand grenade.

The next day, Miller took the hand grenade to school and set it on his desk for an ashtray. Ruark did not object to smoking in the classroom, as smoking was commonplace at that time, but using a grenade as an ashtray did concern him. He stopped his lecture in mid-sentence, looked at the grenade and asked, "You sure that has been defused?"

"Oh yes, it's okay. I just use it as an ashtray," assured Miller. The class turned to look at the grenade and laughed. The young man to Miller's left reached over, picked it up, studied it, smiled at Miller with a crooked smile, and placed it back on his desk.

Miller spent many hours in the classroom. He had little time between classes, and it wasn't easy lugging a stack of heavy, burdensome books while climbing stairs to and from classes, both to attend and to teach. Teaching was a requirement in the fellowship program and he spent many hours preparing his lectures and studies. Hard work had paid off so far: he had been an All District football player, valedictorian, received a full ride to T.C.U., and now had an opportunity to study under men who were thought of highly by colleagues in their fields. What Miller did not realize at the time was these men were greatly impressed with him as well.

twenty-three

They Would Work Side by Side

General Leslie Groves ignored the success at the Naval Research Laboratory. After all, the President's orders were to alienate the Navy from the development of atomic energy. The Army withheld uranium oxide and deprived the Naval Research Laboratory of all information regarding atomic energy. Their efforts caused unnecessary delays, but failed to stop Abelson's team; they succeeded despite the costly attempts to derail the Liquid Thermal Diffusion Process.

In the spring of 1943, the small pilot plant at the Naval Research laboratory produced and shipped 236 pounds of uranium hexafluoride with partial isotopic separation to the Metallurgical Laboratory in Chicago. The material received was of enormous importance because the electromagnetic device was the only other effective source of separated uranium.

Later in 1943, another review of the Liquid Thermal Diffusion Process at the Naval Yard was ordered. This time, the review board not only endorsed the Navy's work, but advised a plant expansion. This report did not go ignored. The team at the Naval Research laboratory had worked independently from the Manhattan Project, and they had succeeded. On November 17, 1943, authorization was obtained to build a larger 300-unit pilot plant at the Philadelphia Naval Yard where cooling water, building space and experienced engineers were readily available.

With war raging all over the world, General Groves felt the urgency to get the bomb completed with each passing day to halt the incomprehensible massacre of innocent men, women and children. Late in the summer of 1943, he announced that the gaseous diffusion plant would provide only 50% instead of 100% enrichment as feed material, and the other 50% would come from Y-12, the plant providing uranium-235 using electromagnetic separation. The principal use of the Liquid Thermal Diffusion Process was as a source for other plants.

§

In late November 1943, Mildred Lucille Moseley received the telegram every mother dreaded. The telegram was from the Marines. Travel expenses would be paid in full if she or a close relative would like an opportunity to visit Cecil, her son. The telegram implied, but never said, Cecil's condition was fatal. Miller was on his way.

He knew his brother had been wounded sometime between November 20 and November 23, 1943, during the operation against the Japanese in the Battle of Tarawa Atoll, but his injuries ended up being non-life-threatening.

When Cecil approached the shore of Tarawa Atoll, part of the Gilbert Islands, he saw Japanese heavy guns lining the shore. In all of the previous battles, Japan did not put up much of a fight. But this time was different. This time they were well-supplied. This time there were 4,500 Japanese soldiers fighting, and this time they were determined to win. The *Colorado* and the *Maryland* had destroyed most of the Japanese guns while additional ships and planes bombed the island. The U.S. thought they had won, or was close to it, but when their Higgins boats failed to clear the reefs due to the neap tide, the U.S. Marines had to crawl over jagged coral and avoid Japanese gunfire to make the beach. On the fourth day, the Japanese launched a suicidal banzai attack and fought to almost the last man; 17 surrendered. 1,009 marines and 687 Naval soldiers lost their lives. America was outraged. In their eyes this was too large of a loss for a seemingly unimportant little island.

In just 76 hours, the Japanese killed more Marines than had been killed during the entire six month Guadalcanal Campaign.

A few of the Marines refused to go to shore, deserting their fellow soldiers and hiding in the ships. After the extremely deadly battle, which the U.S. eventually won, dead bodies lay everywhere. A group of Marines were ordered to stay behind for the horrific job of burying the dead.

Cecil had been shot during the battle, but was given the responsibility of commanding and transporting the deserters back to Honolulu for later transport to San Diego. He was told where to berth the ship in Hawaii since he was the highest in command, yet he didn't hold a high position. He knew the odds of reaching Hawaii were slim because of Japan's Kamikaze pilots, but Cecil made it. Though shot up, he was very much alive and managed to berth the ship as instructed despite the lack of maneuvering space in the harbor. Afterwards, he was taken to a hospital ship for healing and rest.

As Cecil lay recuperating at West Loch, Pearl Harbor, the Navy busily crammed landing craft surrounding the hospital ship with 50-gallon drums of fuel, hand grenades and ammunition in preparation for the next planned attack against the Japanese at the Marianas Islands, code named "Operation Forager." On the afternoon of May 21, 1944, as doctors finished changing Cecil's bandages, several loud explosions rocked the harbor and an inferno quickly spread amongst the ships. Somehow, by a cigarette or a spark from a welder—it was never determined—fuel and ammunition began to explode. Body parts were thrown hundreds of feet. Vessels drifted aimlessly while pieces of metal and other debris flew through the air. Men who jumped from burning ships were killed or injured when they were run over by rescue vessels arriving at the scene. As fuel and ammunition continued to explode, flames caught neighboring ships on fire. Men were swallowed alive by the raging fires and blown apart by continued explosions. After the horrific accident, nine landing ships had been destroyed and many more had been damaged. 163 were dead and 396 lay wounded. Cecil was among the wounded and not given much chance of surviving.

"Cecil was hurt worse in the explosion than he was by the Japanese," Miller later recalled. "The explosion and disaster embarrassed the Navy."

Miller was immediately put in contact with an ace pilot, a man known as the best of the best and who could maneuver his small seaplane safely through violent enemy territory. The pilot was Ensign Myron Melton Truax. Truax would later receive a Navy Cross for serving as a pilot in the vicinity of the Island of Okinawa, where he spied on and courageously dove toward an enemy ship as they viciously targeted his plane. His air assault and skillful hits caused severe damage to the enemy vessel. Later, he found himself greatly outnumbered and attacked by a group of enemy aircraft. He successfully shot down six enemy planes and he received another Navy Cross, which was one notch below the Medal of Honor. He was part of twenty strikes that caused immense damage to enemy military installations and received the Distinguished Flying Cross. In an additional fifty-five air strikes that destroyed Japanese installations and aircraft, he received five Air Medals. Truax was the pilot assigned the task of delivering Miller through enemy territory to his brother's side in Honolulu.

Of all the unbelievable and miraculous occurrences, Miller had grown up with Melton Truax at the Masonic Home in Fort Worth.

There was one cardinal rule at the Home. If you ran away, nobody came looking for you. You were history. You could not come back. In those Depression days there were more applications than there was space for children in the school. Melton's father had been dead only a year when his mother sent him there. He had a great attachment for his father and missed him dearly. He was nine years old. After three days he ran away. Knowing he would head home, Bill Remmert, dean of boys, called his mother and asked her to bring him back. She did. Mr. Remmert talked to him at length and asked him to give the Home a chance. Two weeks later he was on the road again. Mr. Remmert had taken a liking to him. Once more he broke the rule and had him sent back. This time he told Melton there were no more chances. Run away again, he would stay gone. Melton did stay.

Melton and Miller knew the trip would be extremely dangerous. Japan attacked any and all U.S. aircraft and ships. They refueled in Mexico, where the Japanese had little interest, and sent the bill to the U.S. government. But later they were forced to hide in an area where numerous shade trees grew out of the water for camouflage. With the use of cameras with telescopic lenses and recorders, they eventually landed safely on a sea carrier waiting for them in Hawaii.

Myron Melton Truax ended his career with two Navy Crosses, the Distinguished Flying Cross, five Air Medals, the Bronze Star, a Presidential Citation, and many other awards as an aviator aboard the *U.S.S. Essex*. But when Truax returned home, he put his medals in a drawer and he never spoke to anyone about his heroic acts. "To him, the heroes were his buddies who didn't make it back," said Bill Walraven. Shortly, after Truax died, the airfield at the Corpus Christie Naval Air Station in Texas was renamed Truax Field. "He would be miffed at all those who had exposed him as a hero," said Bill.

twenty-four

My Brightest Student

Miller's life was about to change. He didn't know it at the time, but the next class he walked into would introduce him to a whole new world, a world only a select few would ever experience.

Miller, along with every student sitting in that packed classroom, had looked forward to this one particular class with great expectation. It would be taught by Albert Einstein's collaborator and friend, the well-known American-Israeli Physicist, Nathan Rosen. He was the first American-born physicist to work as Einstein's assistant. The professor stood quietly with arms crossed, watching the students slowly fill every available seat.

He was an ordinary-looking man with a receding hairline and a long nose upon which round spectacles rested. Anyone passing him on the street probably would not have given him a second glance. But there he stood, the man who had assisted and partnered with Albert Einstein at the Institute for Advanced Study in Princeton, New Jersey.

Einstein had personally requested the help of Rosen when he was a 26-year-old new fellow at the Institute. He, along with 49-year-old Boris Podolsky, whom Einstein had met at Caltech, were assisting Einstein when Rosen mentioned abnormalities he had discovered in Einstein's research associated with entangled wave functions. Nathan Rosen, Albert Einstein and Boris Podolsky's collaboration resulted in one of the most famous theoretical articles ever written on quantum mechanics, and it became the most important paper Einstein wrote after fleeing Germany and moving to America in December, 1932. The article was titled "Can Quantum-Mechanical Description of Physical Reality Be Considered Complete?" This paper was later referred to as the Einstein-Podolsky-Rosen paradox, or the EPR paradox. Miller did not realize at the time that Nathan Rosen would play a huge part in shaping his own fate.

Rosen had previously left the United States in 1936 to work in the Soviet Union at the University of Kiev. When he returned to the United States, he began teaching at the University of North Carolina at Chapel Hill. There were a few Americans who silently questioned his allegiance. As a student of Nathan Rosen, Miller never saw any ties to the Soviet Union. Rosen's students were well aware of his connection with Einstein and Podolsky, as well as other high dignitaries, and they were awed to study under him.

§

The Physics department was located about a block from the edge of the University's property and only one block from a small grade school.

As Miller and Dr. Ruark prepared their lectures, Dr. Ruark's little girl traipsed in. She had just started school and was told to walk home every day unless the weather was bad. On those days, the professor would drop everything and drive her home. That day, his daughter took the shortcut to the Physics Department. As tears rolled down her cheeks, she begged her father to drive her home. He phoned his wife and said, "Hello Grace, this is Ruark, I have the girl here, she wants me to drive her home and I am too busy. There is no appreciable external precipitation." Miller witnessed firsthand the personal side of men few would ever know. He quietly left the room while Ruark and his daughter worked out the details.

§

Early in 1944, work on the Manhattan Project was in full force. Albert Einstein had pressured his superiors to allow him to bring in Nathan Rosen as his personal assistant. When approached, Rosen agreed with one stipulation: "I want to bring along my brightest student." Einstein had complete confidence in Rosen's judgment and knew that if Rosen championed this young kid, then he too wanted him on the Project; he knew he would be a perfect fit for the caliber of sophisticated scientists working on the Manhattan Project. That student was Harrison Miller Moseley. The team working on the Manhattan Project had to consist of only the best and brightest to bring this experiment to reality ahead of the Germans. There was no room for anyone on the Project who could not perform.

The next day, Miller arrived at class earlier than usual and it seemed as if Dr. Rosen had been waiting for him. As soon as Miller sat down, Rosen walked over and sat down on the top of the desk next to his, leaned toward him and said, "Miller, I would like to see you in my office, after class."

"Okay, sure," Miller replied. Following class, Miller walked down the hall to Rosen's office and found the door open.

Rosen looked up and saw Miller in the doorway. "Miller, come in and have a seat," the professor said, standing up. Miller had barely sat down when Rosen leaned forward, rested his forearms on his desk and said, "Miller, I have a very important question I want to ask, and I hope you will take careful consideration before you give me your decision. I would like for you to join Einstein and myself on the Manhattan Project. Take some time and consider the offer. It would offer great experience into chemical research and include a small salary from the Navy." At that time, a brand new, large pilot plant had been completed at the Naval base in Philadelphia. As Miller sat, the implication of what Professor Rosen had just asked him sank in. He accepted immediately. Nathan Rosen had just asked Miller to work with him on a project that included Albert Einstein. Miller had no idea what lay ahead.

As a 22-year-old kid, Miller had been asked to join the most highly respected group of scientists in the United States of America working on the most important mission in the world. As a result of his assignment, Miller's fellowship was put on hold. Before he knew it, he was on a train with Nathan Rosen headed to Washington, D.C. It was a long way from Fort Worth, Texas. As they began conversing, Rosen said, "Miller, while I taught in the Soviet Union I did not speak Russian very well. I never understood why every time I referred to one of my past lectures, the class laughed. I later learned I had confused a couple of words and had instructed the class to refer to 'my boring lectures.'"

As the train sped its way north, Rosen handed Miller a couple of books to study. Miller flipped through the books and noticed they described a new mathematical technique called the Laplace Transformation. Rosen thumped his finger on one of the books and said, "You will need to know this by the time we reach the Naval Research Laboratory in Anacostia." Miller did not waste any time, and when they reached Anacostia, he had educated himself well and was ready to begin work. Rosen brought a lot of experience as well as his great reputation regarding theoretical work. Others admired and listened to what he had to say. Miller joined Nathan Rosen and his circle of scientists working on the liquid separation of the isotopes of uranium.

Miller's Valedictorian Certificate had read:

Certificate of Award as Valedictorian of the Class of 1939 awarded a complimentary subscription to Reader's Digest for one year; beginning with the July, 1939 issue. In the belief that vital contact with the living, quickening thought of our day is essential to continuing education, this subscription is presented not only in recognition of past accomplishment, but in the anticipation of unusual achievement to come.

If "anticipation of unusual achievement to come" was a test, Miller definitely passed. No one could have seen this coming.

Symbolic of the time, when they arrived at the train station in Anacostia, a military band played as military personnel drove Jeeps, motorcycles, trucks, tanks, and more by the hundreds onto the flatbed railroad cars. Three rows of military personnel marched by, and one-by-one, the men stepped onto the train, each carrying one white duffle bag. Military guards walked the tracks with weapons as protection. As the bell clanged and the train began to move, the conductor leaned out of the window and waved back to the men seated in the tanks which were secured to the flatbeds. The men waved back. Not one young man on that train had any idea where the military was taking them.

Philip Abelson, inventor of the Liquid Thermal Diffusion method of separating uranium isotopes, offered the use of his unoccupied apartment to Rosen and Miller the evening they arrived in Washington. He later extended the offer for anytime they needed it as long as Abelson and his wife were not there. This was an extremely generous offer because the apartment was directly across the street from the entrance of the Naval Research Laboratory. "Finding a place to rent in Washington D.C. during the war was almost impossible," said Miller. "The bureaucrats were running the show and their pay and influence was determined by how many people were under them. They used the war as an excuse to hire as many people as they could. Not that it did the war effort any good, but it meant a lot to those who were directing it."

Abelson and his wife no longer lived in the apartment, but kept it for its convenience. Neva Martin Abelson was a distinguished research physician who was quite accomplished herself. While working for Johns Hopkins Hospital, she co-discovered the life-saving blood test for the Rh blood factor with Louis K. Diamond. Abelson told Miller that Neva's work had caused a bit of controversy because she had inoculated a monkey and animal activists were upset.

There he stood in Philip Abelson's apartment. Later that afternoon Rosen asked Miller what he wanted for dinner. Miller wasn't familiar with the area and didn't have a preference. All he knew was he was hungry. About that time, Abelson walked in and asked, "What are you two having for dinner?"

"Hamburgers from the joint next door," replied Rosen.

"A hamburger. Oh, hell. I'll go get the food," said Abelson.

He later returned with three large, beautiful steaks. And there Miller sat, eating steak with two of the most powerful scientists in the world.

§

The day after Miller arrived in Washington, D.C. he was told to report to Ross Gunn.

"I remember when I was introduced to Gunn," Miller reflected. A guard stood at the door to his office. Inside Gunn sat behind a large desk. There were smaller desks in the room covered with stacks of paper.

When Miller walked into his office, Ross Gunn asked, "Who are you?"

"Well, I was told to report here," Miller replied.

"Are you crazy?"

"What do you mean?"

"Well most of us around here are crazy." Then Gunn laughed, and after a short visit he handed Miller his orders.

From the moment Miller walked onto the Project in April of 1944 until his last day, he received all of his orders directly from Ross Gunn and Philip Abelson. From 1927 until 1947, Gunn was a research physicist on the staff of the U.S. Naval Research Laboratory. In 1934 he was appointed technical advisor for the entire laboratory and in that role he interacted with important Naval personnel. Miller was considered important Naval personnel. Later, Ross Gunn was simultaneously Superintendent of the Mechanics and Electricity Division, Superintendent of the Aircraft Electrical Division, and Technical Director of the Army-Navy Precipitation Static Project. He was also Technical Adviser to the Naval Administration.

Since 1943, the Manhattan Project had the complete support of President Roosevelt, military leadership and the services of some of the nation's most distinguished scientists, but Rosen had failed to mention that Miller would work directly under the commanding officer of the Naval Research Laboratory.

Miller witnessed Gunn's brilliance, his down-to-earth side and his comical side.

While walking across the Naval Yard, Miller and Rosen had the thrill of observing Gunn examining what many said was a spaceship, approximately 42 feet long.

The rocket had crashed in the English Channel and Gunn had it delivered to the Naval Yard. "He must have been a little crazy," said Miller, "because Gunn walked out, looked at 'the spaceship' and noticed green spots all over it. He put his finger on the green spots and tasted it! Put his finger back in his mouth and tasted it! As if tasting the consistency of this object would tell him something." As they stood and watched they were unable to hear or understand what Gunn was saying or discovered. It wasn't their project, but it was entertaining to watch.

Miller was under the impression he would work beside Rosen on

Theoretical Physics calculations for the majority of his assignment. However, Ross Gunn immediately sent him to work for Philip Abelson. The phenomenon of Liquid Thermal Diffusion would become a huge part of Miller's life.

The men in the Naval Research Laboratory were the pioneers. There was no instruction manual. "For the case of pure substances, almost nothing was known. However a considerable amount of experimental work and theoretical study had been devoted to a special case of liquid thermal diffusion, the Soret effect," said Miller.

One day, while working, Abelson said, "Miller, I was instantly interested in the uranium project from the moment I learned of its existence shortly after Neva and I had moved to Southern California." The project had three production facility sites located in valleys away from towns to provide both security and a controlled environment in case of explosions.

Rosen worked with Miller and Abelson on many occasions, and he frequently invited Miller to join his family for dinner at their home. After Miller walked into their home, he carefully stepped over Rosen's sons, Joseph and David, as they played on the living room floor.

§

Miller successfully passed the rigorous top security clearance. The secrecy of the entire project was drilled into their heads. The program and the future safety of the United States and the world depended on the success of the Manhattan Project, and it was their responsibility to live by the command, "What you see here, what you do here, what you hear here, when you leave here, let it stay here," and they sincerely lived by the rules. Family members, including spouses, never knew they worked on the Project. The scientists used code words, such as "material" instead of "bomb." Every movement they made had to be deliberate and careful, yet at the same time they had to work as fast as they could. Living in constant secrecy irritated many because it required working and living in secluded locations with the resultant hardships when dealing with contractors and suppliers.

The scientists were under tremendous pressure because of the enormity of their job and the imperativeness of their success. The accomplishment or failure of the team would not only be representative of the United States, but it meant life or death to millions all over the world. A seriously limited number of employees on the project were privy to the purpose of their work. Miller knew. Without officially informing this small group of scientists, those working beside Abelson knew the enormous potential energy they were producing had to be for the development of a powerful bomb. But they were among the extreme few who knew their purpose. Young men were losing their lives daily, and the hope was that the success of this project would significantly limit the number of lives lost.

During one of Miller's numerous trips to Washington, D.C., Rosen said, "Miller, when we get there, I'll take you over to see Einstein."

Miller replied, "I don't care to go."

Miller very much wanted to visit Albert Einstein, but at that time he felt he lacked the needed experience and knowledge in Theoretical Physics, and he feared he would look like an idiot trying to carry on a conversation with him.

If Rosen had known Miller's concerns, he probably would have driven straight to his good friend. Einstein probably was eager to meet the young man his colleague had described as "his brightest student." This young kid in graduate school had been asked to join an elite group of great minds on the most important project in the world, yet he remained humble. Miller thought once he obtained experience, he would shake Einstein's hand. He later regretted his answer because the opportunity never came again.

"We had an old boy in Carolina," Miller later recalled. "Otto Von Stuhlman, a German who did not care too much for Jews. I mentioned my close encounter with Einstein, and he said, 'Moseley, while I was in Europe I stopped by to visit Einstein. I was somewhat surprised to find

Einstein's house in such an unkempt mess. But, what I found to be even stranger, Einstein was in his backyard without any clothes on!'"

§

Miller felt Nathan Rosen was a great teacher, but he learned more from his association with him on the Project than he did from the classroom. With the numerous experiments in the laboratory, there were occasional blowouts. When this happened everyone was instructed to evacuate the laboratory immediately and not return until it was safe to do so.

Every scientist working in the Naval Research Laboratory was required to walk into a small room that was about 15 feet in diameter. One-by-one, with the door tightly closed behind them, each scientist was subjected to brief exposure to the ultra dangerous uranium hexafluoride. "It was pretty strong, but generally it would be over in a short amount of time," Miller said. Then the door opened and the next scientist in line stepped inside. "It was felt important, at the time, that each scientist was aware of the sensations, to know the smell, if a leak were to occur," explained Miller. Generally, if an accident occurred, the scientists were slow to leave the laboratory until their research was completed. "The trouble was if you waited too long, it sank under the skin and formed a compound that was painful and dangerous. If you quickly showered, you did not get this problem."

Every morning Miller picked up his protective clothing and walked toward the laboratory where guards stood at the door. He seldom wore his gas mask.

Inside the Naval Research Laboratory, the huge, evenly-distributed columns gleaming in the sodium vapor lighting rose 48 feet from the ground and made everyone who entered the laboratory aware of the ultra hazardous dangers threatening the life of every scientist. The column was the key to the Liquid Thermal Diffusion Process.

Miller knew the equipment, how it was constructed, the promises and the dangers, and he explained it well in the document *The Master Liquid Thermal Diffusion* for the U.S. Atomic Energy Commission in 1946.

The column was in the form of three long vertical coaxial cylinders, two of which bounded the space in which the working fluid was kept. The central tube, made of nickel, was heated by condensing steam (introduced at the top) on its interior wall. The outside of the nickel tube and the inside of the second tube (copper) bounded an annular space about 0.025 cm wide that was filled with process fluid. The copper was cooled by the circulation of water flowing upward between it and the outer iron pipe.

The vertical walls of the container are close together and kept at two different temperatures. The density of the fluid near the hot wall is decreased, whereas that near the cold wall is increased, and convection set in, causing the fluid near the hot wall to rise and that near the cold wall to descend. This will cause two streams of fluid to flow past each other and, at the same time, exchange molecules of the two species because of the thermal diffusion. The stream near the hot wall catches the molecules moving toward that wall by thermal diffusion and carries them upward, whereas near the cold wall molecules of the other kind are carried down by the convection flow there. The result is that one kind of molecule accumulates near the top of the container whereas the other kind collects near the bottom.

The inner, or hot, wall was maintained at a temperature that varied in different experiments from about 150 to about 320°C, and the outer, or cold, wall was kept at a temperature near 70°C. When a column is filled with uranium hexafluoride, the process or working fluid, and kept under the conditions described, isotope separation takes place.

The columns were hung vertically, supported on a steel framework.

Steam was introduced at the top of the column, and condensate was removed at the bottom. A cooling water inlet was located at the bottom of the column, with the outlet at the top.

Although all steam piping and the columns themselves were insulated, the amount of heat released into the large room was high enough to make operations very uncomfortable and difficult.

Before Miller or anyone could begin any enrichment of uranium, the equipment had to be thoroughly checked to insure no leaks existed anywhere in the equipment. It was a time-consuming and overwhelming task which could only be performed by experienced personnel.

The handling of the process fluid required some special techniques. Suitable packing materials were not developed for UF6 until late in the project. Efforts were therefore directed toward the development of packless devices. Valve action was obtained by freezing the process fluid. This was easy because most of the connecting lines carrying UF6 were of small bore and the melting point of the substance was 64.1°C.

Miller did it all. He climbed the ladder located behind the columns. Bags of dry ice were scattered along the platform. Located roughly seven feet from the top of the columns was a three foot wide platform which wrapped all the way around the columns as a floor for the scientists to work. "It was strategically placed so the input sample ports located four feet from the top were directly in front of the scientists for easy access while standing on the platform. There were no safety rails," Miller said. There was that one guy who could be found periodically napping on the platform. Somehow he never rolled off the edge.

Miller removed samples of process fluid every two to four hours while the column was in operation and under pressures of 500 to 1500 psi.

To begin, Miller froze a small section, 5 cm in length, of the process fluid by holding dry ice onto the tube. After a plug had formed in a

1/8-inch I.D. tube that would not fail under the 1500 psi pressure, Miller could safely remove the cap from the tube and attach a sampling tube. When the frozen plug thawed, liquid flowed into the sampling tube. At first the samples taken were as large as 50 g, later they were reduced to 10 g, and finally, as a result of the intervention of theoretical physicists, they were diminished to 1 g. Miller could simply grip the tube, and if it was hot to the touch, he knew the liquid had entered the tube. He immediately silver soldered the cap back onto the end of the input valve. The cap had to be completely sealed on the tube else hazardous chemicals would escape.

To get back to the ground where the sample port was located, he slid down a fireman's pole. Steam was introduced at the top of the column, and condensate was removed at the bottom. A cooling water inlet was located at the bottom of the column, with the outlet at the top. The constant need for reaching the platform and returning to the floor could become exhausting. The fireman's pole was a welcome relief. Miller stepped over, wrapped his legs around the pole and quickly dropped to the floor with ease.

Timing was everything. If Miller removed the sample tube too soon or failed to silver-solder the end securely, the dreaded white cloud of material would erupt, serving as a warning the sample had been lost, time had been wasted and temporary emergency evacuation was essential. Miller never experienced such a blowout during Liquid Thermal Diffusion enrichment.

Most of the analytical work with uranium was performed at the University of Minnesota on Nier mass spectrographs, by Alfred O.C. Nier himself.

However, he did experience one major blowout. As they worked side by side one day, Abelson asked Miller his opinion in regards to a special experiment he had been contemplating. Miller listened to his preconception of the possibility of achieving a greater return of separated isotopes working with the material in a gaseous state rather than with liquid and he agreed with Abelson's assumption. He knew there were risks, but thought the experiment could achieve the anticipated results.

Abelson went on to say he wanted Miller to be the scientist who conducted the experiment since he would be unable to take part himself. However, Abelson knew the experiment would be in the best hands possible. He prepared the column ahead of time and had Nier flown in from Minnesota to analyze the product.

Miller climbed the ladder as he had done so many times before, stood on the platform and worked with extreme caution. Since they were unaccustomed to conditions pertaining to the gaseous state, Miller wore every piece of protective covering offered. As he worked, Miller heard the phone ring down below on the floor. Rosen quickly climbed the ladder to get a status report from Miller. At that moment Miller suffered his one and only blowout. All efforts were lost. Rosen quickly slid down the pole to the floor and updated Abelson, who was disappointed. Miller and Rosen evacuated the laboratory and threw their clothes into a washing machine. "That was the only time that I know of that Abelson ever tried experimenting with gas," Miller said.

Later, E. P. Ney and J. H. McQueen constructed a mass spectrograph for use in the pilot plant at Philadelphia.

To reduce the chance for accidents, an automatic procedure was implemented using a cam timer and solenoid valves, which was a huge safety improvement.

> *In operation, an automatic timer first froze the capsule outlet and unfroze the inlet that communicated with the columns. This permitted UF6 to enter the capsule at full system pressure, which was indicated on the gauge. The inlet was then frozen and the outlet opened, allowing the contents of the capsule to pass out into the product pots. All these operations were automatic and were carried out by a cam timer.*

With new automation, Miller could set a timer before leaving for the day. "One evening, a new facilities director came through the laboratory and threatened to shut the place down," Miller said. He told Miller to turn everything off before leaving. Miller explained it was necessary to leave the timer on for the safety of the plant. The man insisted until Miller stated, "The entire system will be destroyed if you do not allow it to run overnight and you will be blamed." The facilities director relented.

Although the method was titled "liquid thermal diffusion," in many of the experiments and plant operations, part of the process fluid was at temperatures above critical, meaning the method was a combination of gaseous *and* liquid diffusion at times.

Any desired degree of isotope separation could be obtained from a column by sufficiently increasing its length. This procedure was impractical due to the awkwardness of such equipment. Nathan Rosen developed the NRL pyramid scheme for further separation. Columns were connected in series to enhance enrichment of uranium beyond that produced by a single stage.

Large quantities of uranium hexafluoride, UF6, had to be maintained in reservoirs at 1,550 psi. To minimize serious operational hazards, the bulk handling of UF6 was done in the transfer room, a separate building especially designed to minimize potential risks.

§

Problems were escalating to a point of crises with the other three processes. The only difficulties arising from the Liquid Thermal Diffusion process were the lack of steam or cooling water. The Naval Research Laboratory was expanded to increase isotope studies, with the objective of providing an alternative method in the event that the magnetic or gaseous diffusion methods failed. At this time, the Navy's accomplishments were regarded as insurance, a backup method if the magnetic and gaseous diffusion methods failed.

In April 1944, General Groves received a letter from Robert Oppenheimer with a solution to the crises. The plant at the Naval Yard in Philadelphia would be completed in July and ready to produce enriched uranium. He suggested expanding Abelson's Liquid Thermal Diffusion project yet again.

> *Pursuant to attached letter of June 3 from Gen. Groves, JBC and W. K. L. [Warren K. Lewis] Discussed with E. O. L. & the top [Oak Ridge] Tennessee people the relation of the NRL process (later to be called the Abelson-Gunn process) to the electromagnetic process. It was agreed that the use of the expanded Phila. [Philadelphia] plant to produce 0.70% feed was of first importance and by itself would increase the output before July 1, 1945 appreciably. The question was also raised of building a NRL plant to operate on the [boiler] house of the [gaseous] diffusion plant at Tennessee. It was pointed out that for small enrichment this process was economical but for large enrichment almost impossible because of coal consumption and long hold-up time. It was recommended to Gen. Groves that a plant be built at Tennessee to feed in the electromagnetic plant enriched material thereby perhaps doubling the output of providing insurance against failure of the [gaseous] diffusion plant to come in on time.*

Suddenly, the Navy's work was considered invaluable.

Their success could no longer be denied. On June 26, 1944, General Groves, accompanied by Richard Tolman, W. I. Thompson of the H. K. Ferguson Co. and Lt. Col. M. C. Fox, arrived at the Naval Research Laboratory to obtain all the available information concerning work on the thermal diffusion process. Officials of the Manhattan District concluded that the Liquid Thermal Diffusion process could be administered in the atomic bomb program. Blueprints of the Philadelphia installation were turned over to them and General Groves issued instructions that the Oak Ridge installation was to be built as an exact copy of the Philadelphia plant. Its primary use would be to serve as a feeder for the electromagnetic process. Groves ordered the construction of another 2,142-column diffusion plant to be built in Oak Ridge, Tennessee, known as S-50. It would be an exact duplicate of the plant at the Philadelphia Naval Yard. Time had been wasted, but Leslie Groves finally acknowledged that the Navy was doing it right.

Major General Groves had the unrealistic endeavor of pushing laboratory research into design, construction and operation of an atomic weapon in a little over two years. The scientists involved in the Project knew their work was of the utmost importance to the government, but they knew nothing more.

Groves immediately bought all of the uranium ore in the United States and attempted to monopolize the world supply. He separated the Manhattan Project into three-parts:

The atomic bomb would be designed and assembled at Los Alamos, New Mexico, under the direction of Robert Oppenheimer.

Uranium isotopes would be separated at massive plants at Oak Ridge, Tennessee, using gaseous barrier diffusion and mass spectrometers.

Large reactors would be constructed at Hanford, Washington, near the Columbia River, and remote-control plants were to be constructed for separating plutonium from radioactive fission products.

Under the security program called "compartmentalization," the scientists in each of these plants did not know what was going on elsewhere. Abelson's efforts at the Naval Research Laboratory were conducted in collaboration with, and were facilitated by, Ross Gunn. As Chief Technical Advisor to the Naval officer commanding the laboratory, Gunn had clout.

Initiation of the Manhattan Project consumed immense material, financial and scientific resources. The price tag would total over $2 billion. But the S-50 2,142 column plant's construction and operation costs would be accomplished with a total expenditure of about one percent of the total cost of the Manhattan Project.

As World War II dragged on, the success of the program grew imperative.

§

Miller continued producing samples from the diffusion columns regularly. The output from this larger pilot-plant increased the output by 20 percent and the purity of the output was also improved by approximately 20 percent.

The War Department moved Miller and Abelson between the Philadelphia Naval Yard, Oak Ridge, Tennessee, and Washington, D.C. so much that Miller never knew where they would be the next day. Anacostia was their home base, and their work at Oak Ridge and the Philadelphia Naval Yard was considered "Temporary Additional Duties." "The Army personnel who worked with us on the project reported to Abelson, a civilian. They called him 'Doc,'" remembered Miller.

"Abelson was quite a character," Miller reflected. "One day he said, 'Miller, when Neva and I were in school at Berkley, we were both studying radiation and we irradiated the testicles of a white rat.'"

"What happened?" Miller asked.

"The rat suffered a pronounced personality change."

§

"I don't remember the reason why Rosen and I were staying at Abelson's apartment on this particular day," Miller said, discussing June 6, 1944. "The apartment had twin beds and easily accommodated more than one person. We were sound asleep when E. P. Nye, another friend of Abelson's who also had a set of keys to the apartment, unlocked the door and came in. Rosen and I were sound asleep in the other room when we were startled by the sudden loud radio in the living room. We got up and walked in to see what all the commotion was about. There sat Nye, sitting close to the radio, yet the volume blaring as if he was afraid he would miss something.

"It was D-day! The allies had invaded Europe. Rosen and I joined Nye close to the radio. We knew the U.S. had to invade Continental Europe sometime, somewhere, if we were going to defeat Hitler. Rosen, Nye and I sat close to the radio and listened. It was bound to come. Here it is. That's all we could do."

As they sat in silence around the radio, they learned thousands of paratroopers and glider-borne troops had been dropped behind enemy lines. The invasion had been a long, well-kept secret. For the past five days, men and boys had waited anxiously on 7,000 ships covering the English Channel. The United States flag waved high on many of the ships. Five Army divisions participated, and 11,000 aircraft. A chaplain prayed for God to see the men and boys to safety. General Eisenhower and Field Marshall Montgomery thanked the troops and added, "God be with you." Then at 6:30 a.m., June 6, 1944, the long wait ended.

From the Channel, thousands of small water craft hit the beaches of northern France at Normandy. The bluish black waves crashed into the men and their small boats with fury. The soldiers worked hard to keep equipment dry while bailing freezing water out of the boats with their helmets for fear of sinking. As they neared the beach, shells began exploding all around. Bodies were thrown everywhere. Those who made it to the beach immediately kissed the sand and repeated, "Thank you, God." They pushed forward as machine guns fired straight into them. From above came the welcome sound of aircraft. Help was on its way. It was the 101st and 82nd Airborne. The ground fog was so bad the paratroopers could not see their target, but they had been told not to return. They jumped anyway. Tracers shot at them from every angle.

Miller, Rosen and Nye sat in front of the radio, not moving, as they continued to listen to the reports pouring in. The allies successfully beat Adolf Hitler's plan to occupy all of Europe. The men leaned back in their chairs without saying a word.

§

As Abelson and Miller worked, Abelson mentioned a dinner he had attended the previous night. He and Neva had met a couple of old acquaintances from college for dinner whom Abelson did not particularly care for. It was stressful sitting through dinner as this couple put on airs. Neva had listened to all the "uppity" conversation she could handle for one evening and threw her food on the floor. The shocked couple sat back and didn't seem so "uppity" after that.

Though Miller had only met Neva a couple of times, he felt he knew her extremely well because Abelson spoke of her often.

§

On July 6, 1944, Groves gave the contractor tasked with building the Oak Ridge Liquid Thermal Diffusion plant a completely unattainable deadline of 92 days to build it from scratch. It was impossible to construct a large house in 92 days, let alone a huge, highly combustible processing plant. He not only expected the plant to be built in 92 days, he expected to see scientists busy at work in that plant within those 92 days. This highly unachievable goal was not only completed, the contractor beat the 92 day limit by 21 days! In only 71 days, the contractor built the S-50 plant on the banks of the Clinch River adjacent to the K-25 steam power plant at the Clinton Engineer Works, Oak Ridge, Tennessee. A building 525 feet long, 82 feet wide, and 75 feet high housed the required 2,142 columns assembled on 21 steel racks, and the plant containing ultra-sensitive explosive material was humming along with its workers.

On September 2, 1944, travel from Oak Ridge to Anacostia to Philadelphia by way of train was hectic. Miller had to press through large crowds on the train. Colonel J. Monroe Johnson, the director of the Office of Defense Transportation, had given the public a stern warning to stay off the trains and intercity buses over the Labor Day weekend unless directly connected to the war effort. However, the public turned a deaf ear. Travelers swamped the railroads and buses, the number of which had diminished because tires were hard to come by. Nonetheless, there was an increase in traffic because, for the first time in a long time, gasoline was slowly becoming available again.

However, the Navy received pressure from family members with loved ones fighting in the war to get Miller and any other young men working on the base into a military uniform. Amid all this high energy and manipulation to get Miller into uniform, they left Abelson alone; he was old enough to bypass the time-consuming roadblock. "Abelson enjoyed his freedom out of uniform. When in uniform there was always someone ahead of you telling you what to do. Abelson was in total control and he wanted it to stay that way," said Miller.

On his Application for Commission or Warrant, U. S. Naval Reserve, question 8 read: "State in full your reason for making application at this particular time (include reason for choice of the Navy in preference to other services)." Miller's answer: "Already working for Navy at time of induction into Navy."

It was hard to imagine the remarkable timing of this request. Miller was sent to the U.S. Naval Recruiting Station in Washington D.C. to change his draft location from Fort Worth to Anacostia.

As Miller followed all protocol, the phone rang.

Because of the remarkable timing, Miller's life had just been spared. He and Abelson worked side by side at the plants. But on this day, September 2, 1944, Miller was not side by side with Abelson, rather he was shoulder to shoulder with holiday travelers who did not heed the request of Colonel J. Monroe Johnson. Miller had been ordered back to Washington D.C. on that catastrophic day.

Four civilians and ten enlisted men had been sent to Philadelphia to be trained at the Naval Research Laboratory by Abelson.

In the Recruiting Office, the fellow in charge answered the phone. He suddenly raised both arms and motioned and yelled for everyone to gather close. The news was bad. There had been an explosion at the Philadelphia Naval Yard. Everyone listened intently as the details unfolded. Most had no idea what went on at that laboratory or what it meant. Miller knew. However, "Abelson kept information regarding the project so well guarded that even top Naval officials at the base were unaware of the exact nature of this project." The explosion was in the uranium hexafluoride transfer room. Miller knew all about the transfer room, the highly-toxic and powerful chemicals and the dramatic results that could have happened.

As the nightmare unfolded, Miller realized the extraordinary timing of having been ordered far away from the laboratory on that one horrific day.

Miller boarded a train headed for Philadelphia. When it arrived in Philadelphia, Miller did not stand until most of the crowd had made it out the doors. Then he headed straight to the laboratory.

After returning to the lab, he learned the terrifying details regarding the tragic explosion. Thirteen men had inhaled large quantities of uranium compounds and had suffered whole body acid burns. Abelson had inhaled several caustic lungfuls, but miraculously, he experienced only slight lung damage. Four civilians and four soldiers were rushed to the Naval hospital, where the medical staff sorely needed information from Abelson to diagnoses and treat the wounded. But Abelson vowed to secrecy, would not disclose pertinent information. The onsite medical staff was summoned to the emergency room to assist the frustrated doctors. Sadly, Peter N. Bragg and Douglas P. Meigs were killed. Family, friends and loved ones were never given any explanation as to how they had died.

The accident halted the training in Philadelphia, and a thorough investigation was conducted. The problem wasn't poor construction.

The cause of the accident was the result of the tanks, and the lack of cooperation on the part of Manhattan. The Army's control of nickel production had prevented the Navy from constructing seamless nickel tubes for UF6 storage. Instead, the Navy had to build tanks with a thin nickel liner. When the meeting turned to discussing the safety procedures that the Army had developed, Gunn asked how they had arrived at their calculations. Only to have an Army representative state he was ordered not to disclose that information. Gunn's anger at the Army must have been greatly increased by this time. Not only had the Army excluded the Navy from nuclear research in terms of material and information, but now it was unwilling to share safety information following two deaths. Repairs were quickly made to the Philadelphia plant, and production of enriched Uranium continued.

§

As Miller and Abelson visited together one afternoon, Abelson reminisced about his first intense interest in the separation of isotopes and uranium. He was working for the National Bureau of Standards. Miller remembered Abelson saying his experiments scared his colleagues. Merle Tuve, an associate, feared Abelson would contaminate the Carnegie facilities with high levels of radioactivity, so they quickly found him a new home at the National Bureau of Standards, where John I. Hoover and four other assistants were assigned to his work.

Because of Abelson's success implementing the Liquid Thermal Diffusion Process, the Navy rescued the atomic bomb project. On October 31, 1944, only two months after plant S-50 opened, the first product was successfully removed.

On November 23, 1944, Miller arrived in Washington, D.C. for the official draft process. As he walked into the office, he handed the letter he had received to Lieutenant L.A. King of the United States Navy. The Lieutenant quickly read the letter and said, "Okay, get in line." Miller took his place in a long line of nervous young men ready to serve their country. Then Lieutenant King said, "I will go over the instructions for the oath of office. Listen carefully. I will begin calling names, one at a time. When I call your name, step forward and answer, 'Here.' Answering 'Here' will constitute the acceptance of the oath of office, at which point I will give your assignment. Your assignment will be one of two places: The Great Lakes Training Station or Ambridge." And so the lieutenant began calling names, and one-by-one the men stepped forward and answered

"Here." The lieutenant then followed with either "Ambridge" or "Great Lakes." Everything was running smoothly until he got to Miller's name.

"Harrison Miller Moseley," he called.

Miller stepped forward. "Here."

The room suddenly became eerily quiet as the lieutenant studied Miller's letter. Under "For What Duties is He Recommended?" The letter read, "This officer has a good educational background in physics and is presently assigned to a special pilot plant project. Believe Ensign Moseley is serving the best interests of the Navy in his present assignment." And under performance, the letter stated, "This is the first assignment this officer has had since leaving graduate school and he has proven that he is capable of adapting himself readily to practical applications of theoretical problems. His assignment has been difficult and he has gone about it in an orderly fashion. Ensign Moseley is recommended for promotion with his contemporaries." Finally, the lieutenant looked up, and in a quizzical voice said, "You are going on inactive duty. Report back to the Naval Research Laboratory for assignment." Miller received the rank of Ensign, which is a junior rank of a commissioned officer. The men in line looked around with confused expressions, wondering; "Who is this guy anyway?"

As Miller left the office, the young men continued to watch Miller walk out the door with wonder. Miller immediately returned to Anacostia and reported in. Soon after, he returned to the lab and continued working on the same assignments he had been working on as a civilian. His responsibilities did not change despite being an Ensign in the Navy at the 8th Naval District.

Miller caught the first train back to Philadelphia. He immediately noticed respect not previously shown when he was out of uniform. But with respect came expectation. During his return trip, a group of young drunken sailors climbed onto the train and into the same car as Miller. He had just left his induction into the Navy and now everyone on the train looked sternly at Miller to discipline the discourteous sailors.

Miller stood and spoke to a sailor who seemed reasonably sober. The sailor took Miller's advice and tried to convince the others that Miller was on their side, and to sit quietly.

However, the conductor overheard Miller's plea and called the shore patrol. The patrol was waiting at the station when the train pulled in and they immediately took the sailors into custody.

The newfound respect in the civilian world would not hold true in the laboratory: When Miller nonchalantly walked in wearing his officer's uniform, the guys shrugged it off and it was business as usual.

The builders held up their end of the bargain, now unprecedented expectations came down on Abelson, Miller and all the scientists to deliver the enriched uranium in a phenomenally short amount of time. The pressure to produce became relentless.

The initial process of the operation at the S-50 plant, however, proved to be challenging. Miller's department was considered the most important and therefore the employment department sent qualified applicants to their group for consideration ahead of any other department.

Miller needed a new amplifier/timer capable of handling the uranium hexafluoride and the added columns. The Employment Department sent an applicant who had stated on his paperwork that he had worked for two years at a radio shop. "He's yours if you want him," they told Miller. At the time, Miller sorely needed an individual who could build a particular amplifier required in the regulation and analysis of the uranium hexafluoride. They grabbed him.

But there was a slight problem: during the two years the applicant worked for the radio repair shop, his duty was driving the supply truck. He knew nothing about amplifiers.

The accuracy of the timer could have meant life or death. At a minimum it was needed to achieve optimum output. Miller called a supplier frequently used by the Navy and they had the needed part. Miller understood the seriousness and consequences and was desperate to get the timer working correctly.

The supplier said the part would be on the counter when he arrived at their facility to pick it up. Miller jumped on a trolley and sometime later walked into the shop. The clerk asked for Miller's purchase order. Miller informed the clerk that he had failed to mention the need for a purchase order prior to embarking on the time-consuming trip. The clerk's manager came to the front, saw Miller in his officer's uniform and informed the clerk that the Navy was a large customer. He told the clerk that Miller's streetcar ride had cost more than the part did. "Let the officer take the part with him and mail the purchase order."

Upon returning to the Laboratory, Miller walked to the purchasing department and requested a purchase order. Tayman hit the ceiling. Unaware that Miller had just made a huge impact on the safety of the personnel and equipment as well as an increase in production, he began yelling at Miller. He echoed the need for a purchase order before ordering a part. Miller acknowledged Taymans' imperatives then immediately repaired the timer, securing the safety of many.

§

By March 1945, Miller had played a part in producing enough U-235 at Oak Ridge while Hanford had produced enough plutonium to assemble a bomb in Los Alamos.

§

Miller enjoyed Abelson's stories and he was entertaining to be around, but his greatest challenge was ahead. Abelson scared Miller. He was pleased with their progress, and confided in Miller that he planned to take a little trip out in the country and test an atomic bomb.

"Hold on," Miller immediately responded. Miller was out of character. Instead of his usual quiet demeanor, he spoke up. "You are thinking like a chemist instead of considering the chemical reaction. This is a nuclear reaction and will emit 100 million times more energy than a typical bomb, and the explosion will be violent. You are not going to find a safe area to run a test. You can't just go out and set off an explosion." Miller sat quietly for a few moments, then added, "If you are going to set one off, give me time to get to Texas before you do."

Miller's abrupt, determined response probably shocked Abelson. He obviously held a high regard and appreciation towards Miller's resolution and concern because he never tested the bomb and he never brought the subject up again. But soon the U.S would test a bomb and it would be called "Trinity."

§

On April 12, 1945, at 3:35 p.m., the news of Franklin Delano Roosevelt's sudden death in Warm Springs, Georgia, hit the radio waves and shocked the world. Vice President Harry S. Truman took the oath of office within hours of the announcement. Truman, a farmer and, briefly, a haberdasher, was the last president of the United States who did not have a college degree. President Roosevelt had only contacted Truman twice during their time together in office. When President Roosevelt died, Truman had absolutely no knowledge of the top-secret Manhattan Project.

Shortly after taking the oath of office, Truman was told briefly on the afternoon of April 12 that the Allies had developed a new, highly destructive weapon. Two weeks later, on April 25, the Secretary of War, Henry Stimson filled Truman in on the details.

Shortly upon learning of the United States' enormous achievements in atomic research, Truman informed Joseph Stalin about the probability of using a powerful, secret weapon—the atomic bomb—against the Japanese. Though the development and existence of the bomb was new to Truman, Stalin was already aware of it, having learned about it through espionage.

§

The secrecy beyond the walls of the laboratory became Miller's lifestyle. Personnel on the project had no idea what final product their efforts would deliver. Miller and the Liquid Thermal Diffusion team had an idea. Nonetheless, when he walked out of the laboratory and into his personal life, he kept his mouth shut.

Typically, when leaving the Naval Yard, Miller jumped onto a trolley and headed out the gate. But on July 25, 1945, the sun shone particularly bright, and it was an extremely hot afternoon. His Navy uniform was heavy and quite warm, but he was under orders to wear it at all times regardless of the temperature. As he exited the base, he decided to check out the Officer's Club located just inside the gate. He had always wondered what went on in there. When he stepped inside, out of the bright sunlight, he noticed the room was completely dark. He took his hat off, wiped his forehead with his handkerchief and waited for his eyes to focus.

He could barely see a bar at the other end of the room and he headed that direction. As he shuffled past several tables, he heard, "Dundee Moseley!" It was Harold Ferguson, from the Home. Miller walked over. Harold stood up and they shook hands. Harold's destroyer had pulled into the Philadelphia Naval Yard for a few repairs and to change the camouflage. Miller excused himself so he could get a cold drink at the bar and immediately returned to Harold's table. Miller still couldn't see where he was going, but he managed to make his way to the bar, get his drink and return to Harold's table without bumping into anything. He took a seat and the two friends visited. It was good to see family from the Home. Together they had successfully won "The best work done by any club in the United States" for the boys in the print shop.

"What are you doing in the military?" Harold asked.

"I'm working at Oak Ridge," Miller said.

"Why are you guys working with such high steam pressure?" Harold queried.

Miller was surprised at Harold's question. His friend had been serving in a remote location in the South Pacific and this top secret mission had been the scuttlebutt even there.

§

During the project, security was implemented in many forms. Miller never used the word "bomb" for the entire project. Instead, he used the secret code name "material." The Manhattan Project operated under a blanket of tight security, but Soviet spies still penetrated the program.

Earlier in 1939, the "first efforts to establish security in atomic matters occurred when refugee physicists in the United States attempted to institute a voluntary censorship on publication of papers concerning uranium fission. American scientists did not accept this suggestion initially, but the outbreak of World War II brought home the need for control over publications relating to atomic fission. To formalize a censorship program, the Division of Physical Sciences of the National Research Council in April 1940 established a committee that succeeded in getting most scientists to withhold publication of papers on sensitive subjects, particularly those concerned with uranium fission."

On June 6, 1945, Truman was briefed by the Interim Committee whose function was deciding the use of atomic weapons. The Committee included Vannevar Bush, James B. Conant, J. Robert Oppenheimer, Enrico Fermi, Karl Taylor Compton, Ernest O. Lawrence, and others. Their recommendation to Truman was to drop the bomb as soon as possible and without warning. The Committee feared that if they gave a warning and it was rejected, then the powerful bomb turned out to be a dud, their credibility would be lost.

§

As Miller walked toward the mess hall one afternoon, he asked the maintenance worker if it was closed. The worker said "No." As Miller walked towards the hall, he turned and glanced back at the groundskeeper and noticed for the first time, printed in large letters on the back of his shirt, "German Prisoner of War." The man looked up as Miller strode by. Miller waved at the man and entered the mess hall. It was common to see prisoners of war freely walking all over the base. At that time, Miller contemplated the unusual lax freedom given to the prisoners. They were allowed to walk dangerously close to where the diffusion columns were fabricated, which was just a few feet from the mess hall. German prisoners also worked in the mess hall cleaning cooking utensils. Workers scrambled around the clock to get the columns completed as fast as possible while German prisoners watched freely. The lack of security in areas such as this did not seem rational to Miller.

During this time, Miller's mother worked as a Postmaster and informed Miller that she would be attending a convention in Nashville. Miller reserved a room at The Guest House on the base. Later, he assisted his mother with her favorite hobby: collecting dirt. She had a jar of dirt from every state she had ever visited. The two set out and collected dirt from Tennessee, North and South Carolina and Virginia.

While in Tennessee they stopped to visit one of her childhood friends, Bill Rice. He was Dallas preacher John Rice's brother. As they pulled in front of Bill's home, they saw numerous children standing in his yard and they thought they had the wrong address. As Miller and his mother were about to drive away, Bill and his wife stepped outside and welcomed them. The Rice's had started a home school for deaf children and were teaching the children sign language and the Bible. Their efforts would later become the Bill Rice Christian Summer Camp. They offered Miller and Mrs. Moseley a room for the night. "We would have had to sleep in the yard somewhere due to all the children," Miller recalled. They decided a hotel room was more practical.

twenty-five

The Material

A former student of Oppenheimer's who had worked on the Manhattan Project, Robert Serber, received the honor of naming the bombs. He chose names that were descriptive of the shape of each device: "Fat Man," named after the Fat Man in *The Maltese Falcon*, "*The Thin Man*," from the popular movie series, and "Little Boy," also named after a character in *The Maltese Falcon*.

On July 13, 1945, a steel tower built in an isolated corner of the Alamogordo Bombing and Gunnery Range, 230 miles south of Los Alamos, New Mexico, was completed for the purpose of suspending an atomic bomb one hundred feet above ground. The test was code-named "Trinity."

The scientists were reaching into the unknown and they were worried. Before the bomb was detonated, a second bomb had already been secretly dispatched to the Pacific. Its target: Hiroshima, Japan.

Crews unloaded the test bomb at the base of the tower on July 13, 1945. Three days later, the first atomic bomb was detonated.

The explosion far exceeded all the scientists' expectations, and in those few minutes all pent-up emotions were released as the bomb blast unleashed tremendous energy far beyond anything developed to that point in history. The United States now had the means to end the war and save thousands of American lives worldwide.

The Allies now knew the power of the bomb, and on July 28, 1945, the United States delivered an ultimatum for Japan to surrender. Japan refused.

On a rainy morning in August, one that seemed no different than any other morning, Miller arrived at work as usual in his crisp, starched uniform. He stepped into the building, wiped the bottom of his wet shoes on the matt inside the door and was immediately approached by a slightly out-of-breath officer who grabbed Miller's shoulder and said, "Did you hear? Did you hear the news?"

"What do you mean?" Miller replied.

"We dropped material. We dropped material on Japan."

Earlier that morning, on August 6, 1945, the *Enola Gay*, a Boeing B-29 bomber from the 590th Composite Group, loaded its cargo, a 9,700-pound uranium bomb, nicknamed "Little Boy," lifted off Tinian Island and headed north by northwest toward the Japanese Islands. Its target: Hiroshima. As the plane approached its target, instead of hiding, many Japanese stepped outside to take a look, thinking it was an innocent weather plane. The *Enola Gay*, piloted by Colonel Paul Tibbets, flew over its target. At approximately 8:15 a.m. Hiroshima time, the bomb bay doors flew open and the most powerful bomb in the world fell out of the belly of the B-29. Tibbets immediately dove away to avoid the anticipated shockwaves from the blast. Forty-three seconds later a huge explosion lit the morning sky as "Little Boy" detonated 1,900 feet above the city, directly over a parade field where the Japanese Second Army was doing calisthenics. Though already eleven and a half miles away, the blast rocked the *Enola Gay*. At first Tibbets thought he had been hit by antiaircraft fire. But when he turned to look, the city was hidden by an awful cloud boiling up, mushrooming, terrible and incredibly tall.

"We had no idea the bomb was planned for this day," Miller said.

That morning turned out to be very different from any other morning for everyone. The Japanese probably would not have stopped their aggression without the bomb. It was at that moment Miller knew his work had played a major contribution in changing the course of the war and world history. He played a significant part in the group who built the first atomic bomb, one of the most provocative scientific achievements in the world. Within a matter of minutes the environment changed from fear and anxiousness to worldwide astonished celebration. Miller knew, in part, the world celebrated because of his work. Just the day before, Miller and his colleagues were anxiously trying to enrich as much Uranium-235 as humanly possible. Upon hearing the word, Miller's personal world became much less dramatic. Everyone from the laboratory, across the street and across the oceans were dancing and singing. Just an hour earlier, hopelessness had been felt around the world. Parents feared the worst. But now celebrations were occurring worldwide and Miller knew he had assisted in making these celebrations possible because of the great achievements accomplished by those who had worked day and night to help end World War II once and for all.

As Miller drove home that day, he could see laughing and crying in the rain. Miller never imagined he could ever again feel the excitement he experienced as a football star at the Masonic Home. But this beat it. The world was now free from the horrific outbreak of torture and death it had experienced over the past several years.

On the *U.S.S. Augusta*, in the mid-Atlantic, President Harry S Truman broadcast the following message on every radio station in the United States:

The device was more than 2,000 times more powerful than the largest bomb used to date. An accurate assessment of the damage caused has so far been impossible due to a huge cloud of impenetrable dust covering the target. Hiroshima is one of the chief supply depots for the Japanese army. The bomb was dropped from an American B-29 Super Fortress, known as Enola Gay, at 0815 local time. The plane's crew says they saw a column of smoke rising and intense fires springing up.

The President said the atomic bomb heralded the "harnessing of the basic power of the universe."

But as inconceivable as it was to imagine, it was true; after the horrifying bomb was dropped, the Japanese refused to stop fighting. The celebrations turned quiet. The world returned to their seats next to the radio, and families continued to pray for loved ones and the world. How could the Japanese harbor such intense determination that they would jeopardize the health and safety of their own people?

On August 9, 1945, three days after "Little Boy" decimated Hiroshima, American forces dropped a second atomic bomb, "Fat Man," on Nagasaki. Though the bomb destroyed 30% of the city, the world remained unsure if this bomb would stop Japan's brutality. "Thin Man," the third atomic bomb, was ready if needed. Word finally reached Washington on August 10 that the Japanese, in accordance with Hirohito's wishes, would accept the surrender terms, provided the emperor retained his position. After almost six years of war, on August 14, 1945, Japan surrendered and Truman halted the third atomic attack. On September 2, 1945, Japan signed the act of unconditional surrender. Within half-an-hour of the signing, a convoy of 42 U.S. ships entered Tokyo Bay with 13,000 American troops. By the time the war ended, the population of Stalingrad had fallen from 850,000 to 1,500.

§

On August 15, 1945 President Truman stood outside the White House and declared: "This is the day we have been waiting for since Pearl Harbor. This is the day when Fascism finally dies, as we always knew it would." He expressed gratitude to all allies, but gave special thanks to the United States "without whose prodigious efforts the war in the East would still have many years to run." Later, from Buckingham Palace, the King addressed the nation in a broadcast from his study. "Our hearts are full to overflowing, as are your own." And he stated the effects of the war would remain. In the streets of every town and city shouting, singing, dancing, and fireworks were heard during ongoing celebrations. But there were no celebrations in Japan. Emperor Hirohito gave a radio broadcast blaming the use of a new and most cruel bomb used on Hiroshima and Nagasaki for Japan's surrender.

General Douglas MacArthur briefly addressed the dignitaries on the deck of the *Missouri,* urging them to comply with the terms of the surrender "fully, promptly and faithfully." He continued: "It is my earnest hope and, indeed, the hope of all mankind, that from this solemn occasion a better world shall emerge out of the blood and carnage of the past; a world founded upon faith and understanding, a world dedicated to the dignity of man and the fulfillment of his most cherished wish, for freedom, tolerance and justice."

For the scientists who labored tirelessly on the Manhattan Project, the nature of their work had been a well-kept secret. But following the news of the atomic bomb, there were those at the University of North Carolina who supposed they knew who had been working on the project. In the days that followed, Miller participated in many discussions with high-ranking officials regarding the building of the bomb. At that time he did not realize that he would be considered part of an extraordinary group of people and science behind one of the most pivotal events in world history.

"The greatest marvel is not the size of the enterprise, its secrecy, nor its cost," President Truman said in an August 26, 1945 address, "but the achievement of scientific brains in putting together infinitely complex pieces of knowledge by many men in different fields of science into a workable plan. It was done under high pressure and without failure."

PART IV

twenty-six

Mason Football Joins the Army

On November 17, 1945, the U.S. Army versus Penn State game would be played in Philadelphia, close to where Miller was working and renting a room. He was eager to see DeWitt Coulter in action for the U.S. Army football team. Miller did not get to see too much action from DeWitt. "They took ol' DeWitt out of the game before it was over," Miller said. In fact, the entire first team was only on the field for thirty-minutes, then the subs were sent in. The Navy scouts were impressed with the Army's performance.

```
           ARMY (61)              PENN (0)
Pitzer  ..............L.E.............. Jenkins
Coulter ..............L.T............. Savitsky
Gerometta ..........L.G............ Dickerson
Fuson ................C.............. Bednarik
Green ...............R.G............... Adams
Nemetz .............R.T........ Reichenbach
Foldberg ............R.E............ Sponaugle
Tucker ..............Q.B............. Falcone
Davis  ...............L.H................ Evans
McWilliams ........R.H............... Deuber
Blanchard ...........F.B.............. Martin
           SCORE BY PERIODS
Army  .......................13   7   28   13—61
Penn  ........................ 0   0    0    0— 0
```

Touchdowns—Davis 3, Blanchard 3, Chabot, Grimenstein, Richmond. Points after touchdowns—Walterhouse 7 (placements).

As soon as Miller walked into the hotel lobby where the Army team was staying, he heard, "ATTENTION!"

Coulter turned to salute, but instead a huge grin erupted on his face. He walked over and picked Miller up. "He was a strong boy," Miller recalled. After DeWitt put Miller back on the floor, Miller told the team to "be at ease."

"Once a Sonic, always a Sonic. That's brotherhood under stress, the best of the best," said DeWitt Coulter.

Miller invited DeWitt to a Sonics get-together at his apartment at the Central Y.M.C.A on Arch Street. During the party the conversation, as always, included Home stories. "Whatever Rusty said, we did," said DeWitt. "We never had many players but we believed we could upset any school."

Everyone echoed the excitement they had felt when they ran Rusty's trick plays.

DeWitt leaned in with forearms resting on the table and said, "We will remain close. When you spend as much time together as we did, you're brothers for the rest of your lives."

"We would have tried to go through a brick wall if Russell wanted us to and many times it felt as if we had run through a brick wall," said Miller.

"Russell coached every sport and informed us that we would be running track in the spring," DeWitt leaned back with a slight smile. "I talked Mr. Russell into letting me throw the shot put while everybody else got hot running. I paid Richard Opperman to run after the shot put and return it to me."

"What do you think about all the attention Gordy Brown has been given? I never knew his real name was Hardy," laughed a Sonic.

Jack Bates leaned forward and declared, "I am disappointed and concerned to find incidents and stories that falsify Hardy Brown's character. "We milked cows and played football together," said Jack. "Everyone at the Home thought well of Gordy. Without hesitation, he saved a boy's life during an epileptic seizure on two different occasions while the rest of us stood helplessly by as he prevented a boy from swallowing his tongue. If his personality has changed, it had to have been after I left the Home in 1939. But I doubt it. Gordy is not mean, period."

Everyone agreed.

During the semi-final championship, "We could handle Jumbo Webster and Leete Jackson but that sandstorm was just too much since we were facing it," said Jack. "Miller, you were a 132 pound, sure-blocking, hard tackling, sticky fingered little all-district competitor."

Another Sonic elbowed Miller and laughed, "The other team probably looked at your small size at the start of the game and thought you were one player they did not have to worry about, but at the end of the game, I bet they were extremely worried."

Everyone laughed.

"I remember Lacey Brady and C.D. Reeves blasting the *Reveille* each morning."

They all agreed: the Masonic Home was their spiritual home where their lives were molded by Coach Russell, Mr. Remmert, Mr. Bodiford, Mr. McCaulay, and others.

As the Sonics called it a night, they wished DeWitt good luck on the Army-Navy football game.

The next day after the get-together, Jack Bates wrote DeWitt and asked if he would send two tickets to the upcoming December 1, 1945, Army-Navy football game for Miller and himself. DeWitt responded with two tickets on the 50 yard line on the Army side of the field. The tickets were an extremely generous gift due to ticket scalping. The scalping situation was so bad that both Republican and Democratic senators were appalled that tickets were falling into the hands of scalpers while servicemen were unable to purchase them. The annual contest between the Black Knights of Army and the Midshipmen of the Naval Academy at Annapolis was among the most celebrated rivalries in all of college sports.

§

On December 1, 1945, as Miller and Jack entered the gates of Memorial Stadium in Philadelphia, they had to walk across the field to get to the Army side. The two were in a deep conversation and not paying attention to their surroundings as they stepped onto the event track. Suddenly a motorcycle turned sharply on the track to avoid hitting Miller, and in doing so spun out and ground looped. Miller fell to his knees and looked up: it was Harry Truman. Miller had stepped in front of the lead motorcycle of President Truman's motorcade as it made its way down the track. It caused quite a commotion and Truman had to abruptly stop his horse. In fact it brought the entire motorcade to a complete halt until the officer recovered. Harry Truman and everyone in the presidential convoy laughed about it. Miller didn't think it was very funny at first. After the commotion settled down, Miller and Bates found a little humor in the motorcade wreck, but their excitement was far from over. When they located their seats on the 50 yard line and sat down, they discovered that only eight rows in front of them sat President Harry Truman.

They instantly noticed a lot of pretty girls hanging around their seats. With all the fuss and attention, they had decided their Naval uniforms were the magnet attracting the girls around them. After all, they were the only two in Navy uniforms on the Army side. The two men sat up tall in their seats with smiles a mile wide.

As it turned out, it wasn't their uniforms, and the fleeting hope of admiration soon dissolved when they realized Frank Sinatra was sitting right beside Miller. Miller laughed as he recalled, "We weren't the ones attracting the girls! It was 'old blue eyes.'" Jack Bates leaned over and whispered, "Miller, that woman Mr. Sinatra's with is not his wife."

The 1945 Army-Navy game would be labeled the "game of the century." DeWitt Coulter was honored with All-American on Army's 1945 National Championship team by the national media.

§

Miller's accommodations at the Y.M.C.A. proved to be less than desirable, and when he was given the opportunity to move, he grabbed it. He packed up and moved to 3624 Chestnut Street. He was fortunate. He had never been referred to as Harrison in his entire life until joining the Navy, and Harrison was the name of his new landlord, which made sorting the mail a little tricky.

Now Miller had to catch the trolley from the Naval Research Laboratory in Anacostia to the District of Columbia. It was hard to tell where one boundary ended and the other began, but he knew he reached the border when he was required to change trolleys. The layover between trolleys was two and a half hours. Instead of sitting and waiting, Miller walked 200 yards or so and caught the trolley going east. Each day, as he walked between trolleys, a lone apartment caught his attention. The other apartments were set back from the curb with lush lawns and a sidewalk leading up to door, but this apartment did not have a lawn or sidewalk. It was oddly close to the road. A sign hanging on the door read, "Salesmen and Delivery Personnel,

Please Do Not Leave Deliveries Outside or They will be Stolen. Ring the bell and someone will let you in." He walked past this apartment daily, noting the oddity of its shape and proximity to the road.

§

On February 4, 1946, the public learned that during the development of the atomic bomb a great number of new secret scientific and technical discoveries had been made that would open the world to entirely new industries, and it had been decided to release these secret discoveries to the public.

§

Sometime later, Miller returned to Chapel Hill to take care of some business. It was a beautiful afternoon the day he arrived, so he decided to take a walk to the Arboretum and enjoy his lunch in the shade of the trees. There were several students at the Arboretum that day with the same idea. Amongst the chatter, Miller recognized a familiar and distinctive voice. It was Otha Tiner. Miller walked over, sat down and visited with him for a few minutes. Tiner was with a group of coaches sent to Carolina for a coaching seminar. He mentioned to Miller that he had spent four years living in a dorm at T.C.U. and now lived in the dormitory at the Masonic Home, so when he was asked to participate in the coaching seminar, he was told a dorm room was included in the package. He wanted a break from dormitories and asked if he could rent a house instead. Of course the University was thrilled to have an extra room and one less person to feed.

He invited Miller over that evening, and at the end of the day, Tiner met Miller at Phillips Hall. They walked over to Tiner's car and proceeded down Cameron Avenue and past Fraternity Court. When he turned left onto Pittsboro Street, Miller knew the neighborhood. He turned right on McCauley Street, and within a couple of minutes, they arrived at 404 McCauley Street. When Tiner pulled into the driveway, Miller said, "Good heavens, this is Rosen's house." Miller had visited Rosen and his family on several occasions.

Rosen had moved his family to Philadelphia while they worked on the Manhattan Project and had rented out his house while he was gone. The odd occurrence that the renter was Otha Tiner was unbelievable. And until then, Tiner was unaware he was living in the house of, and paying rent to, "the" Nathan Rosen. Mr. Tiner could now consider himself a business partner of sorts with Rosen. But few could say they were close friends with him. Miller could. After their visit, they pulled out of the driveway, and as they drove away, Miller looked back at Rosen's house and laughed. His life had taken numerous and varied turns, yet each adventure curiously continued to interlace with the others.

§

In April 1946, Dr. Arthur E. Ruark resigned as Head of the Physics Department at the University of North Carolina at Chapel Hill. Rosen immediately contacted Phillip Abelson as he knew, firsthand, what Abelson would bring to the University of North Carolina and suggested he apply for the position. He applied but the politics within the school was a mighty force, and those with the authority of choosing a new Department head probably had someone in mind from within the University because "they informed Abelson another candidate had been chosen based on the lack of time, they felt, Abelson had put forth in his speech for the position," said Miller. He was Dr. Philip Abelson. He could have shown up, stood up and not said a word and enough would have been said for him to get the position.

twenty-seven

Unprotected

"He left me unprotected with Ruark," Miller laughed. Abelson had left for Chicago with regards to a reactor. He was hardly out the door when Ruark declared, "As long as Abelson is away, Miller will work for me."

"Doc did not protect his members while he was away, so underlings such as myself got sidetracked," Miller reflected. "At that time, the War Department had given Ruark a critical task, a task which needed to be exact, a task that would compromise the safety of many, yet the Navy would not disclose pertinent information needed to make exact calculations," Miller remembered. "Ruark would use speculation on 'Operation Crossroads.'"

President Truman had given his approval on January 10, 1946 for the world's first nuclear weapons test. It would take place within the Lagoon of Bikini Atoll and was named "Operation Crossroads" because those involved with the atomic decision-making felt they were at a crossroads.

Raurk was given the task of calculating and evaluating the probable radioactive risks to a large fleet of more than 242 ships consisting of U.S. capital ships, U.S. cruisers, destroyers, submarines, three captured German ships, Japanese ships, 156 airplanes, four television transmitters, 250 cameras, 5,000 pressure gauges, 25,000 radiation recorders, 5,000 rats, 200 pigs, and 204 goats. Many vessels were loaded down with military equipment which included airplanes, Jeeps and tanks and assembled near the islands of the Bikini Atoll. The objective was to study and document the effects of nuclear weapons on ships, equipment and material, and the unavoidable casualties caused by a nuclear explosion. One bomb, Abel, would be dropped from the air and the other, Baker Day, would be detonated from beneath the surface of the water.

The Navy would not disclose the amount of material in the bombs, claiming the amount used was top secret. Ruark was expected to calculate the exact size of the explosions without knowing the size of the bombs. "He had to carry out critical risk calculations to figure the maximum accumulated exposure and contamination in the lagoon water, living aboard support ships and the health risks to those who later boarded the contaminated target ships," recalled Miller "He also had to take into account the many and varied circumstances. For example, some targets had radiation-shielding properties and the amount of personnel activity varied. This costly experiment would be based upon assumed values." Miller laughed. "In other words, a value picked out of the blue."

The test had a tremendous amount of publicity, which included exposing classified, secret weapons to the public which had only been seen by a few men in the inner circles of the Manhattan District, and by those who had assisted in the atomic bomb detonations.

Ruark handed Miller his long list of calculations, asked him to check for any errors and said, "Miller, I hope the Navy can use one of these assumptions."

"Well, I found errors in his calculations," Miller said. "It was an important calculation, and I would say they gave him an impossible problem."

At that point, Ruark handed the ownership of the task to Miller. The calculations weren't easy, and the list was long. But that's precisely why Ruark took the opportunity to grab Miller while Abelson's back was turned, so to speak. He knew Miller was brilliant.

"Raurk gave me the task of refiguring and correcting every calculation in this long list," Miller said. "As I was refiguring the calculations, I just happened to mention, 'That's a volcanic area isn't it?'"

"Yes, and they might start one, too," Ruark replied.

The United States Army Ground Forces, Army Air Forces, Navy, Manhattan Engineering District, civilian scientific institutions, and various branches of the government worked together to bring about the successful outcome of this experiment.

Miller handed the corrected calculations back to Ruark. "Once the calculations were out of our hands, we never knew which calculation was used," Miller said. This was the only task Miller assisted Ruark on, and he never fully knew what role Ruark played on the project.

Thousands of military and scientific personnel worked together at Bikini Atoll. The vessels were strategically placed in a specific array, and the target, the battleship *U.S.S. Nevada*, was placed directly in the center of the fleet of vessels.

500 cameras pointed at the site, from the ground, from ships, from piloted planes, and from drones to capture scientific data and the effects of a nuclear blast on military aircraft and vessels. Seventy-five foot towers were constructed out of thick layers of steel and other materials designed to block radioactive penetration from the remote controlled cameras and specially designed recording devices.

When everything was ready, the President of the United States sent his Evaluation Commission to report findings and status. A large audience consisting of military officers, congressmen, scientists, foreign observers, and journalists had been invited to this secret test and stood as closely as they could be allowed to observe this historical moment. Miller learned the outcome later, but was never told which calculation they used.

Drones were launched and guided from a strategically-placed aircraft carrier. The control of the drones would be taken over by personnel in planes high above the target. Observers waited on ships. The sound of planes overhead was loud and tense. Zero hour rapidly approached. On July 1, 1946, a B-29 nicknamed "Dave's Dream" flew toward the multitude of vessels. Seconds before the explosion, blast gauges had been parachuted into the target area from weather instrument planes.

The bomber was now over the target with one second to go. "Dave's Dream" released Abel. A deafening sound caused the observers to cover their ears and intense, blinding white light erupted from over the target. Onlookers threw their arms over their eyes to protect them. A huge cloud formed above. Film taken from the camera overhead captured a large, several-mile wide, solid cloud. From above, the outer edge of the massive cloud could be seen breaking away and forming an odd ring around the central cloud, similar to the rings around Saturn. From a side angle, a camera on the ground captured the explosion's unbelievable strength as it climbed upward, creating a radioactive mushroom cloud. A camera located on a tower caught its massive strength as it pulled soot from the ships' smoke stacks into the center of the cloud column, which rose to a height of almost eight miles. Military personnel saw the blinding glare fourteen miles away from the target.

After dropping Abel, "Dave's Dream" headed back to base followed by several Air Force photographic planes carrying film that had just recorded one of the most spectacular events in history.

Personnel removed cameras and film from the planes and immediately sent them to photographic centers for processing and distribution. The B-17 drones had been guided straight through the center of the cloud column to collect deadly radioactive dust particles in large filter bags which had been extended from bomb racks for testing.

Mother control planes guided Navy F-6 drones back to Bikini. Once they were close to the ground, the ground officer, who was sitting in a chair at the edge of the flight strip, took over the controls and landed the pilotless aircraft. Crews removing the dangerously radioactive material stood several feet from the contaminated filters, carefully sliding the box with an extended pole to keep a safe distance from the material. The personnel had been drilled regarding the handling of radioactive objects to avoid deadly burns from gamma and beta rays. The pole had extended hooks which were used to open the filter bags from a short distance. Using the long pole they successfully grabbed the door, yanked it off and removed the filters.

Abel had been dropped 2,000 feet west of the bulls eye ship, the *U.S.S. Nevada*, resulting in less than satisfying results. Officers and inspection groups tried to decipher the results of the blast from a safe distance, binoculars in-hand. Smoke bellowed from the aircraft carrier, *U.S.S. Independence*, as torpedo warheads burned. The *Independence* was a skeleton, gutted. There was little damage to the aircraft carrier *U.S.S. Saratoga* except a small fire in the supply stores. Through binoculars, observers viewed the devastation one vessel at a time. The target of the array, the battleship *Nevada*, suffered moderate support structure damage. The aft deck was buckled and the paint on one side had been scorched but not burned.

There wasn't much time to prepare for Baker Day. Between July 1 and July 25, personnel struggled to get everything ready, which included comprehensive inspections, removing all recording data, cleaning the entire fleet, and moving everything back into place.

During this time, Vice Admiral Blandy paid a visit to King Judah, ruler of Bikini, bearing several gifts in appreciation for temporarily deserting their home for the tests.

To prepare for Baker Day, a Naval photographic officer met with numerous photographers and film experts on board the aircraft carrier, *U.S.S. Saidor,* to review instructions before they took off. The sound of control planes roared as they launched from the carrier. Remarkably, everything was ready in time. Engineers from the Manhattan district then boarded the *U.S.S. Cumberland*, the firing ship.

Once inside the master control room on board the *Cumberland*, support personnel locked the door from the outside. There was no way out without outside assistance. Inside, the master switches were thrown. The laboratory was complex, with transmitters and timing recorders working together to record the end result.

From within the closed chamber, a young enlisted Naval aide was heard over the sound system as he counted down the seconds to the blast: 15... 10... 5 ...4 ...3.... 2... 1... fire! The blast was a fantastic wonder. Contaminated seawater sprayed over everything in sight. The same mushroom cloud observed from the airborne bomb rose from underneath the ship. Below the base of the mushroom, water and fog circled the base of the formation and covered the ships. A spectacular water column rose from the ocean into the sky, which caused a ripple effect racing outward from the mushroom until it reached the trees on the island. Radioactive material fell from the great column of lethal water onto the decks of nearby vessels. Immediately following the blast drone boats equipped with special recording instruments were guided through the target area, capturing samples of water and air contaminated with deadly radioactive particles.

Cameras inside the explosion captured a spectacular sight that looked like a cross between the most horrific thunderstorm mixed with huge amounts of contaminated water falling from a massive cloud which dwarfed the ships. Ship hulls a mile away were drenched with foaming water.

Photographic planes returned to their floating bases at sea. Extremely valuable film was removed and sent to the Naval Photographic Center in Washington D.C. for processing.

This historic Operations Crossroads was "the most observed, most photographed, most talked-of-scientific test ever conducted. Paradoxically, it may also be said that it was the most publicly advertised secret test ever conducted."

Baker

Eventually eight ships and two submarines were towed back to the United States and Hawaii for radiological inspection. The others were sunk off Bikini Atoll, Kwajalein Atoll, or near the Hawaiian Islands. The following year, the Navy returned to Bikini Atoll to record and study the long-term effects of radiation.

Shortly after one of the tests, the Evaluation Board of the Joint Chiefs of Staff stated, "To a degree which the Board finds remarkable, the visible phenomena of explosion followed the predictions made by civilian and service phenomenologist's attached to Joint Task Force One."

On September 10, 1946, Harrison Miller Moseley's contributions were once again utilized in a significant report on Liquid Thermal Diffusion, edited by Philip Abelson, Nathan Rosen and John I. Hoover for the Naval Research Laboratory, Physics Special Research Division, Washington D.C.

§

Admiral Hyman G. Rickover was sent to Oak Ridge as the deputy manager of the entire project, granting him access to all facilities, projects and reports.

Even though the admiral knew nothing whatsoever in regards to the details of the scientific research, he had been put in charge of all research, therefore everything would need his approval. Ross Gunn worked for Rickover and advised the admiral in all aspects of research, including what to approve or disapprove; in a nutshell, Gunn called the shots. However, Miller said, "the numerous trips Gunn would be required to make to obtain Rickover's signature would be time consuming and burdensome." Miller worked close enough to Gunn to witness the burdens Rickover imposed on Gunn and the Navy. Congress loved Rickover, but the Navy did not.

§

Years later, after the nuclear bomb attacks on Hiroshima and Nagasaki, Miller attended a meeting in which the main speaker was Harold Urey. Miller could not remember the designated topic that day, but according to Miller, the theme should have been titled, "My Advising the President of the United States."

During the meeting, Miller sat directly in front of Dr. Julius Robert Oppenheimer, technical director of the atomic bomb. Apparently Urey's presentation did not sit well with Oppenheimer. Maybe it was Urey's lack of piety, or perhaps his over-glorified rendition of his actual accomplishments on the project, Miller could only guess. But one thing Miller did know was, "Every time Urey declared, 'I told the president this' or 'I told the president that,' Oppenheimer could be heard laughing behind him, and it was apparent he was unhappy with Urey's presentation."

§

As the aircraft landed, four men stood waiting for a man named William Pollard to step off the plane. Nathan Rosen, Miller and two other graduate students found themselves waiting at the airport to pick up Pollard and escort him to a meeting where he would be the guest speaker.

Pollard had flown to North Carolina in an effort to recruit members to join the Oak Ridge Institute of Nuclear Studies (ORINS). With additional support, he hoped University researchers in the region would be given access to the elaborate facilities and equipment at the Oak Ridge Laboratory.

As Pollard exited the plane, he stopped near the steps, set his small bag on the ground and lit his signature pipe. He was of average size wearing a dress suit and hat. He had been a research scientist on the Manhattan Project and knew little about the purpose of his work until the atomic bombs were dropped. After Rosen introduced Pollard to Miller and the other two graduate students, they returned to the car and were on their way. Rosen and Pollard sat in the front seat and discussed the possibility of gaining access to the elaborate facilities.

§

Miller set up travel accommodations back to D.C. for discharge from the Navy. The trip was not going to be easy. Due to the train schedule, there would be numerous stops and layovers, including a two hour wait in Washington.

A few days prior to leaving, Miller had received the card from a Masonic Home Alumnus stating that Norman Cardwell, or "Ollie" to the Sonics, was aboard the *Abner Reid* when it was hit by another ship. He was now missing in action. Because of his skill and interest in radios, Mr. Remmert had advised Ollie to join the Navy where he would have the opportunity to receive training in the field of radio technology. The card said his sister, Peggy Cardwell, was distraught over the disappearance of her brother, and if a Sonic was in the neighborhood, she extended an open invitation to stop by Peggy's apartment and offer encouragement.

So during his layover in Washington, he decided to visit Ollie's sister. With the card in his pocket, he walked down Constitution Avenue toward the address listed on the card. As he approached her apartment, he thought, "Good heavens, the numerous times I had walked past her home transferring between trolleys." It was the odd apartment close to the curb with the sign on the door which read, "Salesmen and Delivery Personnel, Please Do Not Leave Deliveries Outside or They will be Stolen. Ring the bell and someone will let you in."

Miller rang the doorbell and a rather gruff woman opened the door. Miller asked if he could step inside and visit with Peggy Cardwell. The woman said, "No. No men allowed. This apartment is strictly for women. I'll call Peggy and see if she wants to see you." Peggy soon stepped outside and Miller handed her the card he had received. He asked if there was a place close by where they could talk. She found a seat on a bench under the Washington Memorial. They had just sat down when a gentleman started singing the Army Air Corps Theme Song. When he finished, he introduced himself as Robert Crawford, the composer. When he left, Miller and Peggy began to discuss Norman, but before they could finish a sentence, a second fellow introduced himself as the child of a movie star and proceeded to sing. Peggy managed to tell Miller that Norman had not yet been located. Miller tried his best to console her, but it was hard to talk with all the commotion that day.

When Miller arrived at headquarters, the man in charge immediately said, "You're an hour and a half late." Miller explained the train schedule and the officer understood. He handed Miller his official discharge papers. As Miller walked toward the station with time to kill, he realized there was one place he had failed to visit. He walked up to the guard and asked if he could attend a Congressional session.

"Not right now," the fellow said.

Miller explained it might be his last opportunity.

The guard said, "It should not be much longer. Harry Truman gave a joint address to Congress. Once he exits and the group of spectators are given or denied a photograph with the President, they will leave. At that time, any visitors will be allowed inside."

"It was just as he said," Miller recalled. "Truman came out and everyone followed him down the street." An usher led Miller to a seat he thought had the best view. As Miller sat down, he looked up and it was none other than Vannevar Bush, the man who tried to exclude the Navy from atomic research, on the floor introducing a bill that would offer scholarships to deserving students toward science. When his speech ended, Miller rushed to catch the train home.

§

The fact that the atomic bomb was built in time to end World War II is unbelievable. The scientists worked with brand new theoretical breakthroughs, and before they could grasp or test these new findings, additional breakthroughs were thrown at them. Engineers struggled to put this theoretical work into a machine capable of releasing enormous energy in a short amount of time.

Miller's brilliant mind was used by the top players on the Manhattan Project, a project of immense legacy. His achievements helped usher in the atomic age, where nuclear physics was taken from the laboratory and put into battle resulting in bringing to a close a war of horrific proportions.

§

On July 28, 1948, Miller returned to the University of North Carolina and completed his graduate studies and could translate both German and French.

§

The following articles were published by Miller Moseley, Nathan Rosen and Albert Einstein with the aim of proving Miller's great mind and the caliber and rank of those who depended on him.

Harrison Miller Moseley collaborated and published several articles with Nathan Rosen.

— Are Mesons Elementary Particles.
—The Meson as a Composite Particle.
—Approach to Equilibrium by a Thermal Diffusion Column, [Part] I, Column Closed at Both Ends.
—Neutron-Proton Interaction.
—Liquid Thermal Diffusion.

Nathan Rosen collaborated and published several articles with Albert Einstein.

—Can quantum mechanical description of physical reality be considered complete?
—The Particle Problem in the General Theory of Relativity.
—On Gravitational Waves.

As Miller completed the *Approach to Equilibrium by a Thermal Diffusion Column, [Part] I, Column closed at both ends.* Rosen said, "Miller, add my name to the publication." The actual citation reads, "Main Author: H.M. Moseley. Other Authors: Nathan Rosen."

Shortly after receiving his Ph.D., Miller was expected back in Fort Worth for a visit, but when the time arrived, he never showed up. Mrs. Moseley paced back and forth with worry in her Fort Worth home. She had called his apartment numerous times and had received no answer. She was afraid to leave the house for fear of missing an important phone call. Back in North Carolina, Miller lay on a cot in the emergency room in grave pain, unable to move and unaware of any concern back in Fort Worth.

Hours earlier, Miller had doubled over in pain but was able to make it to the infirmary. The doctor informed Miller he needed to call someone to take him to the emergency room in Durham. Miller called Rosen, who quickly transported Miller to the hospital where he was rushed into surgery for appendicitis. There had been no time to call home, so he had given his mother's number to the hospital staff, who had promised to contact her. They never called. After his surgery, Miller immediately called his mother and explained he was recovering well.

twenty-eight

Home

After receiving his Ph.D. in Physics from the University of North Carolina, Dr. Harrison Miller Moseley was eager to return home to Fort Worth. Before leaving North Carolina, a colleague and good friend expressed concern regarding Miller's decision to leave before having a job lined up ahead of time. But Miller's mind was made up; he had received his Doctorate and was looking forward to returning home. During his drive back to Fort Worth, he remembered leaving Texas for the first time and never had he anticipated it would lead to the most magnificent journey imaginable. He was leaving an extraordinary world behind, Oak Ridge, a city created entirely because of the war.

When he arrived in Fort Worth his first stop was T.C.U. He pulled into the parking lot, parked his car, smashed his cigarette with the toe of his shoe, and began walking across the campus while lighting another. It felt good to be home. He walked into the Physics Department and down the hall towards Dr. Gaines office. Before stepping into Dr. Gaines' office, Miller put his cigarette out in the ashtray attached to the wall. Miller barely had time to say "hello," when Dr. Gaines asked if he would be interested in teaching. The one class Miller was reluctant to take as a student at T.C.U., the Teaching of Physics, would end up being the class that carried him through the next 40 years of his life.

In the meantime a worried colleague in North Carolina had contacted a friend in the Physics Department at Baylor University in Waco, Texas, who was very eager to meet Miller. It took his friend a few days before he was able to reach Miller, but once he did, he insisted that Miller needed to speak to the Dean of the Physics Department at Baylor before he committed to T.C.U. Miller drove two hours to Waco, located the Physics building, walked inside and up the stairs to the second floor, and began searching for the Dean's office. Once there, he walked into the office and was informed the Dean was running behind schedule.

Miller took the opportunity to step back outside and smoke a cigarette. As he stood in the sun, holding the pack of cigarettes in his right hand and tapping the pack into his left palm, he noticed a couple of students glaring at him. Miller thought their behavior was a little odd and continued to remove a cigarette from the package. He looked up, and yet another student walked past with a look of disgust. He lit his cigarette, and as he exhaled, he glanced up just in time to receive more rude glares. It was if the students were deliberately going out of their way to make sure Miller could clearly see their disgust. He decided it was time to return to the Dean's office, so he stepped on the cigarette and threw it in the trashcan. It wasn't until later that Miller learned smoking on the Baylor Campus was forbidden, which was unusual during that era.

In 1950, at the age of 29, Miller decided to stick with the teaching position offered by Dr. Gaines at T.C.U. The news hit Baylor hard and they were extremely upset with his decision. In fact, Baylor and the University of Texas continued efforts to recruit Miller for many years after Miller accepted the job at T.C.U. Shortly thereafter, Miller settled into a garage apartment at 3801 Bellaire Drive in Fort Worth, within walking distance of the campus.

In August 1950, students stood in T.C.U.'s Amon G. Carter stadium behind a long line of other students enrolling for classes, and as they reached the front of the line, the professor sitting at a table was Harrison Miller Moseley.

§

As a 2nd Lieutenant, Miller was required to participate in weekly, mandatory, officer's meetings held in downtown Fort Worth. He never saw any value; the meetings consisted of a speech followed by either an old football game, such as one in which the U.S. Naval Academy beat West Point, or an old World War II film. Miller felt he received one perk when he was put on inactive duty: he no longer was required to attend the meetings.

§

A short time later, Miller returned to Oak Ridge, Tennessee. Together with Nathan Rosen, they were given the responsibility of destroying every bit of paper linked to the project.

Around the same time, Einstein and Rosen made yet another discovery: the mathematical solution for a type of wormhole connecting distant areas in space. They called it the Einstein-Rosen or Schwarzschild Wormhole.

Effective January 1, 1953, Miller was transferred from the Inactive-Status list (USNR-S2) to the Standby Reserve in an active status (USNR-S1).

§

Miller's brother, Cecil, decided to pursue his dream of becoming an Army Air Corps pilot and tour Europe. After Cecil completed the required battery of questions, Miller asked his brother how he thought he did.

"I had to answer what seemed to be trick questions," Cecil said. "For example, they asked, 'Would you fight an alligator?' I thought they were trying to find out whether or not I had courage, so I replied, 'Show me the color of your alligator.' I guess that was the wrong answer. They said I was too dangerous to be allowed in an airplane."

The question may have been related to a new amphibious landing craft referred to as an "alligator," or a "gator," used as carriers for ships to float cargo to shore.

As a result of failing the Army Air Corps aptitude test, he enlisted as a paratrooper in the United States Army on April 3, 1950, and upon doing so he immediately forfeited his 50% disability from the Marines. He dreamed of touring Europe, but, sadly, the Korean War broke out and he never got the opportunity. On February 15, 1951, he was shot in the back and added to the Korean casualty list. On Wednesday night, August 15, 1951, 1,400 Army veterans, including 102 from Texas, reached San Francisco. Army Sergeant Cecil Ray Moseley, from Dundee in Archer County, was among the 91 rotation troops wounded. Eleven were enlisted reserve. But instead of rewarding Cecil the initial 50% disability given for previous injuries sustained, the Army awarded him only 10%. Cecil received the Purple Heart, Distinguished Unit Emblem and Korean Service Medal with one Silver Service Star, United Nations Service Medal, Combat Infantry Badge, Parachute Badge and Expert Badge with Carbine Bar.

§

About this time, Miller moved from the apartment on Bellaire Drive to Rodgers Road in Fort Worth, where he rented a small place significantly closer to the Physics building.

§

In 1954, Ross Gunn wrote Admiral H. G Bowen a letter strongly suggesting Groves and Oppenheimer had ignored the Navy's work in order to promote their own programs. He also stated, "Roosevelt had no business appointing an independent political group to be responsible for atomic energy when there was already an established Navy team and program designed not only to produce a bomb, but who were dedicated to its long range utilization as a military tool and implement of public welfare."

According to Abelson, "Gunn felt the rug had been pulled out from under him, as he was the one who had initiated the first research into atomic energy, only to have control placed in the hands of the S-1 Committee, with the limelight being given to the Army." Gunn's overall opinion was summed up in the statement, "I think we had the hose turned on us!"

§

During the summers of 1955 and 1956, Miller crisscrossed between Fort Worth and Oak Ridge to work on the preliminary stages of a new high speed accelerator for atomic research. When he returned to Fort Worth everyone in the building was well aware of his arrival because he whistled so loudly the doors shook. No student had a problem locating him. Upon hearing Miller's all-too-familiar tune, a student jumped up and ran out of the classroom to meet Miller in the hall. Miller was a little surprised to see the student running towards him, but more surprised when he heard the student's request. He asked if Miller would be willing to serve as the Master of Ceremonies for Ranch Week. Ranch Week was a big event at T.C.U., and the Fort Worth Chamber of Commerce was an enthusiastic participant.

Miller not only accepted the request to serve as the Master of Ceremonies, he took his new position very seriously. He immediately began growing a beard. He failed to mention the growth to one particular person: his mother. That week, Mildred walked into the office and the secretary informed her that Miller had just stepped outside. She was a little surprised Mildred had not run into Miller on her way in. Miller spotted his mother as she walked across the parking lot. He ran across the lawn and stuck his face in her car window. Her scream could be heard blocks away. He stood up to let those who were walking by with concerned looks know that everything was fine. Miller laughed and was able to convince Mrs. Moseley that the bearded man was indeed her son. The faculty bulletin read: "Dr. Moseley has the finest crop of whiskers for 'ranch week' on campus. Judge Roy Bean, who will look a bit like Harrison Moseley, holds court Friday morning, 8-12."

Early Friday morning, Judge Roy Bean, a.k.a. Miller, set up a "shocking" machine he found in the Physics department for those sentenced to the electric chair. A few turns of the handle would deliver a slight shock.

At the conclusion of a mock trial, a student was found guilty and sentenced to the electric chair. Miller attached the machine to the boy's finger and turned the handle. The boy just laughed, seemingly unaffected by the shock. Miller, puzzled over the boy's reaction, decided to try the machine out for himself. He attached the electrode to his own finger and turned the handle several times and almost knocked himself out. He discovered the boy's hands were so thick with calluses that the electric current could not pass through his skin.

The activities for the week had just begun. Jail activities, the appointment of Sheriff, the faculty softball game, a wiener roast, a bon fire, and the carnival all took place that day. Horace Craig posted the following warning in the *SKIFF*, T.C.U's student newspaper.

> *All you low-life sidewinders that ain't wearin' proper duds this Mornin' had better gittum on or ride clear of Sheriff Gilbert Downey and his 20 man posse.*
>
> *The law says ya gotta wear Texas-type togs today, this bein Ranch Week.*
>
> *Sheriff Downey swears all lawbreakers will be jailed.*
>
> *Ride Clear of Downey,*
>
> *That is unless you're a law-abiding hombre, Ranch Week*
>
> *Sheriff Gilbert Downey would just as soon jail a law-breaker as stroke his Handsome beard.*
>
> *And he has a 20-man posse to help him with the big'uns.*
>
> *It's Ranch Week time again.*
>
> *Time to remind you to wear western duds-unless*
>
> *You care to spend a day with Downey.*

The festivities continued through Saturday, with plenty of activities for everyone. Students attempted the sack race, greased pig chasing, pie eating, balloon blowing, tobacco spitting, three-leg race racing, cigarette rolling, sack racing, cigar smoking, egg throwing, Judge Roy Bean's Court, and bar-b-que. Everyone left around 1:30 to make it to the Lone Star Arena for the 2:00 rodeo.

The fun came to an end that evening at Pioneer Palace. WBAP-TV's

Top Western Band played, and coveted awards were bestowed for Ranch Queen and Foreman and the best-dressed Cowgirl and Cowboy. And the most anticipated and enjoyed spectacle was the judging of longest beard. As the bearded Horned Frogs walked across the dance floor, laughter filled the palace. Only students could enter the elite contest, so Miller's beard took back stage and succumbed to bushier competition.

§

In 1957, T.C.U. President Sadler granted Miller a year's leave of absence to help design a new high speed accelerator for atomic research in Oak Ridge, Tennessee. Dr. Sadler stated that "Dr. Moseley's selection for the atomic project was quite an honor." Those who had worked with Miller on the Manhattan Project never forgot his brilliance and they continued to request his assistance.

§

Around June 1957, Miller began his leave of absence from T.C.U to work on the accelerator. "The long range plan for the United States was to build a proton accelerator," Miller recalled. "I designed the double-focusing magnet for the electron model/proton accelerator." Once the magnet was constructed, it was added to the electron model built specifically to carry out a series of tests. Miller felt his work was a waste of time because "the Senator of Illinois wanted the big machine built in his state."

New York Times May 28, 1958, "The position of the Atomic Energy Commission had been that if the high-speed accelerator was built it should be constructed at the Argonne National Laboratory near Chicago." Title of article "Atom Smasher Backed." On June 19, 1958 The New York Times read "Fund Cuts Limit Atomic Research."

§

On April 21, 1959, LTJG Harrison Miller Moseley, USNR was honorably discharged from the Eighth Naval District of the United States Navy.

Days later, as Miller followed Dr. Morgan down the hall, the professor had no need to turn around to see who was walking behind him; he simply raised his head, said "Miller," then turned around. Miller stopped whistling and listened to what the professor had to say. "I walked a visitor into the Physics building the other day and as we walked past your office, he glanced at your nameplate on the door and said, 'Oh, I know Miller Moseley, he's from North Carolina.'" The gentleman was William Pollard. Pollard had visited T.C.U. to pitch the Oak Ridge Institute of Nuclear Studies.

Sometime later, in 1962, Pollard requested Miller's assistance back at Oak Ridge. As a consequence, Miller was granted a sabbatical leave of absence. But first he had to update his security clearance. To Miller's surprise, the F.B.I. questioned his clearance and instructed him to reserve a room at a convenient hotel in downtown Fort Worth to discuss his clearance application.

Miller reserved a room at the Blackstone, but had no idea what the fuss was all about. A few days later, F.B.I. agents began quizzing him regarding his association with Nathan Rosen. Miller had given Rosen as a reference on his clearance, and apparently, while in Israel, Rosen had developed a friendship with a Russian spy who claimed he had fled the Soviet Union because of persecution of Jews. The F.B.I. had been watching both Rosen and the Russian.

According to the F.B.I., Rosen had traveled to Russia and, while there, fell for the dictatorship of the proletarian of the free. Miller informed the F.B.I. that Rosen never seemed interested in Russia's politics nor did he ever observe any political connections. The only remark he'd ever made to Miller was, "It was just another dictatorship."

The F.B.I.'s only interest pertained to his involvement with Rosen. They advised Miller to resubmit additional names of contacts and acquaintances. "My friends must have told them that I was okay and did not have anything to do with Russian spies or anything like that because I was cleared," Miller said, laughing.

He returned to Oak Ridge. The facility itself had changed little. The biggest shock for Miller was when he walked into Mr. Pollard's office. Behind the desk sat a man who had participated in the successful development of controversial radioactive materials and had spearheaded the Oak Ridge Institute of Nuclear Studies for nuclear research—and he was wearing a clerical robe and collar.

Pollard had not only become an ordained priest, but the Director of the Episcopal Church. His two aspirations seemed to Miller to be extreme polar opposites.

"He married a strong Christian woman whose influence must have made a big impact," Miller reflected. After the bomb drop on Hiroshima, Pollard lived with a feeling "close to terror." Pollard remembered the day— it was a Thursday—as he thumbed through the paper to the religious section, and noticed he had just enough time to make the next service. He walked out of the house alone and took a trolley to Trinity Episcopal Church. As the service progressed, he became conscious of a feeling that it wasn't just an empty rigmarole, and when he returned home, he was no longer disturbed and was able to sleep calmly that night. Later he became an ordained Episcopal priest.

After the initial shock wore off, the Atomic Deacon presented Miller with an unusual request. He asked Miller to refer to him only as "Mister." He never wanted anyone to call him Doctor or Reverend, just Mister. The Pollard Technology Center would later be named in his honor.

§

"Dr. Moseley, you have a knack for asking questions on your exams that I hadn't thought important to study," complained one student after finishing a test. "I'm a better student than what the grade indicates. You ask questions about things I did not think were important."

A couple of weeks later, Miller gave the class a quiz. Two students finished the test, stood, turned in their tests and started out the door. One of them turned around and went back inside. About that time, Miller stepped outside and lit a cigarette. The upset student leaned towards Miller and said, "The son of a bitch did it again." At that time his buddy stepped out.

"I had a good laugh at that," Miller said.

§

Apparently, the desire to explore and challenge the unthinkable to the great extent Einstein, Abelson, Rosen, Gunn, and Miller enjoyed was an extremely uncommon occurrence among most college students. While teaching at T.C.U., Miller's energy kicked in. He spent many hours developing a promising scientific experiment to study the absorption of the sun's rays into the atmosphere. Eager to get started, he wasted little time making the preparations. To help complete the experiment, he needed several assistants to man telescopes from sun-up till sun-down to accurately time the process. The results would be published in the *Scientific Journal*, which would be extremely beneficial to a student's career.

Dr. Harrison Miller Moseley received an unexpected jolt: the students preferred to spend the minimum required time in the laboratory, and decided they did not have enough time to contribute to his experiment.

At this time, Philip Abelson had been asked to speak at a T.C.U. faculty luncheon. As Miller introduced Abelson to the faculty he said, "It was the only project in which I could take the entire laboratory apart with a 3/8 inch wrench." After shaking Abelson's hand, Miller took his seat. Abelson walked over to the podium, looked up and said, "Miller was the best plumber I had."

After his speech, Abelson had just a few minutes before he had to rush to the airport. As they walked across the campus, Miller began discussing his excitement over his experiment. He had planned to ask Abelson for his assistance; he knew the experiment was worthy and Abelson would probably be happy to assist. But because of Abelson's rushed schedule, Miller's intent and Abelson's perception resulted in a miscommunication. Abelson asked, "What are you trying to measure?"

Miller laughed and said, "That is something else again." At this point Miller had planned to explain his frustration with his lack of help. However, Abelson took over the conversation at this point, partly due to his need to hurry to airport and partly due to misunderstanding Miller's response.

Abelson thought Miller wanted to keep the experiment secret until it was complete, and said "Okay, okay," and rushed off to the airport. Miller never found the opportunity to explain his intentions, and his experiment never took place. The students missed the opportunity to work alongside a man accustomed to achieving the unthinkable.

§

To say the Manhattan Project was the best-kept secret of the war is putting it mildly. Years after the end of the war, a reporter asked Philip Abelson if he had ever mentioned his work on the Manhattan Project to Neva, his wife, or Ellen, his daughter. "Oh, no, no, no, no," he responded. Abelson, who had received numerous awards in addition to having a mineral, abelsonite, named after him for his contribution to organic geochemistry, never discussed the Manhattan Project at home.

The Manhattan Project was the best-kept secret of the war.

twenty-nine

Unexpected Change

Jesse Spears, a former student and friend of Miller's, had a peculiar favorite pastime: fixing Miller up with the ladies. It became almost comical. Miller would show up for dinner and there sat a different girl. He was eager to find the perfect match for Miller.

"Who is she?" Miller asked one evening.

"It's dinner," replied Jesse.

"Who else will be sitting there when I walk in?"

"My sister-in-law."

Jesse had a sister-in-law, Dene, a native of Derby, England and he was pushing hard to get these two together. He tried numerous times, but Miller wasn't in any hurry. He had never found any interest in the girls Jesse had introduced to him in the past.

Dene had arrived in America on the *Queen Mary* as a war bride.

She found herself in an unexpected situation as a single mother of three teenagers. She married W. A. Bussey and had four daughters, Denise, Cheryl, Karen, and a fourth daughter, a twin who died at three months of age with a heart defect. Sometime later, as the Bussey family vacationed in Mexico, her husband was creating a commotion in the swimming pool. He had a reputation as a jokester, but Dene jumped in anyhow, knowing it was probably one of his charades, and pulled him to the shallow end of the pool. But this time was different, it was no charade. He began projectile vomiting and his chest turned purple. She frantically called for help, but by the time the so-called Mexican ambulance finally arrived, it consisted of a sad truck with a canvas back flap. She watched in horror as her husband slid back and forth on the stretcher as he was transported to the hospital. When they finally reached the emergency room, the medical staff knocked Dene out completely so that she was unable to speak. It was a nightmare. She was unable to reach family and, most importantly, she could not comfort her children. W. A. Bussey died in Mexico at the age of 43 from a massive coronary. The Mexican funeral home was a nightmare as well. Dene said, "If you are going to die, don't die in Mexico."

One afternoon, she and her good friend, Amanda Kubes, spent the afternoon shopping on Main Street in downtown Fort Worth. As they left each store, they found the clerks incredibly inviting. Each replied, "Ya'll come back and see us, honey." In no time, they made another trip downtown. But this time was special. They embraced the invitations and returned for a visit dressed in their Sunday best with gloves and hats. They quickly learned the invitation was strictly a business formality and they laughed for hours.

Miller hemmed and hawed and took his time before accepting the dinner invitation. He had never found interest in any of the girls Jesse had introduced him to in the past, and he certainly did not want to insult a relative. But Jesse was relentless. He described her as a beautiful redhead from Derby, England, a widow with three teenage daughters.

Finally, they met.

"Dene was beautiful and real good company," Miller said.

Jesse's matchmaking days were over. Dene was different and had grabbed Miller's attention. The incurable bachelor was off the market.

The relationship got off to a slow start. "I made a few mistakes during our courtship," Miller recalled. "We met for lunch at a popular restaurant on the North Side where I proceeded to smoke all her cigarettes." From that day forward, he made sure he had plenty of cigarettes.

A few days later, Miller had the entire night planned; dinner at a nice restaurant followed by an evening at the Fort Worth Stock Show and Rodeo. His cousin, Bud, planned to ride in the show that night.

As Miller pulled in front of Dene's home in Haltom City, Texas, her daughters watched from the window as Miller made his way to the front door. They could not believe their mother would go out with anyone who was not their father. A little bit later, as Dene and Miller walked out to the car, Cheryl and Karen remained glued to the window. They began to giggle as Miller and their mother drove off in his 1953 Ford which looked like something out of the "Nutty Professor" due to some sort of chemical damage.

Underneath their giggling, it was painful to watch their mother go on a date with any man other than their father. Cheryl and Karen were in middle school and their older sister, Denise, was in high school. They wanted their mother to be happy, and they liked Miller just fine, but no one could take the place of their father.

As Miller and Dene drove away, the plans quickly changed. "Instead of the Stock show and Rodeo, Dene had a particular restaurant on 7th Street in Fort Worth that she had wanted to try, followed by a movie about some cat," Miller remembered, smiling.

After the movie, Dene pointed to a place and asked, "Do you want to stop here?"

"I did not realize at the time that if an Englishman asks, 'Do you want to do something,' what he or she means is, 'I want to do something,'" Miller said laughing.

During the courtship, both adults had an easier time than the three girls did. They felt abandoned by their father. And now their mother had accepted Miller's hand in marriage. Dene worked for days anticipating and sewing her wedding dress as well as the girls' dresses and hair bows.

Dene and Miller got married in 1967 in St. Andrew's Episcopal Church in Fort Worth.

Miller moved from his quiet, small apartment around the corner from T.C.U. to a nice, large brick home with a large yard to care for, a dog, a cat, and four women, three of whom were teenagers.

The girls struggled through the first year. They weren't comfortable with the changes, and they intentionally made life as rocky as they felt necessary. They wanted their old life back. They had nothing against Miller, it was just different.

It seemed the harder the girls tried to make life miserable for their mother and Miller, the kinder he became.

"He never tried to take our father's place, never bossy or demanding," said Karen. "Whatever he was feeling, he kept to himself. He had the patience of Job."

Little did the girls realize, Miller understood all too well what they were going through. He relived the same pain each time a new child had entered the Home.

He understood.

After a bumpy first year, Karen received a little black terrier named Little Bit. The terrier was a little confused and thought she was a large Doberman hired as Karen's bodyguard.

Every morning, Miller slowly shuffled down the hall in his long, white terrycloth robe, to start a fresh pot of coffee. His slow motions matched his quiet demeanor.

If Karen's bedroom door wasn't completely shut, Little Bit would fly off her bed, run into the hallway and bark like a Doberman. As Miller strolled by, the dog would nip at his heels.

From her bed, Karen would yell for Little Bit to stop.

Through all the commotion, Miller continued down the hall in his nonchalant manner as the dog clenched its teeth onto the bottom of his robe and held on tight. As Miller dragged Little Bit down the hallway and into the kitchen, she heard Miller mutter a faint, "Confound it!" The tiny dog would eventually let go and strut back to Karen's side.

After Miller plugged in the coffee pot and shuffled back down the hallway, Little Bit would dart out again like a moray eel and the flurry would start all over again. Miller calmly continued with Little Bit fiercely holding on.

Throughout it all, Miller never uttered a negative word about the miniature Doberman to anyone. And he never cursed.

As a nursing student at T.C.U, Cheryl struggled in Chemistry, and at one point she felt absolutely lost. Miller tutored her for many hours. "He never lost his temper nor made me feel dumb. He would simply scratch his head and continue until I understood the material," said Cheryl.

Miller provided each girl the opportunity to attend T.C.U. cost-free. Cheryl appreciated the blessings she received because of Miller. She now has a nice career and an awesome husband whom she met as a student at T.C.U.

"Miller brought stability to our lives as the death of my dad left us all in limbo," said Karen, "and what I appreciate about him most is how kind and loving he has always been to my mother. I love both of them very much and I am thankful that they found each other. Miller came into all this with a positive attitude and a mild manner."

"He never forgot the doctrine taught at the Home: to look after orphans and widows," said Dene.

"The girls all married foreigners," Miller said. "Denise Burgess married an Englishman, Cheryl Costells married a Cuban and Karen Messik an Oklahoman."

At a reunion in 1970 in Austin, Texas, with Mr. Rusty Russell in attendance, the boys pulled their chairs out at the same time, said their prayer in unison and began trading food. Mr. Russell leaned back in his chair with pride, for each and every one of his boys had become men of honor.

§

"Whenever we adopted a new textbook, Miller worked through every problem in the book," said Dr. C.A. Quarles, Emeritus Professor of Physics at Texas Christian University. "He was meticulous about organizing all his labs, his lecture notes, his books—everything. As his student, I was always impressed by Miller's well-organized and detailed lectures. He began his lectures in the upper left-hand corner of the blackboard and finished his derivation at the lower right-hand corner of the blackboard in precisely 50 minutes. He always consistently distinguished in his careful pronunciation of the lower and upper case omega so the students could better follow his lecture."

Coca-Cola was a major donor and filled the campus machines. Loyal Dr Pepper drinkers were forced to go off campus. As a symbol of loyalty and commitment, Dr Pepper fans within the Physics Department began to stack their empty soda cans in SWR 324. In the spring of 1989, to celebrate Neil Koone's and Chris Hardage's BS degrees and Miller's retirement, they tore down that wall. "Miller participated in knocking down a huge, wall-to-ceiling pyramid of Dr Pepper cans," said Dr. Quarles.

After 40 years at Texas Christian University, Miller retired in the spring of 1991. Dr. Lysiak, the Department Chair, hosted a reception at the Green Oaks Inn in Fort Worth.

This quiet professor, writing on the chalkboard, standing in front of a room full of students, was an A-list player working with the most-read-about men in history on the most important mission in the world.

The success of the Home, however, at the end of the 40 year span must be determined by the success of those who have been reared in it and have been furnished with its advantages and institution. Our experience leads us to conclude that the Home has satisfactorily met this test. Thos. Fletcher, Superintendent.

§

A telegram sent December 18, 1938 from Mr. J.T. Miller read in part:

If you boys will play the game of life as you have played football this last season you will accomplish great things and will be recognized in the world as great men the same as you have been recognized as great football players.

§

Bill Walraven returned to the Masonic Home in 1985 and wrote:

"A visit to the Masonic Home left me wishing I had not returned for what I found was the little boys building had been torn down and a clump of trees were growing wild in the location and at the other end of campus where the beautiful high school building stood is a beautiful chapel in its place. The old gravel pit where many a sling shot game was played was gone with the expansion of neighborhoods. And the wonderful creek at Cobb Park, which had an awesome, big, bluff with springs seeping out of its clay layers that once offered the boys a cool drink after running and playing in the hot sun, sadly I would never dare take a drink of water now. Beside the roads, people had dumped trash and the noise from the freeway could be heard in the distance.

And where are the horned toads? Those gentle little critters we would play with and later let go? "The next time a red ant bed crops up in my yard, maybe I should welcome the little fellers. I might give a horned toad a home."

§

The boys are still there, just close your eyes and you can see them.

§

"See you in the next life." —The Sonics.

Historical Documentation

Section of S-50 Liquid Thermal Diffusion Plant at Clinton. (Reprinted from Richard G. Hewlett and Oscar E. Anderson, Jr., The New World, 1939-1946, Volume I of A History of the United States Atomic Energy Commission *(University Park: Pennsylvania State University Press, 1962).*

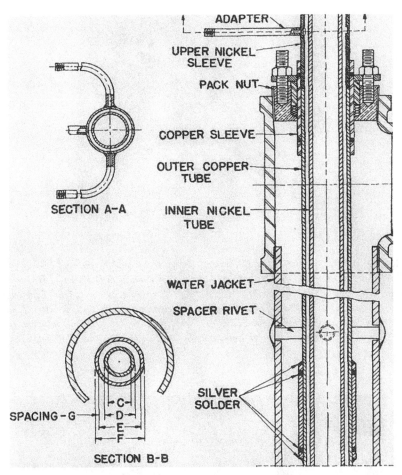

The Liquid Thermal Diffusion column. *(Liquid Thermal Diffusion by H.M. Moseley, J.B. Bidwell, W.N. Blatt, G.Y.Brokaw, M. Drott, F.J. Gradishar, P.N. Kokulis, R.E. Ruskin, J.H. Tayman, W.E. Whybrew, Edited by Philip. H. Abelson, Department of Terrestrial Magnetism, Carnegie Institution of Washington, Nathan Rosen Department of Physics University of North Carolina, John I. Hoover Nucleonics Division, Naval Research Laboratory, Washington, D.C. 10, September 1946 Naval Research Laboratory Special Research Division Washington D.C.)*

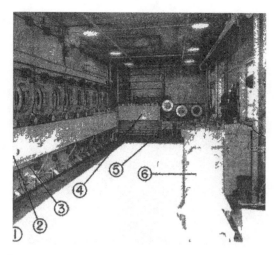

View of transfer room. *(Liquid Thermal Diffusion by H.M. Moseley, J.B. Bidwell, W.N. Blatt, G.Y.Brokaw, M. Drott, F.J. Gradishar, P.N. Kokulis, R.E. Ruskin, J.H. Tayman, W.E. Whybrew, Edited by Philip. H. Abelson, Department of Terrestrial Magnetism, Carnegie Institution of Washington, Nathan Rosen Department of Physics University of North Carolina, John I. Hoover Nucleonics Division, Naval Research Laboratory, Washington, D.C. 10, September 1946 Naval Research Laboratory Special Research Division Washington D.C.)*

S-50 Plant Oak Ridge Tennessee. *(Liquid Thermal Diffusion by H.M. Moseley, J.B. Bidwell, W.N. Blatt, G.Y.Brokaw, M. Drott, F.J. Gradishar, P.N. Kokulis, R.E. Ruskin, J.H. Tayman, W.E. Whybrew, Edited by Philip. H. Abelson, Department of Terrestrial Magnetism, Carnegie Institution of Washington, Nathan Rosen Department of Physics University of North Carolina, John I. Hoover Nucleonics Division, Naval Research Laboratory, Washington, D.C. 10, September 1946 Naval Research Laboratory Special Research Division Washington D.C.)*

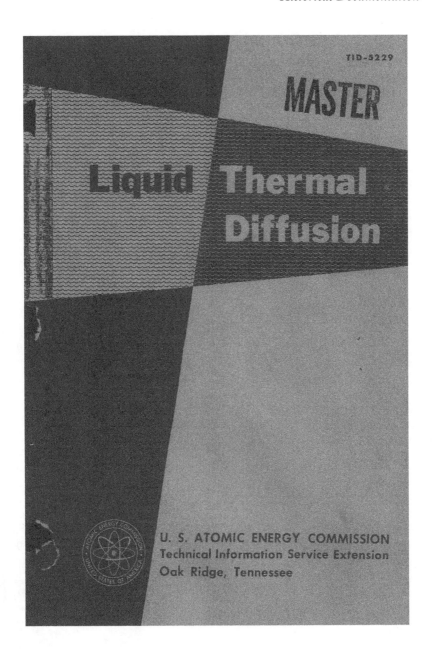

TID-5229

MASTER

Liquid Thermal Diffusion

U. S. ATOMIC ENERGY COMMISSION
Technical Information Service Extension
Oak Ridge, Tennessee

TID- 5229

Liquid Thermal Diffusion

Edited by

PHILIP H. ABELSON

Department of Terrestrial Magnetism
Carnegie Institution of Washington

NATHAN ROSEN

Department of Physics
University of North Carolina

JOHN I. HOOVER

Nucleonics Division, Naval Research
Laboratory, Washington, D. C.

Expansion and Revision
of NNES -IX- I

Declassified 2/12/57

Issuance Date: August 1958

Naval Research Laboratory
Physics Special Research Division
Washington, D. C.
Sept. 10, 1946

380

CONTRIBUTING AUTHORS

J. B. Bidwell
W. N. Blatt
G. Y. Brokaw
M. Drott
F. J. Gradishar
P. N. Kokulis
H. M. Moseley
R. E. Ruskin
J. H. Tayman
W. E. Whybrew

Thermal Diffusion master, written in part by Harrison Miller Moseley. H. M. Moseley was given the responsibility to recount the most pivotal program in United States History, with illustrations, goals, objectives, and actions taken by the A-players. He was responsible for defining the real events and insuring all accounts were included in a master that would become the documented source for historical accounts for the U.S. Atomic Energy Commission.

The top brass knew Miller would accurately provide the details of working with Liquid Thermal Diffusion, including the procedure, the equipment, the cost, and the struggles that only a few knew about first-hand on the most secretive program in the world.

Ensign Moseley has an exceptionally keen mind. Subject Officer has superior intelligence and his knowledge of mathematics and physics and the ability to develop new ideas are of the highest calibre. His performance of technical duties has been outstanding. Recommended for promotion when due.

Miller's evaluation, June 30, 1945. *(Courtesy of National Personnel Records Center, National Archives.)*

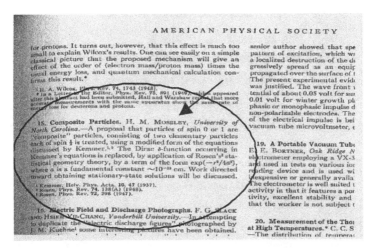

Dr. Harrison Miller Moseley's citation, *Composite Particles. (Courtesy Doug Diesenhaus, Research and Instructional Services. University of North Carolina at Chapel Hill.)*

PHYSICAL REVIEW   VOLUME 80, NUMBER 2   OCTOBER 15, 1950

The Meson as a Composite Particle*

H. M. MOSELEY AND NATHAN ROSEN
University of North Carolina, Chapel Hill, North Carolina
(Received February 28, 1950)

Calculations are carried out along the lines of the work of Fermi and Yang in which the π-meson is considered as a composite particle formed from a proton and an anti-neutron. On the assumption of a vector interaction it is found that the $^1S_0$ state must be excluded because its energy goes to zero as the interaction goes to zero, while the $^3P_0$ state appears to give an acceptable solution. On the assumption of a tensor interaction it is found that $^1S_0$ and $^3P_0$ solutions both exist, but for opposite signs of the interaction. The tensor interaction must therefore be excluded since it would lead to the formation of a composite particle by a proton and a neutron. Using the vector interaction one finds that the ground state is a $^3P_1$, but that there are other states with $j=0$, 1 and 2 lying near it, the proximity depending on the interaction range assumed.

I. INTRODUCTION

SOME time ago the suggestion was made that particles of spin 0 and 1 are composite, consisting of two particles each of spin $\frac{1}{2}$, closely bound to each other.[1] The method of calculation used was essentially equivalent to that of Kemmer in his attempt at a relativistic treatment of the deuteron.[2] Recently this idea was applied by Fermi and Yang[3] to the case of a π-meson, regarded as a composite particle formed by a nucleon and an anti-nucleon. The present paper is devoted to a further consideration of this problem.

II. GENERAL TREATMENT

one can introduce linear combinations of them which will transform like components of tensors of various ranks. Thus, if one takes the Dirac matrices in the usual form,[4] one can write

$$I = \frac{1}{2}(\psi_{12} - \psi_{21} + \psi_{34} - \psi_{43}),$$
$$A_1 = \frac{1}{2}(-\psi_{13} + \psi_{24} + \psi_{31} - \psi_{42}),$$
$$A_2 = (i/2)(-\psi_{13} - \psi_{24} + \psi_{31} + \psi_{42}),$$
$$A_3 = \frac{1}{2}(\psi_{14} + \psi_{23} - \psi_{32} - \psi_{41}),$$
$$A_4 = \frac{1}{2}(-\psi_{12} + \psi_{21} + \psi_{34} - \psi_{43}),$$
$$B_{23} = G_1 = \frac{1}{2}(-\psi_{11} + \psi_{22} - \psi_{33} + \psi_{44}),$$
$$B_{31} = G_2 = (i/2)(-\psi_{11} - \psi_{22} - \psi_{33} - \psi_{44}),$$
$$B_{12} = G_3 = \frac{1}{2}(\psi_{12} + \psi_{21} + \psi_{34} + \psi_{43}),$$
$$I = \frac{1}{2}(\psi_{11} - \psi_{22} + \psi_{33} - \psi_{44}),$$

(4)

Dr. Harrison Miller Moseley and Nathan Rosen, Albert Einstein's collaborator. *(Courtesy Doug Diesenhaus, Research and Instructional Services. University of North Carolina at Chapel Hill.)*

COMPOSITE PARTICLES: PARTICLES OF INTEGRAL

SPIN AS COMPOUNDS OF DIRAC-

TYPE PARTICLES

by

Harrison Miller Moseley

A thesis submitted to the Faculty of the
University of North Carolina in partial
fulfillment of the requirements for the
degree of Doctor of Philosophy in the
Department of Physics

Chapel Hill

1950

Approved by

Nathan Rosen

Adviser

ACKNOWLEDGEMENT

The author wishes to express his gratitude to Prof. Nathan Rosen, at whose suggestion this investigation was made, for his effective direction and constant interest.

Harrison Miller Moseley

Department of Physics

University of North Carolina

December 12, 1949

H.M. Moseley, Dissertation, 1950.

MOSELEY, H. M. (1951). *Composite particles: Particles of integral spin as compounds of dirac-type particles.*The. *ProQuest Dissertations and Theses,* 48-48 p. *(Doug Diesenhaus, Research and Instructional Services.)*

THE
REVIEW OF SCIENTIFIC INSTRUMENTS

VOLUME 29, NUMBER 10

OCTOBER, 1958

Four-Sector Azimuthally Varying Field Cyclotron

H. G. Blosser,* R. E. Worsham, C. D. Goodman, R. S. Livingston,
J. E. Mann, H. M. Moseley,† G. T. Trammel, and T. A. Welton
Oak Ridge National Laboratory,‡ Oak Ridge, Tennessee

(Received July 14, 1958)

An electron model relativistic fixed-frequency cyclotron of the azimuthally varying field type has been constructed for the purpose of testing the orbit dynamics of such a device. An iterative technique used in designing an acceptable magnetic field shape is described in some detail. A brief description of the various components of the device is given as well as an account of the beam phenomena observed in the initial period of operation. Results strongly indicate the feasibility, from an orbit dynamics standpoint, of large proton machines of this type.

INTRODUCTION

DURING the past decade, studies in elementary particle physics at energies below 1 Bev have been performed almost entirely by use of large synchrocyclotrons. As is well known, the synchrocyclotron sacrifices performance (in the form of a low duty cycle) with respect to that of fixed-frequency cyclotrons in order to provide for the relativistic increase in mass of the accelerated particles. This latter effect has in practice limited the f-f cyclotron to the energy range below 25 Mev per nucleon. An alternative method of correcting for the relativistic mass increase without sacrifice of the high performance typical of the f-f cyclotron was proposed in 1938 by L. H. Thomas.[1] Thomas's proposal utilized a magnetic field which, on the average, increased with radius so as to compensate the mass increase, and which had superposed on this main field azimuthal variations of a character such as to provide axial focusing of the beam. Further theoretical studies of the Thomas-type cyclotron were made by Judd[2] at the University of California in the period 1950–1954; this work culminated in the construction and successful operation of two Thomas-type electron cyclo-

trons by Kelly et al.[3] The work was not extended, however, to the construction of a proton machine.

In 1954 Welton undertook a detailed study[4] of the properties of devices of this type with a view toward construction of a large proton accelerator at the Oak Ridge National Laboratory.[5] In this work, it was quickly realized that the concept of the imperfection resonance applied to the Thomas cyclotron just as it does to the alternating gradient synchrotron and that, therefore, the maximum energy attainable in a Thomas cyclotron could quite possibly be limited to that at which the first half-integral imperfection resonance occurred. The periodicity of the magnetic field in the model work of Kelly et al.[3] had been such that the stability limit coincided with the first half-integral resonance so that no information was obtained as to the feasibility of accelerating through this resonance.

In early 1956, design and construction of an electron cyclotron was started at Oak Ridge for the purpose of experimentally studying acceleration through the first half-integral resonance. In the process of building this device, which was named the Oak Ridge Cyclotron Analogue, the design technology of the azimuthally varying field (AVF) cyclotron was considerably refined and

* Now at Michigan State University
† On leave from Texas Christian University.
‡ Operated for the U. S. Atomic Energy Commission by Union Carbide Corporation.

[1] L. H. Thomas, Phys. Rev. 54, 580 (1938).
[2] David L. Judd, Phys. Rev. 100, 1804(A) (1955).
[3] Kelly, Pyle, Thornton, Richardson, and Wright, Rev. Sci. Instr. 27, 492 (1956).
[4] T. A. Welton, Phys. Rev. 99, 1623T (1955); D. S. Falk and T. A. Welton, Bull. Am. Phys. Soc. Ser. II 1, 60 (1956); M. M. Gordon and T. A. Welton, ibid. 2, 11 (1957); 3, 57 (1958).
[5] Proposal for a Southern Regional Accelerator, Oak Ridge National Laboratory Report 57-4-30 (abridged) (unpublished).

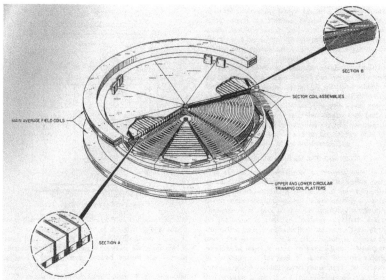

Fig. 11. Sketch of complete coil assembly of the Cyclotron Analogue showing relative positions of the different types of coils. The circular trim

Dr. Harrison Miller Moseley, Four-Sector Azimuthally Varying Field Cyclotron.

Simplified Method for Determing Cascade Impactor Stage Efficiencies, by J.C. Couchman, Ph.D., and H. M. Moseley, Ph.D. EG&G Inc. Santa Barbara Division, Santa Barbara, California, and Texas Christian University, Fort Worth, Texas. *(Courtesy of Doug Diesenhaus Research and Instructional Services, University Libraries. The University of North Carolina at Chapel Hill.)*

THE TEXAS COMPANY Amarillo City, Texas December 13, 1932

Mr. Rusty Russell & Football Team,
Masonic Home,
Fort Worth, Texas

Dear Mr. Russell and Boys:

I just want to express my appreciation to the greatest, cleanest and whole-hearted football team in America. I appreciate you boys and Mr. Russell not only for the games you have won but for the way you won them and the many miracles that you have performed this season.

I think you boys should appreciate and I know you do, the fact that you were honored by having the most outstanding football coach in America.

I am very sorry that you didnot win the Lubbock game; however in my estimation and thousands of others you are recognized as the State Champions. Lubbock's last two touchdowns were due to the bad break of the high wind and cold weather. There is no question but that you out played Lubbock in every respect so long as the breaks were even.

If each of you boys will play the game of life as you have played football this last season you will accomplish great things and will be recognized in the world as great men the same as you have been recognized as great football players.

I havenot had the opportunity of meeting each of you boys personally but I consider each of you a very close friend. I am very much interested in each and every one of you. After finishing school at the Home at any time that I can be of any assistance to any of you I want you to feel free to call on me as I would be glad to do anything possible to assist you. Wishing you all a Merry Xmas and Happy New Year,

I am, An Admiring Friend, *J. Miller*

One of the hundreds of telegrams the team received.

THE TEXAS COMPANY   Archer City, Texas   December 21, 1938

Mr. H.N.Russell ,
Mr. Tiner,
Tom Posey , and boys,

Buster Roach,
Phillip Earp,
Buford Hudgins,
Gene Keel,
Frank Bounds,
Don Stephens,
Norman Strange
Horace McHam,
James Holmans,
Armanante P.Torres,
Jeff Brown,
Jack Bates,
Miller Moseley.

This
is just a small token of my appreciation
and admiration for your great football
Coaching and playing this season.

I still say you can beat Lubbock,and
would have if the wind had not hit for
another two hours.

But boys all through life we must meet
with disappointments.One of the greatest
lessons we can learn is to take our disap-
pointments with a smile.

May each of you play the game of life
and be as successful as you havein your
football playing this season.
    Wishing you a Merry Christmas,
        a Friend,

Miller's Mother
    Mrs Lucille Moseley

Telegram sent to Mr. Russell and the team from Miller's mother.

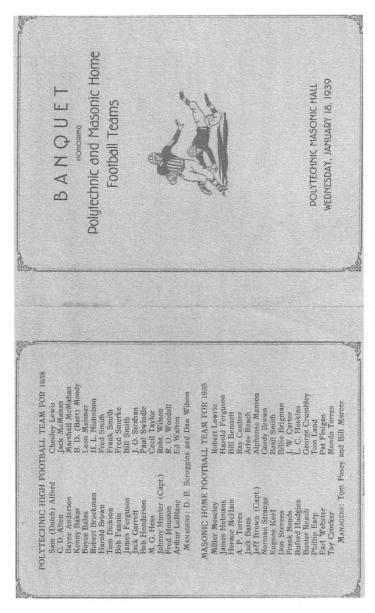

Menu for the football banquet printed for the Masons by the Masons, January 18, 1939.

PROGRAM

Song - - - - - AMERICA
THE EYES OF TEXAS ARE UPON YOU
Led by G. S. GARNETT

Invocation - - - - - - - REV. CAUTHEN

Welcome Address - - - - - - P. B. SWINDLE

Master of Ceremonies - - - - - MIKE BRUMBELOW

Introduction of Guests - - - - MIKE BRUMBELOW

After Dinner Speakers - - - - $\begin{cases} \text{JOE MOORE} \\ \text{TOM FLETCHER} \end{cases}$

PROGRAM COMMITTEE

Dr. JACK GARRISON   HOMER COVEY
H. C. ASHBURN

MENU

GRAPEFRUIT

CELERY

ROLLS

CRANBERRY SAUCE

TURKEY AND DRESSING

GIBLET GRAVY

CREAMED POTATOES

PEAS

SALAD

CAKE   ICE CREAM

COFFEE

Banquet Prepared by Wives and Officers of
Polytechnic Masonic Lodge No. 925

Yearly Football Banquet Menu.

MASONIC HOME FOOTBALL ROSTER, 1938

Name	Position	No.	Weight
Jack Bates	G	23	137
Bill Bennett	T	27	154
Frank Bonds	B	25	142
Billy Brigman	B	17	120
Jeff Brown	T	43	165
Gordy Brown	B	42	137
J. W. Carter	C	36	137
Ray Coulter	E	4	150
Toy Crocker	E	3	126
George Crumbley	G	39	130
Phillip Earp	B	28	131
Harold Ferguson	G	38	148
Pat Finnigan	T	21	146
James Holmans	T	40	155
L. C. Hoskins	E	31	149
Buford Hudgins	B	35	135
Eugene Keel	B	24	150
Tom Land	G	29	136
Robert Lowrie	B	34	128
Alphonse Manson	E	1	145
Horace McHam	G	37	158
Miller Moseley	E	6	132
A. Roach	E	26	135
B. Roach	B	32	135
Basil Smith	B	18	109
Don Stephens	B	41	162
Norman Strange	E	33	137
A. P. Torres	C	22	145
Jack Torres	B	5	132
Earl Webster	C	20	155

STUDENT MANAGERS

Tom Posey   William Mercer

IF

Rudyard Kipling

If you can keep your head when all about you
  Are losing theirs and blaming it on you;
If you can trust yourself when all men doubt you,
  But make allowance for their doubting too;
If you can wait, and not be tired by waiting,
  Or being lied about, don't deal in lies,
Or being hated, don't give way to hating,
  And yet don't look too good, nor talk too wise.

If you can dream—and not make dreams your master;
  If you can think—and 'not make thought your aim,
If you can meet with triumph and disaster
  And treat those two imposters just the same;
If you can bear to hear the truth you've spoken
  Twisted by knaves to make a trap for fools,
Or watch the things you gave your life be broken,
  And stoop and build 'em up with worn-out tools.

If you can make one heap of all your winnings
  And risk it on one turn of pitch-and-toss
And lose, and start again at your beginnings
  And never breathe a word about your loss;
If you can force your heart and nerve and sinew
  To serve your turn long after they are gone
And so hold on when there is nothing in you
  Except the Will which says to them: "Hold on!"

If you can talk with crowds and keep your virtue,
  Or walk with kings—nor lose the common touch,
If neither foes nor loving friends can hurt you,
  If all men count with you, but none too much;
If you can fill the unforgiving minute with sixty seconds'
    worth of distance run,
  And—which is more—you'll be a Man, my son!

Masonic Home football roster, 1938.

Commencement Exercises
Masonic Home and School

Sunday, May Twenty-Eighth
and
Monday, May Twenty-Ninth
Nineteen Hundred Thirty-Nine

School Auditorium

1939 Masonic Home and School commencement program.

Class Roll

JIMMY RUTH ALEXANDER

JANICE ANDERSON

SELMA BELT

FRANK BONDS

CHARLCIE BRANSOM

MARY MARTHA BRICE

JEFF BROWN

TOY CROCKER

PHILLIP EARP

HAROLD FERGUSON

HOMER HAMILTON

JAMES HOLMANS

BUFORD HUDGINS

EUGENE KEEL

MILLER MOSELEY
Valedictorian

ROBERT LOWRIE
Salutatorian

ALPHONSE MANSON

E. A. MAUZY

JUNE MAYO

HORACE McHAM

BILL MERCER

BETTIE MORRILL

DAVID PILLANS

WOODROW PITTMAN

TOM POSEY

MARY NELL REYNOLDS

DON STEPHENS

NORMAN STRANGE

ALICE TEMPELMEYER

JOYE THOMAS

ELLA LOU THORNTON

Sunday, May 28

11:00 A. M.

1. Overture: Bridal Rose .... *Lavallee*
   Orchestra
2. Neopolitan Nights .... *Zamecnik*
3. Hymn 44: I'll Go Where You Want Me to Go
4. Migonnette .... *Baumann*

Senior Orchestra

Selma Belt	June Mayo
Joye Thomas	Ella Lou Thornton
Charlcie Bransom	Mary Nell Reynolds

Don Stephens

5. Invocation
6. Baccalaureate Sermon
   Rev. Wm. D. Daugherty, Grand Chaplain
7. Hymn 42: Give of Your Best to the Master

Monday, May 29

10:00 A. M.

1. Overture Chanson Russe .... *Daniels*
   Orchestra
2. Blue Danube—Processional .... *Strauss*
3. Salutatory: Meet Our Seniors
   Robert Lowrie
4. Narcissus .... *Nevin*
   Senior Orchestra
5. Valedictory: The Challenge to Youth
   Miller Moseley
6. Address to Class
   Sam B. Cantey, Jr., Grand Senior Warden
7. Presentation of Diplomas
8. Awards

Alphonse Manson

Alphonse Manson

E. A. Mauzy

E. A. Mauzy

Horace Wayne McHam
Horace Wayne McHam

William Lee Mercer
"Murphey"
to Dundee

Miller Moseley
Morris Moseley

David Clinton Pillans
David Pillans

Woodrow Wilson Pittman
Woodrow Pittman

Tom Posey
Tom Posey

Don Stephens
Don Stephens

Norman S. Strange
Norman Strange

One of the pages of the 1939 graduating senior cards and signatures Miller has kept for 75 years. Miller had given up and signed his senior card "Morris Moseley," a poke at the press' insistence on misspelling his name in their articles.

397

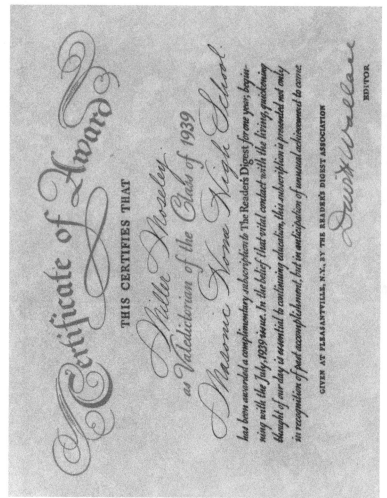

Certificate of Award, Valedictorian of the Class of 1939.

MARCH, 1944   NUMBER 400

THE UNIVERSITY OF NORTH CAROLINA RECORD

THE ONE HUNDRED AND FIFTIETH SESSION

THE GENERAL CATALOGUE

CATALOGUE ISSUE
1943-1944

*Announcements for the Session
1944-1945*

THE UNIVERSITY OF NORTH CAROLINA PRESS
CHAPEL HILL, N. C.

ISAAC HALL MANNING, M.D., *Kenan Professor Emeritus of Physiology.* Student, 1882-1886 (North Carolina); M.D., 1897 (Long Island College of Medicine).

*ISAAC HALL MANNING, JR., A.B., M.D., *Instructor in Medicine.* A.B. 1931 (North Carolina); M.D., 1935 (Harvard).

EDWIN CARLYLE MARKHAM, Ph.D., *Professor of Chemistry.* A.B., 1923 (Trinity College); Ph.D., 1927 (Virginia).

*DONALD FRAZER MARTIN, A.M., *Assistant Professor of Economics.* A.B. 1929 (Davidson); A.M., 1931 (North Carolina).

HANSFORD EARL MARTIN, A.B., *Instructor in English.* A.B., 1942 (Oklahoma).

JOSEPH FRANCIS MARY, S.M., *Instructor in Chemistry.* B.A., 1938 (American University); S.M., 1939 (Va. Polytechnic Inst.).

**HERMAN CHARLES MASON, Ph.D., *Associate Professor of Bacteriology.* S.B., 1932 (Chicago); M.S., 1936, Ph.D. 1939 (Illinois).

ALBERT HENRY MATHES, A.B., *Instructor in Physical Education.* A.B., 1940 (North Carolina).

†ELWYN ARTHUR MAUCK, Ph.D., *Assistant Professor of Political Science and Research Associate in the Institute for Research in Social Science.* A.B. 1932 (Cornell College); A.M., 1933, Ph.D., 1937 (Columbia).

ROBERT IRWIN MEHR, Ph.D., *Assistant Professor of Economics.* B.S., 1938, M.S., 1939 (Alabama); Ph.D., 1943 (Pennsylvania).

EMILY BIDDLE MEIGS, *Assistant Professor of Library Science.* Certificate, 1906 (Carnegie Library School).

HAROLD DIEDRICH MEYER, A.M., LL.D., *Professor of Sociology.* A.B., 1912, A.M., 1916 (Georgia); LL.D. (Florida Southern College).

DANIEL FRANKLIN MILAM, A.B., M.D., M.P.H., *Professor of Nutrition in the School of Public Health.* A.B., 1915 (Vanderbilt); M.D., 1924 (Chicago); M.P.H., 1929 (Johns Hopkins).

AUGUSTUS TAYLOR MILLEN, JR., Ph.D., *Assistant Professor of Physiology.* B.S., 1931, M.S., 1933 (Emory); Ph.D., 1939 (Michigan).

EDWIN SHEPARD MILLER, M.A., *Instructor in English.* A.B., 1925 (Bethany College); M.A., 1930 (Ohio State).

JUAN MIRANDA, *Instructor in Spanish.*

* Absent in military service.
** Absent in military service.
† Absent on leave in government service.

JULIO JOSÉ MONTANO, M.S. Chem. Eng'g., *Instructor in Spanish.* B.S., 1921, M.S. in Chem. Eng'g, 1925 (Nat'l. University of Mexico).

LUCY SHIELDS MORGAN, Ph.D., *Professor of Health Education.* A.B., 1922, M.S., 1932 (Tennessee); M.A., 1929 (Columbia); Ph.D. 1938 (Yale).

RUTH EVELYN DODD MORGAN, M.S., *Instructor in Case Work Practice.* A.B., 1930 (N.C.C.W.); M.S., 1932 (Western Reserve).

WILLIAM GARDNER MORGAN, A.B., M.D., *Associate University Physician and Instructor in Physical Diagnosis.* A.B., 1927 (North Carolina); M.D., 1931 (Pennsylvania).

*JOSEPH LEHRSMAN MORRISON, A.B., *Instructor in Journalism.* A.B., 1940 (North Carolina).

†ROY WILLIAM MORRISON, Ph.D., *Professor of Elementary Education.* A.B., 1916 (Davidson); Ph.D., 1923 (North Carolina).

*JOHN WALTER MORRISS, JR., M.A., *Instructor in Physical Education.* B.A., 1930 (Southwestern Louisiana Institute); M.A., 1937 (Louisiana State University).

ERNST MORWITZ, J.D., and Econ.D., *Instructor in German.* Dr. jur. et econ. 1910 (Heidelberg).

MILLER MOSKIY, B.A., *Instructor in Physics.* B.A., 1943 (Texas Christian).

*OLIN TERRILL MOUZON, Ph.D., *Assistant Professor of Economics.* B.S. in Commerce, 1933 (Southern Methodist); Ph.D., 1940 (North Carolina).

*GEORGE E. MOWRY, Ph.D., *Assistant Professor of History.* A.B., 1933 (Miami); M.A., 1934, Ph.D., 1938 (Wisconsin).

*EDWARD FRANCIS MOYER, A.M., *Instructor in French.* A.B., 1936, A.M., 1937 (North Carolina).

VESTER MOYE MULHOLLAND, M.A., *Instructor in Education.* A.B., 1926, M.A., 1927 (Duke).

CLYDE EDWARD MULLIS, A.M., *Assistant Professor of Physical Education.* A.B., 1938, A.M., 1940 (North Carolina).

HOWARD FREDERICK MUNCH, A.M., *Associate Professor of Education, Instructor in Mathematics.* B.S., 1904 (Adrian College); A.M., 1926 (Chicago).

JOSEPH HAROLD MUSNICK, A.B., *Instructor in Physical Education.* A.B., 1938 (North Carolina).

* Absent on leave in military service.
† Absent on leave in government service.

DESCRIPTION OF COURSES

*DEPARTMENT OF PHYSICS

Professors: A. E. RUARK, O. STUHLMAN, JR., K. H. FUSSLER, E. K. PLYLER (absent on leave)

Associate Professors: NATHAN ROSEN, P. E. SHEARIN

Assistant Professors: R. H. LYDDANE (absent on leave), EUGENE GREULING, E. J. HELLUND

Temporary Staff of Colleagues from other Departments of the University and other Institutions:

M. T. CARLISLE, ARTHUR CRAFTS, W. J. DANIEL, PRESTON EDWARDS, P. C. FARRAR, W. D. HARRELL, GEORGE HENRY, F. H. HUNTER, J. S. JOHNSON, E. C. LEONARD, C. S. MAURICE, ARTHUR WALTNER, W. M. WARD

Instructors: (Early in the year, persons in this list held graduate assistantships, teaching fellowships, or part-time instructorships.) GRIFFIN CARMICHAEL, P. H. EDWARDS, MELVIN EISNER, LAWRENCE FELDMAN, HERMAN GLASER, HERMAN JARREL, GEORGE JENKINS, ROBERT L. LIPTON, H. M. MOSELEY, J. B. NEWMAN, G. D. PEELER, W. S. PLYMALE, IRVING RESNICK, J. B TAYLOR, LUCILE THACKER

Teaching Fellow (part of the year): GRIFFIN CARMICHAEL

Student Assistants: JOHN BARLOW, THELMA BOLICK, GLEN HAYDON, JR., JAMES WALLACE

Courses for Undergraduates

A. RADIO COMMUNICATIONS (3). No prerequisite. Text: Marcus and Horton. Elements of Radio

M. MECHANICS. (3 trimester hours). No prerequisite. Text: Millikan, Coale, Edwards.

A special course in mechanics for V-12 marines, given December 1, 1943 to March 1, 1944. *Four lecture and recitation hours a week.* Mr. Fussler.

PHYSICS I-II, for V-12 Students (10 trimester hours). Covers General Physics in two trimesters. Physics I covers mechanics, heat, and sound and Physics II covers electricity and magnetism, optics and special topics, substantially in accordance with official V-12 course descriptions.

Two lecture, two recitation, and two laboratory hours a week. Lectures and recitations, Messrs. Edwards, Greuling, Ruark, Johnson, Shearin, Fussler; Assistants. Laboratory, Messrs: Fussler, Shearin; Assistants.

PHYSICS 4A. HEAT AND THERMODYNAMICS (3½ trimester hours.) Prerequisite, one year of general college physics. Corequisite, calculus, M-5 in the V-12 program. Text: Cork, *Heat*, and Enswiler and Schwartz, *Thermodynamics.*

Two recitation and three laboratory hours a week. Mr. Hellund; Assistants.

PHYSICS 5A. (Identical with course EE1, official V-12 program). *Electricity and Magnetism* (3½ semester hours). Prerequisite, one year of general college physics. Corequisite, Calculus, M-5 in the V-12 program. Texts: Bialock, *Elements of Electrical Circuits and Machinery;* Smith, *Electrical Measurements in Theory and Application.*

The lectures and laboratory work steer a middle course between the customary, half-year courses given by Physics departments and electrical engineering departments, respectively. Electrostatics, magnetostatics, electrodynamics, D. C. circuits and equipment; single phase and polyphase A. C. circuits and equipment.

Two recitation and three laboratory hours a week. Mr. Plymale:

PHYSICS   271

DEPARTMENT OF PHYSICS

Professors: OTTO STUHLMAN, JR., KARL H. FUSSLER, NATHAN
ROSEN, PAUL E. SHEARIN, *Chairman*
Associate Professors: FRED T. ROGERS, JR., JOSEPH W. STRALEY,
WAYNE A. BOWERS
Lecturer: J. STANLEY JOHNSON
Half-time Instructors: MARY JANE AULD, JOHN BARLOW, ROBERT
J. BLACKWELL, TALBOT CHUBB, WILLIAM BYATT, MELVIN
EISNER, GEORGE JENKINS, EMILY JONES, ROBERT LIDE, MILLER
MOSELEY, ARTHUR WALTNER
Teaching Fellow: ARTHUR LINZ
Technician: NESTORE DiCOSTANZO
Apparatus Custodian: WALTER D. HARRELL

Harrison Miller Moseley, Nathan Rosen, and A.E. Ruark. *(The University of North Carolina Archives.)*

Simplified Method for Determining Cascade Impactor Stage Efficiencies

J. C. COUCHMAN, Ph.D.,* and H. M. MOSELEY, Ph.D.†

EG&G Inc., Santa Barbara Division, Santa Barbara, California, and Texas Christian University, Fort Worth, Texas

A direct method has been devised for measuring cascade impactor stage efficiencies. The method makes use of a special two-stage configuration of the sampler being calibrated. To employ the method, it is necessary only to measure the unnormalized density function of the source and the unnormalized density function of the particles collected on the second of two identical impactor stages. With this method, an impactor stage can be calibrated in a few hours.

Introduction

RECENT NATIONAL emphasis on controlling air pollution has resulted in increased interest in various types of air sampling devices. Principal among these is the cascade impactor. Some of the better-known cascade impactors described in the than cutoff size would be collected on the adhesive, and particles smaller than the cutoff size would be carried along with the air. However, since the probability that a particle of a given size will be impacted on a surface depends, in part, on the distance of the particle from the center of the incom-

Simplified Method for Determining Cascade Impactor Stage Efficiencies. *(Courtesy Doug Diesenhaus, Research and Instructional Services. University of North Carolina at Chapel Hill.)*

Unbelievable

"That dog scared me."

"We were growing boys and needed a new change of clothes at least once a year."

"You will be called, 'New Kid.'"

"We played just about every hour of everyday."

"It's nothing new. We used to run all that stuff."

"A 132 pound, Left End, sure-blocking, hard tackling, sticky fingered little all-district competitor."

"I want to bring along 'my brightest student'."

Dr. Moseley's selection for the atomic project is quite an honor.

"I thought she was real good company."

"It was a great experience, but I can't say I ever fit in with the caliber of people I was working with. I was just doing my job."

"The son of a bitch did it again."

References

Unless otherwise specified, all quotes and anecdotes from Dr. Harrison Miller Moseley were gathered during extensive face to face interviews conducted between the author, Stella E. Brooks, and Dr. Moseley from September 4, 2012 to May 30, 2014. Sources for additional quotes, articles, and papers are cited specifically as follows.

Chapter 2

Knight, Bridget, features editor, Archer County Cemetery records, *Times Record News*

http://en.wikipedia.org/wiki/Great_Depression, retrieved October 2, 2012.

http://www.aclassicmovieblog.com/2012/06/Mary.Pickford...last, retrieved January 1, 2013.

http://www.youtube.com/watch?v=IW4dBODmN9o, retrieved December 1, 2012.

Chapter 4

McCaulay, W.R., *The Masonic Home and School of Texas*. Fort Worth, Texas: Masonic Home Graphic Arts Club, 1938. Page 5, 148.

Douglas, C.L., "Out Masonic Home Way Football's the Thing: They Build Mighty Fine Little Men and Women, Too, Press Writer Finds Out." Courtesy of the *Fort Worth Star Telegram*, Witt, Jim, Executive Editor.

McCaulay, W.R., *The Masonic Home and School of Texas*. Fort Worth, Texas: Masonic Home Graphic Arts Club, 1938. Page 142, 149, 150.

Personally conducted interview: Tom Brady and Richard Opperman, email and telephone, February 5, 2013, October 1, 2012 and October 17, 2013.

Fletcher, T, Superintendent, "Proceedings of the Grand Lodge of Texas." *Report of the superintendent of the Masonic home and school. To the Board of Directors for the Masonic Home and School, 1938-39*. Fort Worth, Texas: Masonic Home Graphic Arts Club. Page 134. *(courtesy of Richard Opperman)*.

Douglas, C.L., "Out Masonic Home Way Football's the Thing: They Build Mighty Fine Little Men and Women, Too, Press Writer Finds Out." Courtesy of the *Fort Worth Star Telegram*, Witt, Jim, Executive Editor.

Chapter 5

McCaulay, W.R., *The Masonic Home and School of Texas*. Fort Worth, Texas: Masonic Home Graphic Arts Club, 1938. Page 151.

Personally conducted interview: Richard Opperman, at his home, Oct 1, 2012.

Personally conducted interview: Richard Opperman, by telephone, October 30, 2013 and February 28, 2014.

Personally conducted interview: Tom Brady, email, Oct 15, 2013 and February 21, 2014.

Unknown author, *The Master Builder*. "Co-operation in the Dining Room." Fort Worth, Texas: Masonic Home Graphic Arts Club, January 28, 1937. Courtesy of Richard Opperman.

McCaulay, W.R., *The Masonic Home and School of Texas*. Fort Worth, Texas: Masonic Home Graphic Arts Club, 1938. Page 158.

http://www.huppi.com/kangaroo/timeline.htm, retrieved October 1, 2012.

Chapter 6

McHam, Horace, *Memories 1899-1999. "A strictly unauthorized trip to Poly Theater."* The Masonic Home and School of Texas, 1999. Page 34.

Personally conducted interview: Tom Brady, email, December 20, 2013.

Walraven, Bill, "Christmas at Masonic Home was far from bleak." *Corpus-Christi Caller-Times,* December 24, 1985. Courtesy of Marjorie Walraven.

Chapter 7

Unknown author, *The Master Builder.* Fort Worth, Texas: Masonic Home Graphic Arts Club, 1934. Courtesy of Richard Opperman.

Personally conducted interview: Bruce Riddle, in his home, March 4, 2013.

Personally conducted interview: Horace McHam, November 24, 2013

Personally conducted interview: Tom Brady, email, September 30, 2012, December 9, 2013, January 10, 2014, February 21, 2014.

Unknown authors, *The Master Builder,* Fort Worth, Texas: Masonic Home Graphic Arts Club, 1934. Courtesy of Richard Opperman.

Personally conducted interview: Dick Vallon, telephone, June 2013.

Walraven, Bill, "Old stories bring back memories of the Masonic Home." *Corpus-Christi Caller-Times,* June 18, 1984. Courtesy of Marjorie Walraven.

Original story told by Harrison Miller Moseley and confirmed by Dick Vallon of the Burkburnett Chamber of Commerce, June 2013.

Chapter 8

Bates, Jack, *Jack Bates Proud to be #23.* Self-published by Jack Bates. Courtesy of Roberta Bates.

Personally conducted interview: Bruce Riddle, in his home, March 4, 2013.

Personally conducted interview: Tom Brady, email, October 30, 2013, November 15, 2013, February 10, 2014, February 11, 2014 and February 22, 2014.

Personally conducted interview: Tom Brady, email, October 30, 2013 and February 11, 2014. Confirmed with Joe "Rocky" Wilkie on February 11, 2014.

Tommye Hurst, *The Master Builder.* "Winchellisms." Fort Worth, Texas: Masonic Home Graphic Arts Club, April 14, 1938, et. al. Courtesy of Richard Opperman.

Torres, Armando "Jack", *Memories 1899-1999. "In Search of Fruit."* The Masonic Home and School of Texas, 1999. Page 40.

Personally conducted interview: Richard Opperman, telephone, December 1, 2013.

Chapter 9

The Master Builder. Fort Worth, Texas: Masonic Home Graphic Arts Club, 1937. Courtesy of Richard Opperman.

http://en.wikipedia.org/wiki/Public_works, retrieved November 13, 2012.

Moseley, Cecil, *The Master Builder,* "Robbing the Hogs." Fort Worth, Texas: Masonic Home Graphic Arts Club, 1938. Courtesy of Richard Opperman.

Moseley, Miller, *The Master Builder,* "The Boaster Takes A Bow." Fort Worth, Texas: Masonic Home

Graphic Arts Club, January 28, 1937. Courtesy of Richard Opperman.

Unknown author, *The Master Builder*. Title unknown. Fort Worth, Texas: Masonic Home Graphic Arts Club, April 27, 1933. Courtesy of Richard Opperman.

Personally conducted interview: Horace McHam, telephone, October 10, 2012.

Personally conducted interview: Tom Brady, email, November 23, 2013 and November 26, 2013.

Walraven, Bill, "Old stories bring back memories of the Masonic Home." *Corpus-Christi Caller-Times,* June 18, 1984. Courtesy of Marjorie Walraven.

Unknown author, *The Master Builder,* "Stop Wasting." Fort Worth, Texas: Masonic Home Graphic Arts Club, 1938. Courtesy of Richard Opperman.

Chapter 10

Personally conducted interview: Tom Brady, email, June 15, 2012; September 30, 2012; March 14, 2013.

Personally conducted interview: Richard Opperman, at his home, June 1, 2012.

Harrison Miller Moseley quote confirm by Horace McHam, Tom Brady, and Richard Opperman.

Chapter 11

Personally conducted interview: Tom Brady, email, September 30, 2012.

Courtesy of the *Fort Worth Star Telegram,* Jim Witt, Executive Editor.

The Holy Bible, 1 Samuel 17.

Chapter 12

Courtesy of the *Fort Worth Star Telegram,* Jim Witt, Executive Editor.

Chapter 13

Courtesy of the *Fort Worth Star Telegram,* Jim Witt, Executive Editor.

Chapter 14

Courtesy of the *Fort Worth Star Telegram,* Jim Witt, Executive Editor.

Bates, Jack, *Jack Bates Proud to be #23.* Self-published by Jack Bates. Courtesy of Roberta Bates.

Unknown author, *The Master Builder,* "Don't Give Up." Fort Worth, Texas: Masonic Home Graphic Arts Club, 1938. Courtesy of Richard Opperman.

Personally conducted interview: Tom Brady, email, October 17, 2013 and February 21, 2014.

Chapter 15

Courtesy of the *Fort Worth Star Telegram,* Jim Witt, Executive Editor.

Courtesy of the *Longview Journal*

Chapter 16

Courtesy of the *Fort Worth Star Telegram,* Jim Witt, Executive Editor.

Chapter 17

Courtesy of the *Fort Worth Star Telegram,* Jim Witt, Executive Editor.

Bates, Jack, *Jack Bates Proud to be #23.* Self-published by Jack Bates. Courtesy of Roberta Bates.

Chapter 18

Courtesy of the Fort Worth Star Telegram, Jim Witt, Executive Editor.

Personally conducted interview: Tom Brady, email, January 29, 2013 and March 2, 2014.

Fletcher, T. *Proceedings of the Grand Lodge of Texas,* "Proceedings of the 1938-39 Report of the Superintendent of the Masonic Home and School." September 30, 1938 to October 1, 1939," Department of Printing. Page 10. Courtesy of Richard Opperman.

Pillans, David, *The Master Builder,* "How My Printing Training Has Prepared Me to Face the World." Fort Worth, Texas: Masonic Home Graphic Arts Club, 1938. Courtesy of Richard Opperman.

Bonds, Frank, *The Master Builder,* "How My Printing Course Has Helped Me." Fort Worth, Texas: Masonic Home Graphic Arts Club, 1938. Courtesy of Richard Opperman.

Earp, Philip, *The Master Builder,* "What Printing has Done for Me." Fort Worth, Texas: Masonic Home Graphic Arts Club, 1938. Courtesy of Richard Opperman.

Walraven, Bill, "Ziggy; The Stray Dog That was Anything but Ordinary," original story provided by Marjorie Walraven.

Unknown author, *The Master Builder,* "To the Graduates." Fort Worth, Texas: Masonic Home Graphic Arts Club, 1938. Courtesy of Richard Opperman.

Pillans, David, "Who's Who in The Masonic Home Graphic Arts Club." Fort Worth, Texas: Masonic Home Graphic Arts Club, 1938-39. Courtesy of Richard Opperman.

Chapter 19

http://en.wikipedia.org/wiki/World_War_II, retrieved, November 14, 2012.

Courtesy of Fehner, Terrance R. and Gosing, F. G. Courtesy, "The Manhattan Project." Page 2.

"Liquid Thermal Diffusion" by H.M. Moseley, J.B. Bidwell, W.N. Blatt, G.Y.Brokaw, M. Drott, F.J. Gradishar, P.N. Kokulis, R.E. Ruskin, J.H. Tayman, W.E. Whybrew, Edited by Philip. H. Abelson, Department of Terrestrial Magnetism, Carnegie Institution of Washington, Nathan Rosen Department of Physics University of North Carolina, John I. Hoover Nucleonics Division, Naval Research Laboratory, Washington, D.C. September 10, 1946. Naval Research Laboratory Physics Special Research Division Washington, D. C. Liquid Thermal Diffusion. A revised and expanded version of NNES-DC-1. The liquid thermal diffusion method for the separation of isotopes is described. The discussion includes the experimental aspects of the method, description of equipment, and the theoretical aspects of the process as applied to the design, development, and performance criteria. A short history of the liquid thermal diffusion method from 1940 to 1945 is presented along; with a survey of relevant literature prior to 1940. The remainder of the report is concerned with theoretical aspects. (J.R.D.). osti ID: 4311423, report numbers: TID-5229; NRL-0-2982, Technical Report. Decl. February 12, 1957. TISE Issuance date: August 1958. Naval Research Laboratory, Washington, D.C., sponsoring USDOE, subject: Physics; Isotope separation; Laboratory equipment; Liquids; Performance; Planning; Thermal Diffusion. Page 5.

Courtesy of the USMA Library, *Official Web Site*: http://energy.gov.

Chapter 20

Courtesy of the *Fort Worth Star Telegram,* Jim Witt, Executive Editor

"Liquid Thermal Diffusion" by H.M. Moseley, J.B. Bidwell, W.N. Blatt, G.Y.Brokaw, M. Drott, F.J. Gradishar, P.N. Kokulis, R.E. Ruskin, J.H. Tayman, W.E. Whybrew, Edited by Philip. H. Abelson, Department of Terrestrial Magnetism, Carnegie Institution of Washington, Nathan Rosen Department of Physics University of North Carolina, John I. Hoover Nucleonics Division, Naval Research Laboratory, Washington, D.C. September 10, 1946. Naval Research Laboratory Physics Special Research Division Washington, D. C. Liquid Thermal Diffusion. A revised and expanded version of NNES-DC-1. The liquid thermal diffusion method for the separation of isotopes is described. The discussion includes the experimental aspects of the method, description of equipment, and the theoretical aspects of the process as applied to the design, development, and performance criteria. A short history of the liquid thermal diffusion method from 1940 to 1945 is presented along; with a survey of relevant literature prior to 1940. The remainder of the report is concerned with theoretical aspects. (J.R.D.). osti ID: 4311423, report numbers: TID-5229; NRL-0-2982, Technical Report. Decl. February 12, 1957. TISE Issuance date: August 1958. Naval Research Laboratory, Washington, D.C., sponsoring USDOE, subject: Physics; Isotope separation; Laboratory equipment; Liquids; Performance; Planning; Thermal Diffusion. Pages 7-8.

Chapter 21:

Personally conducted interview: Tom Brady, email, September 30, 2012, October 18, 2013, October 17, 2013 and November 15, 2013.

Courtesy of the *Fort Worth Star Telegram,* Witt, Jim, Executive Editor.

http://old-time.com/Halper/Halper43.html, "Radio in 1943", retrieved January 18, 2014. Courtesy of Halper, Donna L. Assistant Professor of Communication, Lesley University, Cambridge, MA.

Walraven, Bill, *The General said "Nuts": Firsthand Accounts of Wartime Heroism, Horror, and Honor.* Corpus Christi, Texas: Javelina Press, 2009. Pages 53-54.

http://remindmagazine.wordpress.com, retrieved March 9, 2013.

http://en.wikipedia.org/wiki/Praise_the_Lord_and_Pass_the_Ammunition, retrieved April 24, 2013.

"Liquid Thermal Diffusion" by H.M. Moseley, J.B. Bidwell, W.N. Blatt, G.Y.Brokaw, M. Drott, F.J. Gradishar, P.N. Kokulis, R.E. Ruskin, J.H. Tayman, W.E. Whybrew, Edited by Philip. H. Abelson, Department of Terrestrial Magnetism, Carnegie Institution of Washington, Nathan Rosen Department of Physics University of North Carolina, John I. Hoover Nucleonics Division, Naval Research Laboratory, Washington, D.C. September 10, 1946. Naval Research Laboratory Physics Special Research Division Washington, D. C. Liquid Thermal Diffusion. A revised and expanded version of NNES-DC-1. The liquid thermal diffusion method for the separation of isotopes is described. The discussion includes the experimental aspects of the method, description of equipment, and the theoretical aspects of the process as applied to the design, development, and performance criteria. A short history of the liquid thermal diffusion method from 1940 to 1945 is presented along; with a survey of relevant literature prior to 1940. The remainder of the report is concerned with theoretical aspects. (J.R.D.). osti ID: 4311423, report numbers: TID-5229; NRL-0-2982, Technical Report. Decl. February 12, 1957. TISE Issuance date: August 1958. Naval Research Laboratory, Washington, D.C., sponsoring USDOE, subject: Physics; Isotope separation; Laboratory equipment; Liquids; Performance; Planning; Thermal Diffusion.

http://en.wikipedia.org/wiki/leslie_groves, retrieved April 24, 2013.

Walraven, Bill, *The General said "Nuts": Firsthand Accounts of Wartime Heroism, Horror, and Honor.* Corpus Christi, Texas: Javelina Press, 2009. Pages 38-43.

Chapter 22:

http://www.ask.com/wiki/united_states_declaration_of_war_upon_germany_(1941), January 31, 2013.

Courtesy of the USMA Library, http://energy.gov.

Ahern, Joseph James, *"We had the hose turned on us! Ross Gunn and The Naval Research Laboratory's Early Research into Nuclear Propulsion"* 1939-1946. Courtesy of the American Philosophical Society Library. (NEEDS PUBLICATION).

http://www.atomicarchive.com/History, retrieved April 24, 2013.

http://www.nap.edu/readingroom.php?book=biomems&page=rgunn.html, retrieved February 5, 2013.

Personally conducted interview: Tom Brady, email, September 30, 2012, October 17, 2013, March 13, 2014, March 20, 2014.

Courtesy of the *Dallas Morning News*.

http://www.jesus-is-savior.com/Great%20Men%20of%20God/dr_john_r_rice_man_of_god.htm, retrieved April 24, 2013.

"Ruark resigns from faculty of University", *Chapel Hill Weekly*, April 1946. Courtesy of North Carolina Collections, UNC Library, Chapel Hill.

Courtesy of osti.gov/includes/opennet/includes/med_scans.

http://www.atomicarchive.com/History/mp/p4s1.shtml.

http://en.wikipedia.org/wiki/father_of_the_nuclear_submarine, retrieved October 24, 2012.

Reichelderfer, F. W. (1967). Ross Gunn - The scientist and the individual. *Monthly Weather Review*, 95(12), 815-821. Article provided courtesy of the NOAA Central Library Data Imaging Project

http://energy.gov/sites/prod/files/edg/media/Making_Atomic_Bomb.pdf, retrieved October 24, 2012.

"Liquid Thermal Diffusion" by H.M. Moseley, J.B. Bidwell, W.N. Blatt, G.Y.Brokaw, M. Drott, F.J. Gradishar, P.N. Kokulis, R.E. Ruskin, J.H. Tayman, W.E. Whybrew, Edited by Philip. H. Abelson, Department of Terrestrial Magnetism, Carnegie Institution of Washington, Nathan Rosen Department of Physics University of North Carolina, John I. Hoover Nucleonics Division, Naval Research Laboratory, Washington, D.C. September 10, 1946. Naval Research Laboratory Physics Special Research Division Washington, D. C. Liquid Thermal Diffusion. A revised and expanded version of NNES-DC-1. The liquid thermal diffusion method for the separation of isotopes is described. The discussion includes the experimental aspects of the method, description of equipment, and the theoretical aspects of the process as applied to the design, development, and performance criteria. A short history of the liquid thermal diffusion method from 1940 to 1945 is presented along; with a survey of relevant literature prior to 1940. The remainder of the report is concerned with theoretical aspects. (J.R.D.). osti ID: 4311423, report numbers: TID-5229; NRL-0-2982, Technical Report. Decl. February 12, 1957. TISE Issuance date: August 1958. Naval Research Laboratory, Washington, D.C., sponsoring USDOE, subject: Physics; Isotope separation; Laboratory equipment; Liquids; Performance; Planning; Thermal Diffusion. Page 59, 60 and 11.

Courtesy of the *Fort Worth Star Telegram*, Witt, Jim, Executive Editor.

Chapter 23:

Courtesy of the USMA Library, http://energy.gov.

"Liquid Thermal Diffusion" by H.M. Moseley, J.B. Bidwell, W.N. Blatt, G.Y.Brokaw, M. Drott, F.J. Gradishar, P.N. Kokulis, R.E. Ruskin, J.H. Tayman, W.E. Whybrew, Edited by Philip. H. Abelson, Department of Terrestrial Magnetism, Carnegie Institution of Washington, Nathan Rosen Department of Physics University of North Carolina, John I. Hoover Nucleonics Division, Naval Research Laboratory, Washington, D.C. September 10, 1946. Naval Research Laboratory Physics Special Research Division Washington, D. C. Liquid Thermal Diffusion. A revised and expanded version of NNES-DC-1. The liquid thermal diffusion method for the separation of isotopes is described. The discussion includes the experimental aspects of the method, description of equipment, and the theoretical aspects of the process as applied to the design, development, and performance criteria. A short history of the liquid thermal diffusion method from 1940 to 1945 is presented along; with a survey of relevant literature prior to 1940. The remainder of the report is concerned with theoretical aspects. (J.R.D.). osti ID: 4311423, report numbers: TID-5229; NRL-0-2982, Technical Report. Decl. February 12, 1957. TISE Issuance date: August 1958. Naval Research Laboratory, Washington, D.C., sponsoring USDOE, subject: Physics; Isotope separation; Laboratory equipment; Liquids; Performance; Planning; Thermal Diffusion.

http://en.wikipedia.org/wiki/Battle_of_Tarawa, retrieved September 24, 2013.

http://en.wikipedia.org/wikipedia/commons/6/6e/8-inch-japanese-gun-betio.jpg. Retrieved September 24, 2013.

http://en.wikipedia.org/wiki/File:Cemetry_at_Tarawa.jpg, retrieved September 24, 2013.

Sample, Herbert, A. "Deadly 1944 West Loch Tragedy to be remembered," May 19, 2009. Reprinted with permission of the Associated Press.

Walraven, Bill, "The General said 'Nuts'; Firsthand accounts of wartime heroism, horror, and honor." Pages 97

Chapter 24:

Walraven, Bill, *The General said "Nuts": Firsthand Accounts of Wartime Heroism, Horror, and Honor.* Corpus Christi, Texas: Javelina Press, 2009. Page 97.

Isacson, Walter, Einstein, page 641

Personally conducted interview: Diamond, Susan, email, November 4, 2013

"Liquid Thermal Diffusion" by H.M. Moseley, J.B. Bidwell, W.N. Blatt, G.Y.Brokaw, M. Drott, F.J. Gradishar, P.N. Kokulis, R.E. Ruskin, J.H. Tayman, W.E. Whybrew, Edited by Philip. H. Abelson, Department of Terrestrial Magnetism, Carnegie Institution of Washington, Nathan Rosen Department of Physics University of North Carolina, John I. Hoover Nucleonics Division, Naval Research Laboratory, Washington, D.C. September 10, 1946. Naval Research Laboratory Physics Special Research Division Washington, D. C. Liquid Thermal Diffusion. A revised and expanded version of NNES-DC-1. The liquid thermal diffusion method for the separation of isotopes is described. The discussion includes the experimental aspects of the method, description of equipment, and the theoretical aspects of the process as applied to the design, development, and performance criteria. A short history of the liquid thermal diffusion method from 1940 to 1945 is presented along; with a survey of relevant literature prior to 1940. The remainder of the report is concerned with theoretical aspects. (J.R.D.). osti ID: 4311423, report numbers: TID-5229; NRL-0-2982, Technical Report. Decl. February 12, 1957. TISE Issuance date: August 1958. Naval Research Laboratory, Washington, D.C., sponsoring USDOE, subject: Physics; Isotope separation; Laboratory equipment; Liquids; Performance; Planning; Thermal Diffusion. Pages 5, 11, 26, 27, 35, 39, 40, 41, 60, 61, 63, 70, 71, 73, 79, 80, 81, 82, 83, 84, 85, 86, 87, 88 and 89.

Vogel, Peter, "Transcriptions regarding The Liquid Diffusion Uranium Isotope Separation method, Appendix A." page 26. Official Web site: www.petervogel.us.

Courtesy of osti.gov/includes/opennet/includes/med_scans.

Courtesy of the USMA Library, http://energy.gov.

Abelson, John, *Uncle Phil and the Atomic Bomb.* Page 112.

Ahern, Joseph, James, *"We had the hose turned on us!; Ross Gunn and The Naval Research Laboratory's*

Early Research into Nuclear Propulsion" 1939-1946. Courtesy of the American Philosophical Society Library.

Courtesy of osti.gov/includes/opennet/includes/med_scans.

Courtesy of the USMA Library, http://energy.gov.

Reichelderfer, F. W. (1967). Ross Gunn - The scientist and the individual. *Monthly Weather Review,* 95(12), 815-821. Article provided courtesy of the NOAA Central Library Data Imaging Project

http://www.atomicarchive.com/History/mp/p4s3.shtml, retrieved April 24, 2013.

http://www.atomicarchive.com/History/mp/p4s11.shtml, retrieved April 24, 2013.

http://energy.gov/sites/prod/files/edg/media/Making_Atomic_Bomb.pdf, retrieved October 24, 2012.

Courtesy of The New York Times, *Holiday Travelers ignore ODT Please.* September 2, 1944. http://www.mphpa.org/classic/HISTORY/H-06b5.htm

http://en.wikipedia.org/wiki/Manhattan_Project.

http://www.atomicarchive.com/History/mp/p4s33.shtml.

Courtesy of The New York Times, *Holiday Travelers ignore ODT Please.* September 2, 1944.

http://www.globalsecurity.org.

Courtesy of the USMA Library, http://energy.gov.

Courtesy of osti.gov/includes/opennet/includes/med_scans/VIII.

Manuscript of James Conant, "Historical note on introduction of the Abelson-Gunn process." 1944, July 27.

Chapter 25:

www.atomiarchive.com

Bates, Jack, "Proud to be #23" *(Courtesy of Roberta Bates).*

Chapter 26:

Unknown. Army vs Penn. November 18, 1945. The New York Times archives.

Reprinted with Permission of the Associated Press.

Personally conducted interview: Sherwin, Martin J. email, January 16, 2013.

Courtesy of Wilson Special Collections at the University of North Carolina at Chapel Hill.

Courtesy of osti.gov/includes/opennet/includes/med_scans.

http://www.history.navy.mil

Courtesy of Fehner, Terrance R. and Gosing, "F. G. The Manhattan Project" page 8.

Riddle, Bruce, "Legends, Masonic Home and School of Texas," Vol II, *Dewitt "Tex" Coulter,* Page 3.

Chapter 27:

North Carolina Collection Clippings file through 1975, U.N.C. Library Chapel Hill, Ruark Resigns from faculty of University. Jason E. Tomberlin, North Carolina Research & Instruction Librarian. Wilson Special Collections Library. University of North Carolina at Chapel Hill.

Can quantum mechanical description of physical reality be considered complete? The Einstein-Podolsky-Rosen paradox, or the EPR paradox. Albert Einstein, Boris Podolsky, Nathan Rosen (Princeton, Inst. Advanced Study). 1935. 4pp. Published in Phys.Rev.47:777-780,1935. (In *Wheeler, J.A., Zurek,

W.H. (eds.): Quantum theory and measurement, Princeton U. Press, 1983* pp. 138-141)

The Particle Problem in the General Theory of Relativity. Albert Einstein, N. Rosen (Princeton, Inst. Advanced Study). 1935. Published in Phys.Rev.48:73-77,1935.

On Gravitational waves. Albert Einstein, N. Rosen 1937. 12pp. Published in J.Franklin Inst. 223:43-54,1937.

"Neutron-Proton Interaction." Moseley, Hm; Rosen, N., Physical Review, volume: 71 issue: 11, pages: 835-835, published: 1947, WOS:A1947UB27800043. American Physical Society, Physics. IDS number: UB278. ISSN: 0031-899X.

"Approach to Equilibrium by a Thermal Diffusion Column. Part I. Column Closed at Both Ends." Main Author Moseley, H.M. Other Authors: Rosen, Nathan. October 31, 1948. OSTI ID: 4439221. Subject: Isotope separation; diagrams, enrichment, extraction, columns, mathematics, tables and thermal diffusion. Oak Ridge, Tenn. : U.S. Atomic Energy Commission, Technical Information Division, 1948. Work performed at the Naval Research Laboratory. Date Declassified: August 25, 1948. AECD-2236.

Moseley, H.M. and Rosen, N, "Are Mesons Elementary Particles," Source: PHYSICAL REVIEW Volume: 78 Issue: 1 Pages: 67-67 DOI: 10.1103/PhysRev.78.67.3 Published: 1950. Cited References: Fermi E, 1949, Phys Rev, V76, P1739, DOI 10.1103/PhysRev.76.1739 Moseley HM, 1949, Phys Rev, V76, pA197. Rosen N, 1948, Phys Rev, V74, pA128.

Miller, H.N. and Rosen, N, "The Meson as a Composite Particle," Source: Physical Review Volume: 80 Issue: 2 Pages: 177-181 DOI: 10.1103/PhysRev.80.177 Published: 1950.

Courtesy of osti.gov/includes/opennet/includes/med_scans, VIII.

Courtesy of the USMA Library, http://energy.gov.

http://www.history.navy.mil/faqs/faq76-1.htm.

http://www.osti.gov/includes/opennet/includes/MED_scans/Book%20I%20-%20General%20-%20 Vol.%204-Chapters%202-5.pdf.

Courtesy of ORAU.

Riddle, Bruce, "Legends, Masonic Home and School of Texas," Vol I, *SK2c Norman W. Cardwell*. Page 5.

(http://www.osti.gov/includes/opennet/includes/MED_scans/Book%20VIII%20-%20Volume%20 3%20-%20Auxiliary%20Activities%20-%20Chapter%208-%20Ope.pdf}.

http://energy.gov/sites/prod/files/edg/media/Making_Atomic_Bomb.pdf, The Manhattan Project: Making of the Atomic Bomb, Part VI, the Manhattan Project in peacetime, page 55.

http://en.wikipedia.org/wiki/Harry_S_Truman.

Courtesy of the USMA Library, http://energy.gov.

"Liquid Thermal Diffusion" by H.M. Moseley, J.B. Bidwell, W.N. Blatt, G.Y.Brokaw, M. Drott, F.J. Gradishar, P.N. Kokulis, R.E. Ruskin, J.H. Tayman, W.E. Whybrew, Edited by Philip. H. Abelson, Department of Terrestrial Magnetism, Carnegie Institution of Washington, Nathan Rosen Department of Physics University of North Carolina, John I. Hoover Nucleonics Division, Naval Research Laboratory, Washington, D.C. September 10, 1946. Naval Research Laboratory Physics Special Research Division Washington, D. C. Liquid Thermal Diffusion. A revised and expanded version of NNES-DC-1. The liquid thermal diffusion method for the separation of isotopes is described. The discussion includes the experimental aspects of the method, description of equipment, and the theoretical aspects of the process as applied to the design, development, and performance criteria. A short history of the liquid thermal diffusion method from 1940 to 1945 is presented along; with a survey of relevant literature prior to 1940. The remainder of the report is concerned with theoretical aspects. (J.R.D.). osti ID: 4311423, report numbers: TID-5229; NRL-0-2982, Technical Report. Decl. February 12, 1957. TISE Issuance date: August 1958. Naval Research Laboratory, Washington, D.C., sponsoring USDOE, subject: Physics; Isotope separation; Laboratory equipment; Liquids; Performance; Planning; Thermal Diffusion. Pages 1, 2, 3 and 5.

(www.nautilus571.com/rickover.htm)

http://en.wikipedia.org/wiki/Hyman_G._Rickover

Proceedings of the American Physical Society. *Minutes of the Meeting of the Southeastern section at Clemson College, April 15-16, 1949.*. Vol 76, No. 1, July 1, 1949. page 195, 197. Courtesy of the Wilson Special Collections Library at the University of North Carolina at Chapel Hill, and The Special Collections Library at Texas Christian University.

http://energy.gov/sites/prod/files/edg/media/Making_Atomic_Bomb.pdf, The Manhattan Project: Making of the Atomic Bomb, Surrender, Page 54.

Terrence R. Fehner and F. G. Gosing. Courtesy of The Manhattan Project, page 9.

Caption/citation here The (University Libraries, The University of North Carolina at Chapel Hill), Jason E. Tomberlin, North Carolina Research & Instruction Librarian

Wilson Special Collections Library, University of North Carolina at Chapel Hill and Amy Leslie, T.C.U. special Collections Library.

Courtesy of Doug Diesenhaus, Research and Instructional Services, University Libraries. The University of North Carolina at Chapel Hill.

Casey Madrick, USMA Library. September 3, 2013.

Chapter 28:

Moseley, Harrison Miller, "Composite Particles: Particle of Integral Spin as Compounds of Dirac-Type Particles," Courtesy of Research and Instructional Services, University Libraries at the University of North Carolina at Chapel Hill. Doug Diesenhaus.

"We had the hose turned on us!" Ross Gunn and The Naval Research Laboratory's Early Research into Nuclear Propulsion, 1939 - 1946. Joseph - James Ahern, American Philosophical Society Library.

Dallas Morning News, 16 August 1951, Section II, p.6.

Courtesy of Special Collections at Texas Christian University.

Courtesy of the New York Times, *Fund Cuts Limit Atomic Research*, June 19, 1958.

Courtesy of the New York Times.

Personally conducted interview: Sherwin, Martin J. email, January 16, 2013.

H.M. Moseley, H.G. Blosser, R.E. Worsham, C.D. Goodman, R.S. Livingston, J.E.Mann, G.T. Trammel and T.A. Welton. "Four-Sector Azimuthally varying field cyclotron," Reproduced with permission from Review of Scientific Instruments 29, 819 (1958); doi: 10.1063/1.1716014. Copyright 1958, AIP Publishing LLC.

www.orau.org/about-orau/history/william-pollard.aspx

Personally conducted interview: Nester, Margaret, Boone, email, January 12, 2014.

(www.orau.org/about-orau/history/william-pollard.aspx)

Chapter 29:

Walraven, Bill, "42-year school reunion special this year." *Corpus-Christi Caller-Times,* August 1, 1985.

Courtesy of Marjorie Walraven.

Courtesy of Special Collections at Texas Christian University, "Faculty Bulletin," October 13, 1965.

Washington state magazine, *Philip & Neva Abelson: Pioneers on the knowledge frontier*, by Pat Caraher | © Washington State University, Paul Espinosa, Curator, George Peabody Library, The Johns Hopkins University, September 9, 2013.

Personally conducted interview: Richard Opperman, at his home, June 1, 2012.

Personally conducted interview: Tom Brady, email, September 30, 2012, October 17, 2013, October 18, 2013, November 15, 2013, November 26, 2013 and November 27, 2013.

Personally conducted interview: Cheryl Castells, March 9, 2013.

Personally conducted interview: Karen Messick, March 29, 2013.

Courtesy of Special Collections at Texas Christian University, "Skiff".

Stafford, Ted, Unknown source, Courtesy of Special Collections at Texas Christian University, April 10, 1981.

Caraher, Pat, Washington State Magazine, *Philip and Neva Abelson: Pioneers on the knowledge frontier*, Courtesy of Paul Espinosa, Curator, George Peabody Library, The Johns Hopkins University.

Personally conducted interview: Cherniavsky, Ellen, email, January 21, 2013 and January 24, 2013.

Miller, H.N. and Rosen, N, "The Meson as a Composite Particle," Source: Physical Review Volume: 80 Issue: 2 Pages: 177-181 DOI: 10.1103/PhysRev.80.177 Published: 1950.

Cited References: De Broglie L., 1935, Comptes Rendus Hebdomadaires des Seances de l'Academie des Sciences, V200

Debroglie L, 1943, Theorie Generale Par

Debroglie L, 1940, Une Nouvelle Theorie

Fermi E, 1949, Phys Rev, V76, P1739, DOI 10.1103/PhysRev.76.1739

Kemmer N., 1937, Helv Phys Acta, V10, P48

March A, 1938, Naturwissenschaften, V26, P649

Moseley HM, 1949, Phys Rev, V76, pA197

Moseley HM, Thesis U N Carolina Pauli W, HDB Physik 1, V24, P219

Rosen N, 1948, Phys Rev, V74, pA128

Rosen N, 1947, Phys Rev, V72, P298, DOI 10.1103/PhysRev. 72.298.

Walraven, Bill, "A visit to the Masonic Home".

Reproduced with permission courtesy of Lamar University IL, from American Industrial Hygiene Association Journal, *Simplified method for determining cascade impactor stage efficiencies*, vol 28: Issue: 1, 1967, pages 62-67.

Courtesy of the Dallas Morning News, "Masons Have Power as well as tricks to toss," McClanahan, Bill, 9-14-41, page 18

Personally conducted interview: McHam, Horace, November 6, 2013.

Bates, Jack, "Proud to be #23" *(Courtesy of Roberta Bates)*.

Personally conducted interview: Roberta Bates, telephone, February 3, 2013.

Personally conducted interview: Walraven, Marjorie, telephone, November 17, 2012.

Personally conducted interview: Dr. Abelson, John, telephone, March 1, 2013.

Personally conducted interview: Riddle, Bruce, at his home, March 12, 2013.

http://en.wikipedia.org/wiki/Philip_Abelson

Washington State University Libraries, Manuscripts, Archives, and Special Collections, Pullman, WA., '*Master*', *Liquid Thermal Diffusion*, TID-5229, U.S. Atomic Energy Commission, Technical information service extension, Oak Ridge TN. Courtesy of The Johns Hopkins University.

"Series 2: World War II atomic research, 1942-1956". Courtesy of the George Peabody Library, The Johns Hopkins University.

Personally conducted interview: Dr. Quarles, C.A., telephone, January 10, 2013.

Fletcher, T., Proceedings of the Grand Lodge of Texas, page 142. *(Courtesy of Richard Opperman).*

The Chapel Hill Newspaper, *Former Physics Department Head, AEC Official Dies*, Friday, May 4, 1979, Courtesy of The University of North Carolina at Chapel Hill Collections.

Chapel Hill Weekly. April 19, 1946. North Carolina Collection Clipping File through 1975, UNC.

Riddle, Bruce, "Legends; Masonic Home and School of Texas," Vol III, *Harvey Nual "Rusty" Russell*, Page 2.

Courtesy of osti.gov/includes/opennet/includes/med_scans, VIII. Page 332: Ibid.

Reichelderfer, F. W. (1967). Ross Gunn - The scientist and the individual. *Monthly Weather Review*, 95(12), 815-821. Article provided courtesy of the NOAA Central Library Data Imaging Project

Walraven, Bill, "The General said 'Nuts; Firsthand accounts of wartime heroism, horror, and honor." Pages 98.

Courtesy of ORAU

Reproduced with permission for Physics Today 47(11), 106 (1994); doi: 10.1063/1.2808717.

Moseley, H. M., Blosser, H.G. , Worsham, R.E.,Goodman, C.D., Livingston, R.S., Mann, J.E., Trammel, G.T. and Welton, T.A. *Four-Sector Azimuthally varying field cyclotron,* Reproduced with permission from Review of Scientific Instruments 29, 819 (1958); doi: 10.1063/1.1716014. Copyright 1958, AIP Publishing LLC.

Washington, D.C., "Many Atomic Finds of Value to Industry Will Be Released at Once, Scientists Say" Writer unknown, Special to the New York Times.

Walraven, Bill, *After 'Progress' hits, you can't go back*, 30 July 1985.

Photo by Jason S. Munford

§

Stella Elizabeth Brooks found the inspiration to step out of her comfort zone and into the world of writing upon learning of Dr. Harrison Miller Moseley. Moseley, a man of historical significance, had gone unnoticed for years. After studying his personality and life, she was able to understand his responses, his choices and his silence. Brooks brings to life the emotional and personal journey of a young boy, Harrison Miller Moseley, as he works to turn his losses into becoming a self-sufficient man through academics and football. Miller's senior year, 1938, would test him mentally and physically. Drawing from her numerous exclusive one-on-one recorded visits with Miller, and extensive research, Stella manages to show Miller's emotional side as well as his achievements in the classroom, the football field and during his scientific work on the Manhattan Project.

She was honored with the first and only lengthy interview Miller ever gave detailing his phenomenal achievements and inspirational courage. He vividly described his fantastic life working in the world's most famous laboratory with new details not previously known. His wonderful dry humor and personality brought a special sentiment to his inspirational life. Additional extensive interviews with Miller's childhood friends from the orphanage—Richard Opperman, Tom Brady, Horace McHam, and Bruce Riddle—are included. Stella has two children and lives in Fort Worth, Texas. This is her first book.

§

CPSIA information can be obtained
at www.ICGtesting.com
Printed in the USA
LVHW110856280521
688738LV00005B/12

9 780999 648476